Communities, Performance and Practice

Kerrie Schaefer

Communities, Performance and Practice

Enacting Communities

Kerrie Schaefer
Exeter, UK

ISBN 978-3-030-95756-8   ISBN 978-3-030-95757-5 (eBook)
https://doi.org/10.1007/978-3-030-95757-5

© The Editor(s) (if applicable) and The Author(s) 2022

This work is subject to copyright. All rights are solely and exclusively licensed by the Publisher, whether the whole or part of the material is concerned, specifically the rights of translation, reprinting, reuse of illustrations, recitation, broadcasting, reproduction on microfilms or in any other physical way, and transmission or information storage and retrieval, electronic adaptation, computer software, or by similar or dissimilar methodology now known or hereafter developed.

The use of general descriptive names, registered names, trademarks, service marks, etc. in this publication does not imply, even in the absence of a specific statement, that such names are exempt from the relevant protective laws and regulations and therefore free for general use.

The publisher, the authors and the editors are safe to assume that the advice and information in this book are believed to be true and accurate at the date of publication. Neither the publisher nor the authors or the editors give a warranty, expressed or implied, with respect to the material contained herein or for any errors or omissions that may have been made. The publisher remains neutral with regard to jurisdictional claims in published maps and institutional affiliations.

This Palgrave Macmillan imprint is published by the registered company Springer Nature Switzerland AG.
The registered company address is: Gewerbestrasse 11, 6330 Cham, Switzerland

Acknowledgements

I'd like to especially thank two colleagues who steadfastly supported this project from conception through to completion: Professor Jane Milling and Professor Graham Ley. The University of Exeter has approved periods of research leave to complete this (and other) projects. Research leaves are enabled by colleagues as well as institutions, and the Drama department at Exeter has offered a collegial, generous and stimulating academic home for several years: thank you. I'd like to thank Chloe Bradwell for comments on Chap. 5 and Dr. Jo Ronan for comments on Chap. 6. I'd like to thank an anonymous reader who offered constructive and supportive comments at a critical stage. Thanks to the Palgrave Macmillan team—Eileen, Jack and Imogen.

There are several organisations, and many practitioners and participants to acknowledge and thank. I'd like to heartfully thank acta Community Theatre Company and, in particular, Neil Beddow, Helen Tomlin, Ingrid Jones, Philippa Smith, the Malcolm X Elders and the cast of the *Gas Girls*. Thanks to Big hART and in particular, Scott Rankin, Sophia Marinos, Cecily Hardt, Debra Myers, Elspeth Blunt and the entire (professional and community) cast of *Hipbone Sticking Out*. I travelled to Roebourne (*Ieramugadu*) to research the chapter on Big hART and the *Hipbone* creative development as part of the *Yijala Yala* project. I acknowledge the traditional landowners, Ngarluma and Yindjibarndi language groups, and other language groups responsible for custodianship of the Burrup Peninsula (*Murujuga*) on Yaburara country. I pay my respects to the traditional owners and custodians of these lands, past and present, whose sovereignty was never ceded and who keep alive living cultures. Thank you to Anne Basting, Michael Rohd and Sojourn performers: Shannon Scrofano, Maureen Towey, James Hart, Rebecca Martinez, UWM undergraduate and graduate students (especially Dr. Chelsea Wait), and Milwaukee elders. The Drama Box company offered incredible support for the project. I'd like to thank Hui Ling Koh, Han Xuemei and Kok Heng Luen. Special thanks are due to Jiaying Tay for preparations before arriving in Singapore and Khee Shihui, who set up interviews (with project participants as well as other cultural practitioners for broader context), translated interviews and ethics participant information and consent forms, and engaged with me in her inimitable way as I thought out loud.

My family have provided enormous amounts of love and support. Thanks to my parents, Deidre and Wilhelm Schaefer, my sister, Fiona, and her family, partner, Charlie Davis, and daughter, Ellie Schaefer-Davis. I'd like to dedicate this book to the memory of David Watt, a dear colleague and friend.

This research was undertaken with an Arts and Humanities Research Council Fellowship (AH/J007765/1) grant, a BA/Leverhulme small grant and a National Arts Council Singapore Research and Development Grant.

Contents

1 Enacting Community — 1

2 Historical and Theoretical Perspectives on Community Performance — 15

3 acta Community Theatre, the 'Cycle of Engagement' and a 'Community of [Theatre] Practice' — 47

4 *Yijala Yala*: Big hART Creative Producing Cultural Livelihoods in the Pilbara — 81

5 *The Crossings* (Part of the *Islands of Milwaukee*): The Agency of Older Bodies Enacting Pedestrian Crossings — 125

6 Community Performance in Singapore: Drama Box's *IgnorLAND of Its Time* Performing the 'HDB Nation' at Bukit Ho Swee — 157

7 Conclusion: An Invitation — 193

Index — 199

CHAPTER 1

Enacting Community

Introduction: Contextualising an Approach to Enacting Community

This study emerged in a particular context, and has a specific aim: namely to explore how the re-signification of the concept of community might impact on the theory and practice of community performance. I begin by introducing an aspect of my own experience, as an induction into that context, and that aim.

In the early to mid-2000s, I was a member of the Performance, Community Development and Social Change research group led by my then colleague in Drama at the University of Newcastle, New South Wales, (the now late) David Watt. The group undertook practice-based research projects in community cultural development (CCD; the Australian term approximating community performance). Some of these interdisciplinary, cross-sector CCD projects were written up by members of the group, with the aim of explicating how 'arts workers' (the utilitarian term that was used) collaborated with non-arts professionals in local and state government (housing, health, and heritage services), in community organisations and within various constituencies to facilitate developmental changes by drawing on local (situated or embedded) cultural resources.[1] The aim was to articulate through thick description of collaborative performance-making process how community cultural development practices operated, and how culture could be a resource for community development and social change.

Towards the end of this period, the group was approached by a community organisation connected to Windale, a residential suburb in the south of the greater Newcastle metropolitan area with a population of approximately 3000 people, with over two-thirds of housing in the suburb in public ownership. We were encouraged to create a performance about Windale with its residents and

---

[1] See Schaefer and Watt (2006, 2007); Schaefer (2009); Watt (2009).

© The Author(s), under exclusive license to Springer Nature Switzerland AG 2022
K. Schaefer, *Communities, Performance and Practice*,
https://doi.org/10.1007/978-3-030-95757-5_1

to stage the resulting performance in The Civic, a 1500-seat theatre in the city of Newcastle's cultural precinct. The idea was that a high-visibility performance staging a celebration of Windale would counter a particular narrative attached to the neighbourhood over recent years. This narrative crystallised with the publication of a research report analysing public social data (including Census data from 1996 and 2001) at postcode level in order to determine the distribution of social disadvantage in south-eastern Australia (Vinson 2004). The 'Vinson report', as it became known, placed Windale within the top percentile of postcode areas of concentrated social disadvantage. Windale thus became an example of a neighbourhood or 'community' defined as a problem. Local media headlines amplified the findings of the research report reproducing an image of Windale as top of a list of areas of entrenched deprivation, one of the worst postcode areas in which to live in the state of New South Wales.

Vinson's report was instrumental in garnering directed state government investment to support already-existing community-led efforts towards social development in Windale. However, the release of the report was contentious and contested by community representatives, such as Roger Greenan, Secretary of the Windale Community Group, who argued that labelling Windale as "worst of the worst" merely reproduced the standard narrative about public housing spaces (2007, p. 19). This critique acknowledged problems with the research design given that Windale was an anomaly in the state of New South Wales as a suburb with an extremely high proportion of public housing provision given its own postcode (postcodes usually take in several suburbs and tend to have a more mixed public and private housing profile). Geographers also problematised Vinson's research as "a socially abominable, academically flawed and politically unhelpful process":

> one of the most destructive things you can do to a person or a community is to label it with a derogatory tag. Name it, it becomes it. (O'Neill 2007, p. 9)

It was clear that postcode-level analysis on which the research methodology was based did not work in instances such as Windale where the single postcode area was also an area with a large concentration of public housing.

The Drama department offices at the University of Newcastle shared the top floor of a building with Geography. This meant that on our corridor was Professor Phillip O'Neill, who criticised the Vinson report, and Dr Kathy Mee, a senior geographer with a research specialism in public housing. In addition to offering her expertise, Mee directed us to Greg Heys, who was writing a Geography PhD on assets-based community development (ABCD), involving applied research in Windale. Heys offered a different vision of the locality:

> The figures would say that this is the worst-off suburb in New South Wales and Victoria, but when you get to know it, it's a very unique, rich suburb with ordinary people living heroic lives, and it's a great experiment to see how that ordinary working class suburb has had to come to grips with the changes that have

affected it ... and is experimenting with different ways of dealing with those changes. (*Windale: A Work In Progress* 2006)

A former (Labour) Lord Mayor of Newcastle, Heys was also a Bennetts Green Rotarian, the organisation that made the initial approach (through another member) to create a performance with Windale residents that enacted counter-narratives of the suburb, by utilising and showcasing the community's assets. In the outcome, our research group (expanded to include Mee, Heys and CCD practitioner, Brian Joyce) fomented an invitation to work with residents of Windale to create a performance that expressed some of this community-led mobilisation. The emergent practice-based research project became known as 'Windale 2306'.[2]

After initial field visits and meetings, and with some small, start-up amounts of funding from Rotary and the NSW Department of Housing to build relationships and pilot projects, we began on an Australian Research Council (ARC) Discovery Grant application.[3] The aims of the application were to execute and critically evaluate (using participatory action research) a number of performance-based community development projects in Windale, with a view to supporting residents in countering and changing misrepresentations of the suburb as a place of entrenched social disadvantage. Through this exercise, I was introduced to an alternative notion of 'community' circulating in cultural and feminist economic geography. Gillian Rose (1997) adopted Jean-Luc Nancy's (1991a) notion of 'inoperative community' to examine how community arts workers created space for residents of an Edinburgh housing estate to engage in making processes that were so multi-voiced that the project far exceeded any articulation of unified opposition or singular resistance. J.K. Gibson-Graham's *Post-capitalist Politics* (2006)[4] draws on Nancy's re-signification of community from 'common being', understood as "community that is built on already constituted subjects who are brought together in a constructed oneness", to 'being-in-common', or a notion of coexistence (2006, pp. 85–86). Gibson-Graham engage this "ethic of being-in-common, of coexistence with the other" (2006, p. 86) to explore (through a series of action research projects) the economic possibilities for areas variously experiencing the negative impacts of late capitalism.

---

[2] Brian Joyce, then director of the Hunter Writers Centre, Newcastle, became artist-in-residence based in Windale Library. He discusses the process in *Stories from community cultural development, apocryphal or emblematic? Mining the seams of personal practice* (2017). (2017, MPhil, University of Newcastle): pp. 95–118. https://ogma.newcastle.edu.au/vital/access/manager/Repository/uon:28968

[3] Mee and Watt were named chief investigators on the application. I was a named researcher because I had accepted a job offer in the UK (starting April 2007). The application was deemed a 'near miss', and supported by internal research funding (AUD20,000) from University of Newcastle.

[4] J.K. Gibson-Graham is the pen name of feminist economic geographers Katherine Gibson and Julie Graham. The composite name reflects their collective authorial project, which began in 1996 and lasted until Graham's death in 2010.

These ideas of community as 'enacted' or 'performed' provided the primary departure point for the research project. It enabled an alternative starting point to the "limiting research entry point [of] viewing public housing estates as communities with problems" (Mee and Watt 2007). Viewing public housing estates as 'performed' rather than problem communities entailed examining "important moments of past performances of Windale, as well as providing spaces for new performances of Windale(s)" (Mee and Watt 2007) Furthermore, it opened onto the idea of "viewing housing estates as places of possibility" (Mee and Watt 2007). With Windale reconceptualised as open to other performances and possibilities, CCD practice was considered a "viable means of exploring those possibilities" (Mee and Watt 2007). In other words, the way geographers approached an overdetermined place/space such as Windale, seeing that space as performed and as a place of possibility, was commensurate with a CCD praxis based on a dynamic notion of cultural community, formulated by Watt (1991) and reproduced in the application (see also Watt 2009). I will quote from the application at length to show how the approach taken in this book was generated in specific circumstances:

> The notion of 'community' central to CCD has been defined, in one of the formative theorizations within the movement (Kelly 1984, 50–1), as "a goal, a target" of a CCD process rather than as a pre-given, and as "a set of shared social meanings which are constantly created and mutated through the actions and interactions of its members" (i.e. 'performed', in Rose's [1997] sense) who are members through an act of choice rather than an external process of categorisation.
>
> CCD practice is based on three principles:
>
> - Ordinary people are 'makers' of 'culture' rather than merely consumers
> - CCD 'arts workers' are facilitators of the cultural expression of others and thus 'agents of transformation' (Adams and Goldbard 2001, p. 14)
> - 'Making' 'culture' through collaborative and dialogic processes can build and/or consolidate diverse, multivocal 'communities', and thus enhance individual and social wellbeing through creating opportunities for social participation
>
> CCD is now internationally acknowledged as a tool in the promotion of public health and wellbeing (see M. Mayo 2000, for example), particularly in Australia (see Mills and Brown 2004, for a brief survey), which is internationally recognised as having "the best-developed public apparatus for support of community cultural development of any nation on earth" (Adams and Goldbard 2002, p. 189). It is thus unsurprising that CCD projects have been frequently used in public housing estates (see Rose 1997 for work in Scotland), particularly in Australia (see Pitts 2003 [...]). The most high profile example recently has been by the CCD organisation Big hART in the Northcott Estate in South Sydney (see Wright and Palmer 2007) in a project which produced the site-specific performance *Stickybricks* as part of the [2006] Sydney Festival. (Mee and Watt 2007)

I want to stress that this study of community and performance has its genesis in this interdisciplinary, community cultural development, practice-based research approach. While the vagaries of life and research funding may have rerouted my research to a base in the UK, and a more critically distanced and analytical exploration of practice, it has its beginnings in CCD and ABCD research communities in Newcastle, New South Wales, and maintains tendril-like links to Australia via the case study of Big hART, which brings out strong connections between community performance and cultural livelihoods, with cultural livelihoods a concept aligned with ABCD while also rooted in post-sustainable development critical discourse (see Chap. 4).

THE PROBLEM OF COMMUNITY IN/AND POSTMODERNISM: ARTICULATING A PARADOX

Kershaw's (1992) *The Politics of Performance: Radical Theatre as Cultural Intervention* traced the evolution of the alternative and community theatre movement in the UK through phases: beginnings in the 1960s; consolidation in the 1970s; reorientation in the 1980s; and queried fragmentation in the 1990s. The book closed with the sense that the movement had staved off fragmentation through balancing the somewhat contradictory domains of 'cultural democracy' and 'community development' (see pp. 240–242). In 1999, on the cusp of a new millennium, Kershaw's *The Radical in Performance: Between Brecht and Baudrillard* turned to address the problem of community in postmodernity:

> In the post-modern, notions of the common good are frequently viewed, paradoxically, as potentially coercive. Anything that smacks of collectivism, whether in the 'traditions' of conservative thinking or in the 'communes' of left-wing Utopias, is treated with suspicion, so that sometimes even the slightest hint of 'community' becomes a disease of the imagination, a nostalgic hankering after a shared sense of the human that never actually existed. (p. 192)

In light of this "newly negative view of 'community'" produced by postmodern criticism of theoretical metanarratives (see Lyotard 1984), Kershaw identified how critical theory responded by reducing the scope of community to "the temporary and highly localised" (1999, p. 193). This move begged the question, however, of what concept might encapsulate broadly social processes, already in train, producing a sense of the 'global' and a related set of challenges requiring collective action (such as climate change or a pandemic, for instance). At the same time, while pointing out this conundrum, Kershaw engaged Jameson's thesis that postmodernism is "the cultural logic of late capitalism" (1991) to identify another issue. Cultural production, according to Kershaw after Jameson, is closely aligned with the logic of late capitalism and is therefore complicit in the reproduction of an economic system that exploits the material world in its quest for monetary growth. Van Den Abbeele, who we will come to in a moment, expresses this best:

the celebration of difference and the suspicion of absolutes that characterise post-structuralism and postmodernism seem a mere ideological correlative of the ceaseless upheavals and relentlessly splintering effects exerted on the material level under modern capitalism. (1991, p. x)

Kershaw ended up articulating a paradox in which the problems of community in postmodernity were reformulated as a search for radical performance between the political, represented by the (left) theatre project initiated by Brecht, and postmodern simulation, represented by Baudrillard's (1994) theorising which Grace (2002) describes as an "active challenge to the real" (2000, p. 2). This paradoxical formulation, however, displaced the fusion of cultural democracy and community development forged in earlier theories of alternative and community theatre practice. Such displacement has been exacerbated by the emergence of applied theatre in the UK in the late 1990s and early 2000s, a field which nevertheless questions "the dynamics of coercion, control, cohesion and collective power" (Kershaw 1999, p. 194) in theatre and performance practices turned to the social. Meanwhile, practices have gone on developing under the sign of 'community(-based)' in the US, the Netherlands, Australia and elsewhere with a focus on 'communities of difference' and negotiating 'difference' through coalition building (see Kuftinec 2003, pp. 37–39), and the ongoing project to strengthen relations between culture and social democracy (Watt 1991 after Kelly 1984 and Shelton Trust 1986; McConnachie 1998; Haedicke and Nellhaus 2001; Cohen-Cruz 2005, 2009). Eugène van Erven's (2001) identification of community theatre as plural global practices was reiterated by Jan Cohen-Cruz at the 2011 International Community Arts Festival (see Cohen-Cruz and Van Erven 2013, pp. 140–141). These developments render the re-signification of community necessary. And, so, I turn to a theoretical project that began in the late 1980s that sweated similar questions to those raised by Kershaw, and that did so by maintaining focus on the changing concept of community.

Re-signifying Community: From Common Being to Being-in-Common

Shortly before Kershaw articulated the joint problem of community in postmodernity and post-modernism's complicity with late capitalism, setting the question of the radical in performance in terms of a paradox between a liberatory or emancipatory project and postmodern simulation, a 'theory collective' "was similarly exploring "the contemporary crisis of community" (Van Den Abbeele 2001, p. xiii) while maintaining sharp focus on community. Van Den Abbeele claims:

> [N]o sociopolitical thinking can do without some theory of community [and that] the urgency of rethinking that category requires the elaboration of a discourse that does not fall into the trap of an immanentism, whose pernicious

effects have marked the political history of the twentieth century and whose preclusion of the value of difference makes it untenable before the contemporary exigency of articulating the demands of a host of new social movements [...] none of which [...] are simply subsumable or even foreseeable under the traditional aegis of class struggle. (1991, p. xiii)

The Miami Theory Collective (MTC) introduced Nancy's work after *La Communauté désœuvrée* (translated as The Inoperative Community (1991a)[5] into what was becoming a productive dialogue, that moved beyond Kershaw's political/postmodern paradox. Explaining how Nancy's notion of community differs from traditional notions of community, Van Den Abbeele states:

Community, as Nancy wants to revive the notion, is neither a community of subjects, not a promise of immanence, nor a communion of individuals in some higher or greater totality (a State, a nation, a People, etc.). It is not, most specifically, the product of any work or project; it is *not* a work, not a product of projected labour, not an *oeuvre*, but what is un-worked, *dés-oeuvré*. It *is* what is given and what happens to "singular beings," the exhibiting or presenting of their singularity, which is to say the copresenting of their *finitude* as the very basis or condition for their commonality. (1991, p. xiv; original emphases)

I want to explore the impact of this fundamental rethinking of community that has its genesis with the work of Jean-Luc Nancy (1991a, 2000), for whom a central idea is that "there is no common being, but there is being *in* common" (Nancy in Gibson-Graham 2006, p. 85). For feminist economic geographers J.K. Gibson-Graham, Nancy's significant achievement is in dissociating community from its "traditional recourse to common being" (2006, p. 85) and associating it, instead, with being-in-common or the "question of being-with and of being-together (in the sense of the world)" (Nancy in Gibson-Graham 2006, p. 85). According to Nancy, this notion of 'community' opens up new questions concerning the "community of being, and not the being of community [or] the community of existence, and not the essence of community" (in Van Den Abbeele, p. xvi). This reversal of common-sense thinking about Being beginning with single individual subjects is replaced by coexistence of inter-dependent social beings that is also expressed in terms of a "relational theory of identity" (Bond 2011, p. 782). Welch and Panelli (2007) point to the inherent dynamism in Being as a form of relational identity or coexistence:

---

[5] The Miami Theory Collective formed following the publication of Jean-Luc Nancy's *La Communauté désoeuvrée* (1986), which was based on a 1983 article which earned a book-length response from Maurice Blanchot, *La communauté inavouable/The Unavowable Community* (1984). The collective consisted of a reading group (1986–1988), conference (1988) and publication, *Community At Loose Ends* (1991), which was a 'loose' translation of Nancy's text (see Van Den Abbeele 1991, p. xiv) expressing the central idea of 'a revisionist understanding of community as being "at loose ends"' (p. xiii–xiv).

this co-existence does not infer a collective of singulars in some unified 'society' or common-being 'community'. Rather being singular plural posits connection *as opposed to* sameness; a togetherness [...] '"linked" ... [but] [...] not unified' (Nancy 2000, 33). [...] [T]he potency of 'connection' and 'between' exists in a conception of community as a connection of beings-in-common that distances at the very moment that it appears to bind. (pp. 350–351; original emphasis)

Gibson-Graham have harnessed Nancy's concept of 'being-in-common' in the context of developing a 'postcapitalist' political project based on re-signification and enactment of what they call the 'community economy' (2006, pp. 79–100). They argue that what is called the capitalist economy is actually the tip of the iceberg of productive activity. Beneath the surface is a wealth of productive activity that is not recognised as economic activity because it isn't capitalist but is social or relational activity. This is the community economy. It holds all productive activities and social relations that the capitalist economy is built on and that are necessary and essential to its operation. At the same time, the capitalist economy denies this (inter-) dependence with the community economy. The keystone of Gibson-Graham's post-capitalist politics is to make explicit this implicit or effaced interdependence on social relations, thereby, resocialising commerce. It is "a counter-hegemonic project of 'differently politicising' the economy" (2006, p. 84). And it seeks to action this community economy to enact a more just society cognisant of diverse or plural productive activities and social values, beyond the purely monetary.

Gibson-Graham stress that community economy is not an alternative space. Thinking through Nancy entails resisting the desire "to draw on normative ideals of community as fullness and a positivity" (2006, p. 86) exemplified in appeals to the small scale, the self-sufficient, the homegrown, the locally oriented and so on. These appeals recentre "a commonality of being, an ideal of sameness" that serves to supress economic difference: "any ethic of being-in-common, of co-existence with the other, is relegated to a remnant" (2006, p. 86). Gibson-Graham value Nancy's thinking as it establishes an understanding of community not as a pregiven entity, an already-specified content, form, function or quality, but as an ethical and political space of decision-making. Community then is a site of potential insofar as "the multiple possibilities that emerge from the inessential commonality of negotiating our own implication in the existence of others" gives way to "the becoming of new and as-yet unthought ways of being" (Gibson-Graham 2006, p. 88). Given Kershaw's foregrounding of the close relationship between cultural and economic production, it seems appropriate to explore the role of arts and culture in relation to the community economy.

Providing a Research Context for 'Community'

An extensive discourse critiquing community has arisen since identification of the crisis of community in postmodernism. The term has gone from being 'warm and fuzzy' to 'overtly negative' (Kuppers 2007a, p. 9). Community has been dismissed as nostalgia for a more 'organic, traditional and ascriptive' past way of life (Mackay 2006, p. 6) and, relatedly, as a romantic project that has been captured by mainstream governmentality (Joseph 2002; McAvinchey 2013). The exclusionary propensity of community, after Young (1990), has been replayed (Nicholson 2005), as has its tendency to impose uniformity of identity on subaltern or hybrid subjectivities (Nicholson 2005).

Performance scholars are, justifiably, wary of uncritical notions of 'community'. Mackey and Whybrow, for instance, in a special issue of *Research in Drama Education: Journal of Applied Theatre and Performance*, claim that the association between site, place and applied theatre "has, perhaps in its refraction through notions of 'community', sometimes suffered from being seen critically to be allied with nostalgic and teleological impulses" (2007, p. 1). Noting that there is a broad spectrum of applied theatre work, they point to one in which "Effectively, […] the work aspires to […] the establishment or cementing of a given collective identity or community-belonging", and assert that it is in relation to this type of practice that, rightly or wrongly,

> the charge of an implicit paradigm of nostalgia has been brought: the practices concerned are supposedly intent primarily on establishing the sense of an integrated, homogenous identity within a targeted host community, and therefore guilty of imposing a form of misconceived idealism or limitation. (2007, p. 2)

Such valid criticisms of uncritical, 'nostalgic' or 'romantic' notions of community raise immediate and urgent questions centred on how we might write and talk critically about community performance practice today.

At the same time, there is reluctance to abandon the term 'community'. Rose, after Williams, notes that "community" remains one of the "most powerful terms through which collective identity can be named and collective action legitimated" (in Rose 1997, p. 185). Delanty notes that "virtually every term in social science is contested, and if we reject the term *community* we will have to replace it with another term" (2003, p. 2; original emphasis). He argues:

> Community is relevant today because, on the one side, the fragmentation of society has provoked a worldwide search for community, and on the other, […] cultural developments and global forms of communication have facilitated the construction of community. (p. 193)

Martin Mulligan, an Australian sociologist based at RMIT's Globalism Institute, leads on from Delanty to assert that community is both "aspirational and contestable", and that, as something imagined, constructed and negotiated, the arts have a significant role to play in creating community (2013, p. 105). Mulligan's more recent writing on community is underpinned by research commissioned by public and third-sector/charity bodies investigating CCD practice in Australia in connection with public health and wellbeing (Mulligan et al. 2006) and in supporting the operations of local governance (Mulligan and Smith 2010). As part of this analysis, he has developed an enhanced analytical framework for understanding communities as "grounded", "way-of-life" and "projected" (Mulligan et al. 2006). According to this schema, a projected community represents "neither embeddedness in particularistic relations nor adherence to a particular way of life, but rather the active establishment of a creative space in which individuals engage in an open-ended process of constructing, deconstructing and reconstructing identities and ethics for living" (Mulligan et al. 2006, p. 18). The notion of projected community is very similar to Rose's notion of community as 'enacted'. So it is that, in addition to perhaps more traditional ways of understanding community as geographically located (grounded) or based on shared identities and interests (way of life), there is now a third way.

Nancy's widely influential re-signification of community has been both a point for criticism of community and participatory arts practice (see Kwon 2002; Bishop 2012)[6] and a point for developing an enhanced understanding of the politics and ethics of community performance practice, as distinct from the model of marginalised 'communities' articulating an oppositional world view in resistance to the powerful (Rose 1997, p. 201; see Kuppers' (2007b) exploration, informed by Nancy (2000), of the 'singular plural co-essence of being' in an ongoing community performance project, called *The Olimpias*). Given the rapid emergence of the field of applied theatre and the tendency, perhaps, towards uncritical or nostalgic notions of community-based practice within it, there is an urgent need to re-examine sites, contexts, methods and processes of community theatre and performance practice after Nancy's and others' critical theories of community linked to "negotiating and exploring interdependence rather than attempting to realise an ideal" (Gibson-Graham 2006, p. 86). In the following chapter (Chap. 2), I unearth and trace a similarly dynamic notion of community in and across community cultural practices. For the purposes of

[6] Both Bishop and Kwon draw on Nancy's notion of inoperative community to critique community and participatory arts practices. In her analysis of participatory art, Bishop is critical of work that attempts to create 'community'. Bishop wields Nancy's notion of inoperative community rather bluntly to argue that community is a defunct concept and to reinforce her argument that the role of art in society is to produce aesthetic critique rather than alternative spaces of social conviviality. Kwon draws on Nancy to argue that community is impossible to define in any operative sense and is, therefore, best avoided. Community artists could too easily find themselves agents of political (left/right) propaganda or government welfare. Kwon cautions artists to maintain a critical distance from community. Instead, she proposes the collective projective enterprise, which "involves a provisional group, produced as a function of specific circumstances instigated by an artist and /or cultural institution, aware of the effects of these circumstances on the very conditions of the interaction, performing its own coming together and coming apart as a necessarily incomplete modelling or working out of a collective social process" (2002, p. 154).

this book, this overall need for re-examination might resolve itself into two leading questions:

1. How is 'community' enacted in community theatre and performance practices?
2. How might the critical re-signification of community as enacted contribute to the praxis of community theatre and performance?

References

Adams, D and Goldbard, A. (2001) *Creative Community: The Art of Cultural Development*. New York: Rockefeller Foundation.

———. (eds.) (2002) *Community, Culture and Globalisation*. New York: Rockefeller Foundation.

Baudrillard, J. (1994) *Simulacra and Simulation*. Ann Arbor: The University of Michigan Press.

Bishop, C. (2012) *Artificial Hells: Participatory Art and the Politics of Spectatorship*. London: Verso.

Bond S. (2011) 'Being in Myth and Community: Resistance, Lived Existence, and Democracy in a North England Mill Town', *Environment and Planning D: Society and Space* 29 (5), pp. 780–802.

Cohen-Cruz, J. (2005) *Local Acts. Community-based Performance in the United States*. New Brunswick, N.J. and London: Rutgers University Press.

Cohen-Cruz, J. and Van Erven, E. (2013) 'A Field Ready To Leave Home: Notes from the ICAF Seminar' in Van Erven, E. (ed.) *Community, Art, Power. Essays from ICAF 2011*. Rotterdam: Rotterdams Wijktheater, pp. 140–180.

———. (2009) *Engaging Performance. Theatre as Call and Response*. London; New York: Routledge.

Delanty, G. (2003) *Community*. London and New York: Routledge.

Gibson-Graham, J.K. (2006) *A Postcapitalist Politics*. Minneapolis: University of Minnesota Press.

Grace, V. (2000) *Baudrillard's Challenge. A Feminist Reading*. London; New York: Routledge.

Greenan, R. (2007) 'Windale's sorry street label a sticking point', *The Newcastle Herald*, 3 March, p. 19.

Haedicke, S and Nellhaus, T. (eds.) (2001) *Performing Democracy. International Perspectives on Urban Community-based Performance*. Ann Arbor: University of Michigan Press.

Jameson, F. (1991) *Postmodernism, or, the Cultural Logic of Late Capitalism*. Durham, NC: Duke University Press.

Joseph, M. (2002) *Against the Romance of Community*. Minneapolis: University of Minnesota Press.

Joyce, B. (2017) *Stories from Community Cultural Development, apocryphal or emblematic? Mining the Seams of Personal Practice*. MPhil Dissertation, University of Newcastle, NSW.

Kelly, O. (1984) *Community, Art, and the State: Storming the Citadels*. London: Comedia.

Kershaw, B. (1992) *The Politics of Performance. Radical Theatre as Cultural Intervention*. London and New York: Routledge.

———. (1999) *The Radical in Performance: Between Brecht and Baudrillard*. London and New York: Routledge.

Kuftinec, S. (2003) *Staging America. Cornerstone and Community-based Theatre*. Carbondale: Southern Illinois University Press.

Kuppers, P. (2007a) *Community Performance. An Introduction*. London and New York: Routledge.

———. (2007b) 'Community Arts Practices: Improvising Being Together', in Kuppers, P and Robertson, G. *Community Performance Reader*. London and New York: Routledge, pp. 34–47.

Kwon, M. (2002) *One Place After Another: Site Specific Art and Locational Identity* Massachussetts: MIT Press.

Lyotard, J-F. (1984) *The Postmodern Condition*. Manchester: Manchester University Press.

Mackey, S. (2006) 'Community. Performance Related Fray', *Performance Research*, 11(3), pp. 25–29.

Mackey, S and Whybrow, N. (2007) 'Taking Place: Some Reflections on Site, Performance and Community', *Research in Drama Education*, 12(1), pp. 1–14.

Mayo, M. (2000) *Cultures, Communities, Identities*. London: Palgrave Macmillan.

McAvinchey, C. (2013) *Performance and Community: Commentary and Case Studies*. London: Bloomsbury.

McConachie, B. (1998) 'Approaching the 'Structure of Feeling' in Grassroots Theatre', *Theater Topics* 8 (1), pp. 33–53.

Mee, K and Watt, D. (2007) *Windale 2036*. Australian Research Council Discovery grant application.

Mills, D. and Brown, P. (2004) *Art and wellbeing: a guide to the connections between community cultural development and health, ecologically sustainable development, public housing and place, rural revitalisation, community strengthening, active citizenship, social inclusion and cultural diversity*. Surry Hills, NSW: Australia Council.

Mulligan, M. (2013) 'Thinking of Community as an Aspirational and Contestable Idea: A Role for the Arts in Creating Community', *Journal of Arts & Communities*, 5(2/3), pp. 105–118.

Mulligan, M., Humphery, K., James, P., Scanlon, C., Smith P. and Welch, N. (2006) *Creating Community: Celebrations, Arts and Wellbeing Within and Across Local Communities*. Melbourne: VicHealth and Globalism Research Centre.

Mulligan, M. and Smith, P. (2010) *Art, Governance and the Turn to Community: Putting Art at the Heart of Local Government*. Globalism Research Centre, RMIT University. Available at: http://mams.rmit.edu.au/fc1d0uu0zhpm1.pdf, (Accessed 12 July 2015).

Nancy, J-L. (1991a) *The Inoperative Community*. Minneapolis: University of Minnesota Press

———. (1991b) 'Of being-in-common', in Miami Theatre Collective (ed.) *Community at Loose Ends*. Minneapolis: University of Minnesota Press, pp. 1–12.

———. (2000) *Being Singular Plural*. Redwood City, California: Stanford University Press.

Nicholson, H. (2005) *Applied Drama and the Gift of Theatre*. Basingstoke: Palgrave Macmillan.

O'Neill, P. (2007) 'Rocked by resort to pilloried postcodes' *The Newcastle Herald*, 12 March, p. 9

Pitts, G. (2003) *Public Art Public Housing*, North Richmond Community Health Centre, Cultural Development Network (Victoria), and Neighbourhood Renewal, Department of Human Services.

Rose, G. (1997) 'Performing Inoperative Community. The Space and Resistance of Some Community Arts Projects' in Pile, S. and Keith, M. (Eds.) *Geographies of Resistance*. London and New York: Routledge, pp. 184–202.

Schaefer, K and Watt, D. (2006) 'Nobbys Newcastle. Place, History, Heritage, Identity and Performance', in McAuley, G. (Ed.) *Unstable ground. Performance and the politics of place*. Brussels: Peter Lang, pp. 125–148.

———. (2007) 'Not Going Quietly. The Royal on the Move Procession', *About Performance* 7, pp. 117–131.

Schaefer, K. (2009) 'The Birabahn/Threlkeld project: place, history, memory, performance and coexistence,' in Haedicke, S., Heddon, D., Oz, A. and Westlake. E.J. (Eds.) *Political Performances: Theory and Practice*. Amsterdam; New York, NY: Rodopi, 2009, pp. 311–330.

The Shelton Trust (1986) *Culture and democracy. The Manifesto*. London: Comedia.

Van Den Abbeele, G. (1991) 'Introduction', in The Miami Theory Collective (ed.) *Community at loose Ends*. Minneapolis: University of Minnesota Press, pp. ix–xxvi.

Van Erven, E. (2001) *Community Theatre. Global Perspectives*. London: Routledge.

Vinson, T. (2004) *Community Adversity and Resilience: The distribution of social disadvantage in Victoria and New South Wales and the mediating role of social cohesion*. Richmond: Jesuit Social Services.

Watt, D. (1991) 'Interrogating 'Community': Social Welfare Versus Cultural Democracy', in Binns, V. (Ed.) *Community and the arts: History, Theory, Practice: Australian Perspectives*. Leichhardt, NSW: Pluto Press, pp. 55–66.

———. (2009) 'Local Knowledges, Memories, and Community: From Oral History to Performance', in Haedicke, S., Heddon, D., Oz, A. and Westlake. E.J. (Eds.) *Political Performances: Theory and Practice*. Amsterdam; New York, NY: Rodopi, 2009, pp. 189–212.

Welch, R. and Panelli, R. (2007) 'Questioning Community as a Collective Antidote to Fear: Jean-Luc Nancy's 'Singularity' and 'Being Singular Plural'', *Area*, 39(3), pp. 349–356.

Windale: A work in progress. (2006) Background Briefing, Australian Broadcasting Corporation (ABC) Radio National, 4 Jun. Available at: https://www.abc.net.au/radionational/programs/backgroundbriefing/windale-a-work-in-progress/3325628 (Accessed: 17 May 2020).

Wright, P and D. Palmer. (2007) *People Now Know Me for Something Positive. An Evaluation of Big hART's Work at the John Northcott Estate*. Murdoch university. Available at: https://researchrepository.murdoch.edu.au/id/eprint/2908/1/People_now_know_me_for.pdf (Accessed: 17 June 2019).

Young, I.M. (1990) *Justice and the Politics of Difference*. Princeton, N.J.: Princeton University Press.

CHAPTER 2

Historical and Theoretical Perspectives on Community Performance

Introduction

Theatre and Performance Studies academics tend to agree that community-based theatre and performance is a contemporary practice, even if some practices are 'invented traditions' (Kuppers 2007, p. 20). Van Erven identifies the more immediate forerunners of community theatre as, "the various forms of counter-cultural, radical, anti- and postcolonial, educational and liberational theatres of the 1960s and 1970s" (2001, p. 1). He asserts that "improvisation-based, collectively oriented" theatre practices emerged initially (as *creación colectiva*) in South America in the early 1960s before similar practices developed independently on each continent (2001, p. 2). Kuppers specifically locates community performance in relation to the countermovements that emerged in twentieth- and twenty-first-century art (2007, p. 16). She engages multiple historical narratives connecting community performance to folk culture revivals and avant-garde, 'everyday', animator and 'service-based' art movements (2007, p. 16).

Kershaw has identified a risk in pinpointing too specific an origin in his work on the alternative and community theatre movement in the UK (1960s–1990s). In particular, he notes that accounts that privilege the 'myth of 1968' (see, for instance, Itzen 1980)—"the idea that the alternative theatre movement was born out of the great social and political upheavals of 1968" (1991, p.70)—speak more to attempts to establish authority (based on 'being there, then') in the process of constructing a new cultural elite. Adopting Sandy Craig's (1980) circumspection, Kershaw asserts that the 'myth of 68' has tended to exclude exploration of historical continuities and broader social-cultural reconstruction of alternative theatres (1991, p. 71). His own account of the British alternative and community theatre movement is set within the post-war period and draws on Raymond Williams' notion of 'the long revolution' (1961) to denote a set of wider political (democratic) and sociocultural formations that follow on from the Industrial Revolution in that specific period (1991, p. 71). I will return to this point, because I want to locate what Milner refers to as Williams' cultural materialist 'research project' (2002, p. 148)—it is more searching than doctrinal—as central to development of theories of community performance practice.

In terms of the spatiality of community performance, Van Erven (2001), Kuppers (2007) and Cohen-Cruz and Van Erven (2013) document and analyse transnational, or global, domains of practice. Kershaw's account of the alternative and community theatre movement in the UK argued that its efficacy lay in generating oppositional popular culture as (a small) part of a diffuse international countercultural movement. Recent historiographies of US community-based theatre and performance characterise the practice as 'local acts' (Cohen-Cruz 2005) intentionally crafted in the wake of the national civil rights movement. These 'local acts', according to Kuftinec (2003), participate in re-imaging the 'imagined community' that is the nation (Anderson 1983) from the grassroots, decentring representations of national (US) identity in the process of staging it. Mapping long antecedents of community-based theatre and performance, Cohen-Cruz (2005, p. 9) reminds us that, in the settler colonial nation, First Nations performance precedes community-based performance, while Kuftinec points to modes of performance (civic pageantry) that sought to assimilate new immigrants into quite restrictive, and even coercive, modes of citizenship (2003, p. 30). Recently, Kershaw (2016) attempted to suture disrupted histories of applied theatre (after community theatre) in the UK and community-based performance (after grassroots theatre) in the US by coining the expanded term, applied theatre and community performance. This transcontinental connection adds another dimension to the spatial contours of community performance from the local, or grassroots, to the national, and the transnational, or global.

Reconstruction of transcontinental (UK/US) continuities emphasises the alternative (counter)cultural formation in which community and grassroots theatres emerged and from which subsequent iterations of applied theatre and community-based performance practices 'expectably' diverged (Kershaw 2016, p. 16). This construction tends to downplay the complexity of community performance as government funded or as work (arts working). While the beginnings of community arts in Britain, Europe (the Netherlands), the US and Australia may have been rooted in a countercultural milieu, the development of practices has been, as Heddon and Milling assert, "largely underpinned by government funding through Arts Councils and other national funding agencies" (2006, p. 133). Jeffers and Moriarty's multi-voiced history of community and participatory arts in the UK similarly narrows its frame of overview of the "long and varied roots of community arts" to "the beginnings of the development of formal ties between the arts and the state" in mid-nineteenth-century Britain (i.e. within welfare reform in the Victorian era) (2017, p. 11). Gibson pinpoints mid-nineteenth-century British and Australian government support for arts programmes in terms of a concern for "the utility of art in 'civilising' a [working class] population" (2001, p. 33). This has, as all four authors note (excluding Gibson for a moment), set up a struggle between forces for the democratisation of arts and culture—"an improving, but limited, conception of community arts" which nevertheless earned the sector government funding in the 1970s (Heddon and Milling 2006, p. 133)—and forces for 'cultural democracy', a concern for people to have opportunities to produce their own art, not simply as artefacts but as active, living or ordinary cultures (see Jeffers and Moriarty 2017, p. 57). This right to 'freely participate in the cultural life of the community' is recognised in Article 27 of the Universal Declaration of Human Rights (1948).[1] Cultural policy studies analysts, such as Gibson, for whom there is no outside the text of Foucauldian governmentality, tend to view tensions as a struggle between economic (creative industries) and social (cultural development) forces within cultural policymaking.

Itzen has noted that community theatre practitioners identified themselves (through The Association of Community Theatres, TACT) as distinct from members of the Workers' Theatre Movement of the 1930s, constituted by collectives made up of mainly unemployed workers "who wanted to use their self-acquired performing skills in the struggle for socialism" (1980, p. 177). Community theatres of the 1970s were founded by "professionals" with "formal theatre training" who "aimed to make a living from the work" while actively contributing to the "the larger class struggle" by "means of changing dominant concepts of culture" (Itzen 1980, p. 176). Already in this characterisation of the practice, it is possible to see the construction of community theatre as work (arts working) *and* as part of the struggle for 'cultural democracy' and democratic cultural policy, debates which will be detailed below. In the US in the 1970s, Don Adams and Arlene Goldbard turned a public art programme to employ artists to engage in neighbourhood renewal projects (reminiscent of the Federal Theatre Project of the Great Depression era) into an ongoing concern for 'cultural democracy' and community cultural development that subsequently attracted philanthropic funding (see Adams and Goldbard 2001, 2002; Goldbard 2006). Such contextual complexity (and contradiction) is deeply embedded in community performance practice and best examined in the specific case studies of practice that follow this chapter.

In this chapter, I examine the (contested) concept of community that underpins an ecology of theatre and performance practices variously known as community theatre, community-based theatre, community-based performance, community performance, community arts, community cultural development and/or community arts and cultural development. Rather than provide a history or historiography of community(-based) theatre or performance,[2] I aim to

[1] https://www.un.org/sites/un2.un.org/files/udhr.pdf
[2] There are a number of extant texts that already offer histories or historiographies of community-based practices, and I draw on them here. Sonja Kuftinec's *Staging America: Cornerstone and Community-based Theatre* (2003) offers 'historiographic perspectives' on the community-based theatre in the US, although, as she says, she is more interested in how Cornerstone's community-based theatre practice stages the nation (from local, grassroots) than with archiving the theatre

trace and interweave theories (theoretical debates) underpinning the emergence and, in some cases, disappearance (see Kershaw 2016) of this theatre and performance practice since the 1960s. As already indicated in the Introduction (Chap 1), the focus of this book is on the period post-2000, questioning the thesis of fragmentation of the alternative and community theatre movement given the purported incorporation of countercultural opposition within postmodernism, and the conceptual hollowing out of community with the poststructuralist critique of the self-identical subject and celebration of difference. In this chapter, I question how the term 'community' has been defined, debated and developed in reference to theorising community performance. I am ready to admit that it may be a fool's errand to attempt to 'pin down' terms as weedy as culture and as notoriously vague as community, yet I am interested in the concept of cultural community *and* in how performance practices enact or negotiate community (see Kuftinec 2003, pp. 10–11). Moreover, as Watt (1991) has noted in relation to an instance of misappropriation and redirection of 'community theatre' (see below), it is important to outline critical histories and theories of community and theatre/performance given contemporary relevance in practical[3] and policy[4] contexts.

As stated, I aim to link the development of thinking and writing about community performance with the post-war British intellectual formation of 'left culturalism' as it evolved, especially via the work of Thompson on 'class' and Williams on 'culture'. The term 'culture' is a "linguistic weed" (Hartman in Milner 2002, p.11), and Milner himself has observed that the notion of 'class' has "suffered a strange death" (Milner 1999, p. 109). Yet these terms have a wide application in the discussion of the alternative and community theatre movement, since much literature on community theatre, community-based

---

form (p. 24). Her historiographic perspectives track the evolution of community-based theatre across Progressivism and Pageantry (civic theatre) in the early twentieth century; Representation and Grassroots Theatre; Socialism, Identify Politics and Community Specific Theatres; and Radical Coalition Building and the American Festival Project (pp. 26–40). Jan Cohen-Cruz's *Local Acts: Community-based Performance in the United States* (2005) similarly traces the 'early antecedents' of community-based performance into a movement in the 1970s from which the field of community-based performance emerged in the post–civil rights era of the 1980s. Jeffers and Moriarty's edited collection, *Culture, Democracy and the Right to Make Art: The British Community Arts Movement* (2017), offers multiple historical perspectives on the British community and participatory arts movement. This text augments Kate Crehan's history of formative community arts organisation, Free Form, in *Community Art: An Anthropological Perspective* (2011). I'd also add Alan Filewod's *Committing Theatre: Theatre Radicalism and Political Intervention in Canada* (2011) to this list, although the Canadian terminology tends to be 'popular theatre' so as not to confuse the practice with amateur theatre, which is known as community theatre across North America (hence the US term, 'community-based').

[3] See, for instance, the reconnection of Applied Theatre and Community Performance (Kershaw 2016) or the International Community Arts Festival https://www.icafrotterdam.com/

[4] See, for instance, see, the notion of 'cultural community' in Arts Council England's Let's Create strategy, 2020–2030: https://www.artscouncil.org.uk/publication/our-strategy-2020-2030

performance and community arts makes reference to the work of E.P. Thompson and Williams. From this intellectual formation, in which class is the central point of social difference, develops 'cultural materialism' as an ongoing research programme (tied today, perhaps, to anti- or alt-globalisation (Milner 2002, 180)). Cultural materialism was the background against which an understanding of community theatre emerged and evolved. I refer to four key moments in this process: Owen Kelly's (1984) theorisation of community in community arts after the (left) culturalist notion of class; Kershaw's discussion of the alternative and community theatre movement in the UK using the concepts of ideology and hegemony to articulate the generation of oppositional popular culture as part of a broad countercultural movement; Hawkins' and Watt's conflicted discussion of community arts/community cultural development in Australia as democratic cultural policy (Hawkins), and dynamic community and cultural democracy (Watt); and the intervention of McConnachie who contests Kershaw's approach that identifies ideological transaction as central to community theatre, bringing instead the notion of 'structure of feeling' (from Williams) to explain the central dynamics of community in grassroots theatre in the US. These four points take theorising up to 1998 and into 2001 with the reproduction of McConnachie's text in Haedicke and Nellhaus' *Performing Democracy: International Perspectives On Urban Community-Based Performance* (2001). In the postscript to this chapter, I briefly outline the post-2001 scene of community performance. Year 2001 was a watershed year for community performance in terms of new literatures produced and a new international organisational formation. Now, however, I turn to explicate concepts of class, culture, power and community, and examine how these concepts participate in configuring theories of community performance.

The 'Cultural Turn': Left Culturalism and Class

'Culturalism' is a term used to characterise the 'cultural turn' taken by British (Marxist) historians, literary and cultural theorists, in particular Thompson (1963) and Williams (1958, 1961). Taken together, their writings in the 1950s and 1960s comprise a radical intellectual formation with a shared, central focus on "social class ...[as] the central marker of what we have since come to know as 'difference'" (Milner 1999, p. 108). The intellectual formation is shaped by two key features: the first is a "'classist' critique of the unitary conception of culture" inherited from the English (Cambridge University-based) literary critic, F.R. Leavis (Milner 1999, p. 108), and the second is a shift towards "a 'culturalist' understanding of class as constituted pre-eminently in class consciousness" (Milner 1999, p. 111). These early British cultural studies theorists were critical of purportedly 'objective' notions of class reduced to a 'category' or 'structure' (Milner 1999, p. 111) (over)determined by an economic base, namely the means and relations of production. For Thompson (1963), the making of the English working class is a historical, active, relational and conscious process. Class consciousness formed dynamically as "experience of the

Industrial revolution as it was lived by different working groups" (Storey 2012, p. 49) clashed with and was mediated by extant "political and cultural traditions" (p. 49) drawn on to navigate determining conditions (see Milner 1999, p. 111). Acknowledging limiting structures, Thompson stresses experience and agency in the growth of class consciousness:

> class happens when some men [*sic*], as a result of common experiences (inherited or shared), feel and articulate the identity of their interests as between themselves, and as against other men (sic) whose interests are different from (and usually opposed to) theirs'. (in Storey 2012, 49)

Class is, for Thompson then, "a social and cultural formation, arising from processes which can be studied as they work themselves out over a considerable historical period" (in Storey 2012, p. 49). While Thompson's notion of class consciousness, the translation of un/common experience into a social and cultural formation, is focused on the past and offers "a history [of English working classes] from below" (Storey 2012, p. 50), it also provides a conceptual touchstone for defining more contemporary notions of cultural community and for articulating the work of generating community through cultural practice (see Kelly, Hawkins and Watt, below).

While Thompson conceptualised class as "a cultural process as much an as economic phenomenon" (Milner 2002, p. 54), Raymond Williams developed a broad-based 'analysis of culture' (Storey 2012, p. 44), and within that analysis he identified the significant role of dominant class-based interests in shaping cultural production, dissemination and consumption. Williams' thinking was influenced by the then dominant approach to literature studies at Cambridge University led by F.R. and Queenie Leavis in the tradition of Matthew Arnold. This approach articulated culture in terms of a 'Great Tradition', a canon of literary works held by an educated minority to be a store of universal value and authority. Knowledge of this literary culture marked the bounds of enlightened civilisation and its other/s (such as 'mass' democracy, which would be associated with cultural decline or degradation, or anarchy). Williams did not directly critique Leavis' thinking but, rather, developed an expanded analysis which included a contrasting, socially active definition of culture.

According to Williams, cultural traditions, including Leavis' 'Great Tradition', select certain elements from the cultural record and elevate these as a 'selective tradition', one that is nevertheless institutionally validated (legitimated) and held to be universally applicable. A selective tradition, according to Williams, is linked to "the dominant or hegemonic culture" as "an intentionally selective version of a shaping past and a pre-shaped present, which is then powerfully operative in the process of social and cultural definition and identification" (Williams in Milner 2002, p. 90). In *Culture and Society*, Williams analysed the extent to which cultural production and consumption are influenced by the social relations of production. He distinguishes between middle-class culture as 'individualist' and working-class culture as 'collectivist', or 'social'. As Milner notes, "this argument led directly to [Williams'] defence of the 'collective democratic institution' as the central 'creative achievement' of working-class culture" (2002, p. 111). Taken more expansively, it suggests that culture is much broader than works of art or literature, and can be social institutions, social relations or sets of practices. Negatively, it suggests that there are two oppositional or binary cultures, which is a more static rendering of cultural process than elsewhere in Williams' work, and also ties common culture to (one specific) working-class culture. Watt (below) picks this apart in articulating the difference between community cultural practice as cultural democracy distinct from (pseudo-) social work. In fact, with the term 'structure of feeling', Williams invents terminology to describe how new social formations might emerge from within the whole of actual or lived experience. Milner states that with the concept of "structures of feeling" Williams identifies forms of cultural pre-emergence which foreshadow challenges to dominant or residual cultural formations. In other words, structure of feeling identifies "those particular elements within the more general culture which most actively anticipate subsequent mutations in the general culture itself; in short, they are quite specifically counter-hegemonic" (Milner 2002, p. 94). Bruce McConnachie (below) deploys this term to describe the centrality of a sense of community in grassroots theatre practice.

In the end, Williams does make a definitive break with Leavis when, according to Storey, he "insists on culture as a definition of the 'lived experience' of 'ordinary' men and women, made in their daily interaction with the texts and practices of everyday life" (Storey 2012, p. 48). Williams' conception of culture as ordinary and as 'a particular way of life' presses the case for a "democratic definition of culture" (Storey 2012, p. 48). According to Milner, "Williams relocates the common culture from the idealised past it had occupied in Leavis to the not too distant, still to be made, democratically socialist future" (2002, p. 125). These notions of class and culture, developed in the 1950s and 1960s in advance of cultural studies, play a key role in the articulation of cultural community and community-based cultural practices.

From a Culturalist Notion of Class Towards a Notion of Dynamic Community

A direct line from a culturalist notion of class to a culturalist notion of community was drawn by British community artist, Owen Kelly, in *Community Art and the State: Storming the Citadels* (1984). Kelly is a central yet contentious figure within British community arts because he was highly critical of the way the movement pragmatically engaged with government funding for community arts (community arts was initially funded for a short period by the Arts Council of Great Britain after the Baldry report, 1974). Kelly argued that with the introduction of government funding for community arts, community artists lost control of their movement and it was gradually redirected away from questioning "the role of art in society, and the relationship between cultural and political struggle" (1984, p. 14) and towards alignment with state (professional) social welfare services. Kelly's argument has been contested (Crehan 2011) and elaborated in broader context (Jeffers and Moriarty 2017). I am placing Kelly here as a touchstone that provides a link between culturalist notions of class and community. Kelly forwarded this idea of community in the second half of his polemical text in outlining a renewed political programme for community art. That programme did not come to fruition, partly because it wasn't popular amongst a majority of community artists (Jeffers and Moriarty 2017, pp. 59–60; p. 137) and, mainly, because the Thatcher government's reorientation of cultural policy towards economic outcomes favoured more commercial and entrepreneurial arts/cultural enterprises (see Crehan 2011, pp. 85–86). Community artists working with urban working-class constituencies found it difficult to secure a niche in this corporate-sponsored, major arts institution-centred, mega popular (bums on seats) cultural events space. It wasn't until the election of New Labour in 1997 and another reorientation of cultural policy that community and participatory arts again found space in which to flourish.

In a statement that resounds with Thompson's notion of class as historical, active, conscious and relational, Kelly states:

> The kind of community to which I am referring … is an active and self-conscious process. For a group of people to be defined as this kind of living community it is not sufficient that they live, work and play in geographical proximity; nor that to an observer they have habits, goals and achievements in common…it is also necessary that the members of a community acknowledge their membership and that this acknowledgment plays a recognised part in shaping their actions.…Community then is not an entity, nor even an abstraction, but a set of shared social meanings which are constantly created and mutated through the actions and interactions of its members, and through their interactions with wider society. (1984, pp. 49–50)

Heddon and Milling have pointed out similarities between this "dynamic model of community-consciousness" (2006, p. 131) and the process of conscientisation—a socially oriented, problem-posing approach to critical processing of lived experience—central to Freirean pedagogy that underpins educational drama (and applied theatre). Kelly suggests a dialogical edge to community insofar as "the process of communication is in fact the process of community – … the offering, reception and comparison of new meanings, leading to the tensions and achievements of growth and change" (1984, p. 50). Most importantly, for Kelly, however, is that community is a dynamic process: "community grows as its members participate in, and shape its growth and it grows because of its members' participation" (1984, p. 50). It is, in other words, not set in the past (in traditional ways of life) but is future oriented insofar as the community produced by "a group of people engaged in a process of collective creativity" is a "goal, a target, rather than a starting point"… [it is what] "a group is working towards; that is, what community a group is participating in bringing into being" (Kelly 1984, p. 51).

I will pick up this notion of dynamic cultural community again, directly, in reference to debates within Australian community cultural development. Now I want to move on to how culturalist notions of class and community have been seeded in understandings of the alternative and community theatre movement after Kershaw (1991, 1992). This cultural interventionist model of practice, in which theatre professionals actively constructed communities as non-traditional theatre audiences for their work, may not seem to share much in common with Kelly's idea of dynamic cultural community. However, Kershaw's characterisation of alternative and community theatre as interventionist is, at the same time, heavily reliant on processes of constructing symbolic 'community' and negotiating ideological meaning and cultural participation to co-produce oppositional popular culture.

COMMUNITY THEATRE AS AN 'IDEOLOGICAL TRANSACTION' BETWEEN A THEATRE COMPANY AND THE COMMUNITY OF ITS AUDIENCE

Kershaw's *The Politics of Performance: Radical Theatre as Cultural Intervention* (1992) was developed from his two-volume PhD Thesis, *Theatre and Community: Alternative and Community Theatre in Britain 1960–1985. An investigation into cultural history and performance efficacy* (1991). Although it drops the word 'community' from its title, the book follows the PhD in examining community theatre as part of the radical theatre project that was, itself, a small contributing part of the international countercultural movement of the latter half of the 20th century (1992, pp. 32–36). Community theatre was at its peak in terms of the number of identified companies and their geographical reach in the mid-1970s, acccording to Kershsaw (1991, p. 205). In returning to this body of work, I wish to focus on the symbolic construction of community that theatre companies engaged in as they intervened in social spaces, constructed audiences from communities of location and/or interest, and opened participatory processes of theatre-making with the aim to challenge the status quo through direct opposition or subversive acts.

Kershaw seems to imply that the move outside of traditional theatre spaces by practitioners was not necessarily an explicitly political rejection of the capitalist 'culture industry' after, for instance, Adorno and Horkheimer (1944/2002). While noting that "cultural institutions and products are clearly central to the maintenance of ideology" (1991, p. 16), Kershaw simultaneously asserted that culture, including theatre and performance, is "frequently the locus for ideological struggle in society" (p. 16). His thesis was that in actively seeking out new, non-traditional contexts for performance as "opportunities to relate to a widening spectrum of different types of community", professionally trained theatre practitioners were engaged in a larger ideological and counter-hegemonic cultural project, contributing to the generation of an "oppositional popular culture" (1991, p. 13).

Central to Kershaw's analysis of how alternative and community theatre generated not just theatre but counterculture are the concepts of ideology *and* hegemony (1991, p. 15), making his analysis typical of British cultural studies. The concept of 'ideology' derives from French philosopher Althusser's radically structuralist reading of Marxist theory. He postulated that the social formation is an assemblage of the economic, the political and the ideological. Political and ideological systems are subordinate to the dominant economic system, in the capitalist mode of production. Ideology operates on the level of human *consciousness*, interpellating concrete individuals into subjects of the system. In other words, while individuals have a stake in the system, the system also produces an overarching set of ideas that accommodate subjects to their structural economic subjugation. Kershaw avoids the over-determinism of Althusser's structuralist position by drawing on post-structuralist theory and the perspective that there is not a single, dominant social order but a set of dominant ideologies that tend to be mutually reinforcing (1991, p. 15).

The other important concept here is hegemony, which comes from the work of Italian Marxist philosopher and activist, Antonio Gramsci. Milner argues that Gramsci's theory of hegemony presented the

> possibility of a mid-way position, somewhere between class practice Marxism and ruling ideas Marxism where working class consciousness could be analysed as neither necessarily virtuously heroic nor necessarily hopelessly duped. (Milner 2002, p. 49)

Gramsci's thinking, according to Milner, managed to break down the distinction between structuralist notions of ideology over culturalist conceptions of experience:

> The term hegemony denoted those processes by which a system of values and beliefs supportive of the existing ruling class permeates the whole of society. Hegemony is thus a value consensus, very often embodied in common sense, but constructed, nonetheless, in the interests of the dominant class. ... At the same time, hegemony as culture is a matter for political and moral contestation. Hegemony is never in principle either uncontested or absolute, but is only ever an unstable equilibrium, ultimately open to challenge by alternative social forces. (Milner 2002, pp. 49–50)

Kershaw offered a sophisticated analysis of alternative and community theatre, one based on marrying cultural materialist and post-structuralist notions of culture as experience and agency with a vision of culture as a set of structures legitimating class power, exerted via mutually reinforcing ideologies. For Kershaw, the 'status quo' tends to operate as commonsensical and natural, but it is also open to contestation, opposition, subversion and change, with cultural practice as a site of potential ideological opposition to that status quo (1991, p. 24).

This is where the term 'community' becomes critical. Deferring from an earlier formulation of community theatre that drew on Victor Turner's notion of 'communitas' to argue that community theatre restored social and relational bonds in an increasingly fractured post-modern Europe,[5] Kershaw defined community after an alternative theorisation also from within symbolic anthropology. Anthony P. Cohen (1985) argued that community (he is critical of Turner's notion of *communitas* as a unifying identificatory process, see p. 55–56) is an experiential phenomenon that is constituted in social interaction via management of symbolic boundaries "people construct community symbolically, making it a resource and repository of meaning, and a reference of their identity" (p. 118). Kershaw therefore viewed community as something of a "conceptual lynchpin", marking the interactive space between everyday lived and felt experience, and larger more abstract social structures. He argued that community theatre creates a space of ideological transaction—a space of symbolic exchange of meaning and values—between a theatre company and the community of their audience, typically defined by location or identity/interest. Bringing together a 'symbolic' repertoire drawing on theatrical and social conventions, Kershaw asserts that theatre companies devised

> complex theatrical methods in order to circumvent outright rejection and to establish ideological negotiations in the most unpromising environments. … The whole panoply of performance came into play as part of the negotiation, and all aspects of performance were subject to radical experiment. (Kershaw 1991, p. 13)

After cultural intervention and community construction, participation was a key element:

> If identification allows the company to become a part of the community, participation may validate its questioning of the community's ideological identity. The former is the foundation, the latter the main building material, for the structure of performance efficacy. (Kershaw 1991, p. 516)

Kershaw appeals to the notion of counterculture to hold together the cultural politics of community theatre. It is notable that in this account of community

---

[5] Kershaw's notion of community as an interactive social space contrasts with an earlier notion of community presented at the 1983 Theatre and Communities/Council of Europe Workshop, organised by Peter Hulton and Alan Read, and held in the Department of Theatre, at Dartington College of the Arts, Devon, in April 1983. The Workshop plenary concluded its enquiry into the "contribution theatre practice can make to the welfare of the community in which it occurs" with the observation that "theatre practice clearly has something valuable to contribute to the continuous regeneration of the spirit of community" in the context of modern European society subject to processes of fragmentation (5 and 6, Working Papers No.16 http://spa.exeter.ac.uk/drama/eda/documents/europe.pdf).

theatre as cultural process class is already decentred. It is not the primary point of social difference, and community theatre is not concerned, primarily, with the cultural politics of working-class 'solidarity'. Community theatre is theorised with an awareness of the 'new social movements' and 'the cultural effects of other kinds of cultural difference' (sex/gender/sexuality, race, ethnicity, age). The notion of counterculture designates a socially diffuse formation whose central ideological premise is opposition to hegemony by a utopian idealism.

Theorising Community Arts in Australia: Nostalgia, Cultural Activism and Democratic Cultural Policy

In their study of the British community arts movement, Jeffers and Moriarty (2017) argue that it is "necessary to distinguish" community arts and community theatre "as separate entities" (p. 23). They argue for this differentiation on the basis that, firstly, community artists "saw themselves as part of a national movement" in a way that makers of alternative (including community) theatre did not and, secondly, because "although theatre… played an important role" within the cross-art form that was community arts, it "was more often the innovative combinations of performance and visual arts … that provided the distinguishing hallmark of community arts" (p. 23). In the section above, I have referred to community theatre as part of the alternative theatre movement, which was nonetheless influenced by the simultaneously occurring community arts movement, particularly in the development of participatory modes of cultural practice for *and* with communities (see Kershaw after Khan 1992). Nonetheless, there is a lack of distinction between these fields of cultural practice in Australia and elsewhere. Moreover, however separate or contentious in their own context, concepts and practices elaborated within the British community arts movement have been adapted and debated within a local Australian context, and that has flowed back into definitions of community devising (see, for instance, Heddon and Milling 2006, pp. 131–132).

In her oft-cited book, *From Nimbin to Mardi Gras: Constructing Community Arts*, Hawkins asserts that the concept of community arts is an "official invention" (1993, p. 18) defined by governmental discourse disputing the consensus at the time (see Binns 1991) that community arts was "part of a long history of radical cultural activism" (1993, p. 18).[6] She labels such thinking "left romanticism" because it tends to underplay the significant involvement of government patronage in constructing the field of community arts. For Hawkins, there was only one way to read community arts in Australia, and that was "as one of several movements towards more democratic cultural policy"

---

[6] Hawkins' analysis of community arts is contained within a critique of Australian cultural studies that attempts to anchor the 'undiscipline' of Cultural Studies to the 'real world' via a focus on cultural policy (culture and governance). This subfield of 'cultural policy studies' is associated with the work of Tony Bennett (and others) at Griffith University.

(p. 22). This was to take issue with both 'nostalgic' and 'activist' discourses of community arts (p. 19).

Sociologist Gerard Delanty observes that "the discourse of community has been dominated by a narrative of loss and recovery", based on the persuasive notion that "modernity destroys community which must be recovered and realised in a new form" (2003, p. 25). Hawkins points to this discursive strain in some versions of community arts, where the invocation of community depends on an analysis of modernity as the loss of an idealised, past way of life which artists seek to re-create:

> People have lost their essential creativity, intimacy with neighbours, traditional symbols and sense of long-term origins and objectives. All these losses are expressed as components of the traditional community which can be recovered and re-established via new forms of artistic practice. (2003, p. 20)

Activist discourses of community arts are, she grants, more critically sophisticated than this. Grounded in "the radical welfare (community development) movements of the late 1960s and early 1970s", the activist discourse of community arts emphasises the powerful potential of "associational life" and "the struggle for the decentralisation of power (from the centralised/centralising state) and self-determination" (1993, p. 20). According to Hawkins, British community artist and polemicist, Owen Kelly, best articulates this thesis when he asserts that "community ... understood as shared activities and goals" acts as a bulwark against

> the domination of the centralised state ... [which] constitutes one of the major obstacles to achieving the kind of democratic and equitable access to the means of cultural production which community artists have claimed as their ultimate aim. (Kelly 1984, p. 49, cited in Hawkins 1993, p. 20)

According to Hawkins, this activist thesis advances a notion of community as

> not something to be magically recovered, but a goal to be struggled for. It is not something to be manufactured by outside professionals but emerges out of collaboration and shared commitment and expression. (1993, p. 20)

She notes, further, that this definition of community is not fixed according to geographical location (or any other essentialist categories); it is, in fact, 'dynamic' allowing for "the idea of communities of interest" (1993, p. 20). While pointing to potential in cultural activist discourses of community, Hawkins cuts off this possibility. Instead, she returns to a local (national) debate concerning the tendency of left-wing theorists in Australian cultural studies to uncritically celebrate postcolonial and nationalist popular culture as a form of political opposition (to a dominant colonial, i.e. British culture). Drawing on Bennett's criticism of a romantic notion of 'popular culture' as "the emergent cultures of oppressed groups or classes" characterised as "inherently oppositional" and as "active cultural expression rather than passive cultural consumption" (Bennett in Hawkins 1993, p. 100), Hawkins asserts that advocacy for community arts as cultural activism tends to be in just this vein. She cautions against accounts of community arts which would uncritically celebrate and romanticise community arts as oppressed, working-class/ordinary people consciously making their own popular and oppositional culture, rather than consuming high art or mass/commercial culture (US popular culture ranks with high culture exported from Britain as resistable).

According to Hawkins, community arts are government subsidised art, and need to be critiqued as such. Even as a class-based culture (an oppressed culture producing an oppositional popular culture), a position which she queries, community arts are not morally above critique. Like a lot of cultural studies of the time, Hawkins' analysis aims to move beyond the reductive, binary characterisation of community arts, construed as a type of class-based cultural activism. In so doing, she forecloses prematurely any analysis of community arts as being implicated in hegemonic struggle, preferring to examine its construction in and through governmental cultural policy and funding, and the associated discourse.

While critical of the cultural activism thesis, Hawkins argues that community arts is a democratisation of cultural policy:

> the introduction of notions of access and participation into the objectives of the Australia Council generated a series of tensions about what could be considered a cultural activity, about audiences whose interests were not acknowledged in existing funding practices, about different discourses of value and different methods for disbursing grants. (1993, p. 23)

Within this cultural policy context, the profound ambiguity of the term 'community' acted not as a euphemism for fantastical notions of 'ordinary' people or working-class collectivity and solidarity, but "to claim a new concern within arts funding for all those previously unrepresented 'others'". The community arts programme, according to Hawkins,

> generated a proliferation of new constituencies; it fostered a pluralism that not only fractured the illusion of a singular public for the arts but also eventually forced a recognition of cultural difference. (1993, p. 23)

Community in this cultural policy context implied not a common working-class struggle, but difference, in terms of constituencies traditionally excluded from arts funding, and plurality. Here again, class is not the only marker of social difference (as with Kershaw), and 'community' cannot be used in a monolithic sense to describe a single (working) class-based culture.

In the end, Hawkins' evaluation of the Community Arts Programme, from its inception in 1973 to the end of the study timeframe in 1991,[7] including an extended analysis of community arts practices, reaches ambiguous and contradictory conclusions. On the one hand, Hawkins claims that the community arts programme led to a more equitable arts funding landscape producing "methods and rationales for disbursing grants that are more democratic than the search for excellence" (1993, p. 167). Furthermore, Hawkins views the community arts programme as producing a shift from a concern with access and participation, based on a deficit model of cultural participation in which non-participation in public arts provision is construed as cultural lack, towards recognition of cultural difference and plurality. In other words, the programme is "a significant example of the value of cultural participation as a resource for the expression and affirmation of social difference" (1993, p. 167). In this vein, Hawkins acknowledges that community artists developed a "significant body of skills in facilitating collaborative cultural production", including capabilities "to express plural authorship, to establish democratic mechanisms for skilled and unskilled creatives to work together, and to collapse the social distance between producers and consumers" (1993, p. 159).

On the other hand, Hawkins contends that community arts have been overly concerned with "political process and community development" at the cost of developing a "dynamic aesthetic able to explore and critique the nature of the social order" (1993, p. 164). This evaluation insists that community arts are good at building community and bad at making art, and is based on the tendency towards producing didactic art in opposition to both high art *and* commercial mass production. Following the emerging "cultural industries approach", which attends to the central place of cultural consumption in people's everyday lives, Hawkins concludes that community arts is "a cultural programme whose moment has passed" (1993, p. 166), within a larger argument for a radical overhaul of cultural policy, itself, aimed at dislodging art as a separate realm distinct from the diverse cultures of everyday (popular) consumption. According to Hawkins, community arts' inability to shake off notions of cultural disadvantage (known as the deficit model), evident in its limited aesthetic as a didactic form opposed to experimentation and mass-produced commercial culture, implicitly affirms the hegemony of high culture (1993, pp. 166–167).

While the limitations of this position in exploring the dynamic creation of community that community arts practise so well are evident, Hawkins was one of the few cultural (policy) studies theorists to analyse practice, and I shall be drawing on her work to assess the 'affirmative aesthetics' of practices in some of the following case study chapters (see Chap. 3).

---

[7] In 1987, the Community Arts Board was reformed as the Community Cultural Development (CCD) Committee.

Theorising Community Arts in Australia (Part 2): Dynamic Community and Cultural Democracy

In his all-inclusive history of Australian theatre since the 1950s, Geoff Milne asserts that while "it is true that the term 'community arts' gained currency through its official usage at Australia Council level", some elements of community theatre preceded the Australia Council's 'invention' and these "were undoubtedly politically influenced in their incubation (if not altogether in their creation) and in their practice, much of which was left leaning" (2004, p. 220).

He outlines developments using a 'wave' metaphor. Community theatre emerged in the second wave (1966–1981) from a debate concerning 'cultural democracy' and the 'democratisation of the arts', in which the former prevailed with the addition of the Community Arts and Development Committee to the Australia Council's arts boards in 1973. Milne characterises community theatre practice of the second wave in terms of three broad categories: (1) radical and political action, (2) participation and local response, and (3) social amelioration and social welfare via Community Youth Support Schemes.

Community theatre in Milne's third wave (1981–1999) grew buoyed by a decision to redistribute funding away from the professional mainstream state theatres to the robust alternative—small to medium scale—sector. The important Art and Working Life programme was established in this period. But the move to apply a funding ceiling on state theatres was strenuously contested. In the following backlash, the mainstream sector harnessed its political influence and power to force policy reversals that saw the controversial return of key criteria of excellence and professionalism (2004, p. 335). By the end of the 1990s, only ten identifiably community theatre companies were left standing. Death Defying Theatre reinvented itself at Urban Theatre Projects in the western suburbs of Sydney (see van Erven's analysis of the company 2001, pp. 206–242), so proving itself, perhaps, more nimble than Street Arts, established in 1982 in West End, Brisbane, which collapsed in 1991 (Artistic Director Pauline Peel's principles of CCD practice—in Pitts and Watt (2001)—are applied in Chap. 4). Nevertheless, during this time—in the late 1980s and early 1990s—there was a noticeable shift, observed by Watt and Milne after him, from a 'theatre of disadvantage' in which cultural and/or social disadvantage played a key role in definition, to a 'theatre of difference' which moved towards more specifically defined notions of cultural difference, as in the work of Doppia Teatro, and Kooemba Jdarra, multicultural and Indigenous theatres. This was a shift away from deficit model of culture towards recognition of cultural difference and diversity.

The return of dominant values of excellence and professionalism towards the end of the third wave of Australian theatre, and an attempt at appropriation of 'community' by a mainstream company, led Watt to elaborate the notion of community as cultural democracy in community arts. As he explained, there had been little urgency to define community while the development of community arts in Australia was "oddly and inextricably linked with the government agencies which funded it" (1991, p. 55). Watt was prompted to outline the critical project of community arts practice drawing on seminal texts from the UK community arts movement, namely Owen Kelly's *Community, Art and The State: Storming the Citadels* (1984) and Shelton Trust's *Culture and Democracy: The Manifesto* (1986).[8] He viewed the theoretical explication of community in community arts practice as a "bulwark against both marginalisation as social work and against a similarly dangerous appropriation…[by] bastion[s] of the dominant culture" (1991, p. 56). He asserted that this exercise remained strategically useful as long as 'community' remained a key term in a funding category within the Australia Council for the Arts. Watt's essay is valuable because it unpacked the longer British intellectual tradition that informed Kelly's critical account of the British community arts movement and was implicit in Shelton Trust's manifesto. Watt showed how community arts criticism draws on this tradition while adapting and updating aspects of it.

Watt aimed to differentiate between community arts as cultural democracy and social welfare, and argued that the notion of a dynamic community was central to articulating the difference between community arts as social change or as an instrumental tool of social policy. Watt contended that the notion of 'community' that, according to Kelly, the collective working methods of community artists sought to create as "a target or goal, rather than a starting point" (1984, p. 51) owed much to E.P. Thompson's 'culturalist' (historical, conscious, active, relational) notion of class. As Kelly had stated:

> [f]or a group of people to be defined as [a] living community it is not sufficient that they live, work and play in geographical proximity; nor that to an observer they have habits, goals and achievements in common … it is also necessary that members of a community acknowledge their membership, and that this acknowledgement plays a recognised part in shaping their actions. … Community grows as its members participate in, and shape, its growth; and it grows because of its member's participation. (Kelly 1984, pp. 49–50)

In his turn, Watt noted the dynamism in this understanding of community:

> the interactions within a group of people who choose to see themselves as a community continually alters the nature of that community so that it is always in a state of becoming and therefore growing and thus avoids the stasis of a 'thing' to be serviced. (1991, p. 61)

While the notion of a dynamic community closed down the problem of breadth of meaning that left community open to misdescription and appropriation, it did not fully resolve the problematic elision of community with nation and

---

[8] The Shelton Trust was a national organisation formed after the Association of Community Artists, the representative body of community artists, went regional. Shelton Trust became the organisation responsible for national conferences and a magazine publication, *Another Standard*, in which this manifesto was published. A member of The Shelton Trust collective, Owen Kelly continues to lead discussions on cultural democracy in a podcast series made with Sophie Hope: https://miaaw.net/

state (1991, p. 62). It was this problem that had led Raymond Williams to argue that 'community' was a dangerous term.

Watt asserted that the Shelton Trust *Manifesto* was an attempt to avoid these conundrums of 'community' by clarifying the rhetoric of community arts via a new set of terms, revolving around the notion of cultural democracy. Watt termed the manifesto 'post-Gramscian', because central to it was Gramsci's notion of cultural hegemony, understood as a 'common sense' consensus reinforcing the domination of a ruling class. Cultural hegemony was now operating within the system of late capitalism, which was concerned with "a method of ordering consciousness necessary to ever increasing production" and, in the process, with "opening up distances between people then described as natural" (1991, p. 62). Watt locates cultural democracy as a critical point in breaking down these distances via participation in the production of culture, and thus of social meaning. Cultural activism can therefore be explained as a project of countering the hegemony of dominant cultural practices which render people passive consumers of an imposed cultural commodity: "work on the cultural front serves to replace an imposed monolithic culture with cultures which emerge from communities of people, and reflect democratic modes of social relations" (1991, p. 63). Watt believed that the notion of dynamic community within a struggle for cultural democracy over cultural hegemony was essential and necessary to understanding community cultural practices:

> Static notions of community are seen as impositions, usually categorisations by a dominant culture concerned to maintain itself as monolithic by exercising its power to define and thus subsume subgroups. Dynamic notions of community, on the other hand, allow the creation of purposive communities of interest which, by the process of self-definition, resist being thus subsumed ... this autonomy introduces the possibility of internal negotiation as a basic mode of social interaction, and they are consequently potentially democratic and alterable. The commitment to democracy as a principle is then seen as leading to the possibility of broad alliances between autonomous groups working to undermine the dominant culture through an insistence on common access to the processes of creating meaning and value within the culture. (1991, p. 64)

Watt's analysis goes a long way towards articulating a theoretical understanding of community arts, including theatre. While this analysis had moved away from Williams' 'culturalist' analysis of class-based social relationship, it remained within his broader cultural materialist project which was, according to Milner, "essentially politico-institutional" and concerned primarily with how to "create and strengthen the institutions of political, economic and cultural democracy" (2002, p. 179). It marked a difference from Kershaw, since there was less emphasis on theatre company and community as separate entities, engaged in an ideological transaction between company and community and the broader society. For Kershaw, this generation of popular oppositional culture is contained within a countercultural movement. Watt focused more on dynamic cultural-social alliances that might form and that were more broadly counter-hegemonic, replacing an imposed, monolithic culture. Watt tied the concept of a dynamic community to cultural democracy as part of socialist, participatory democracy.

Grassroots Theatre in the US: From 'Ideological Transaction' to a 'Structure of Feeling'

The appropriation of community arts by the dominant culture as the former emerged to challenge aesthetic legitimation and cultural formation was an issue across the board—in the UK, Australia and the US. In the US, the threat of cultural appropriation prompted a re-evaluation of grassroots or community-based theatre through a conference organised by the Theatre Arts Department at Cornell University in association with leading theatre organisations, Roadside Theatre (Dudley Cocke) and Junebug Productions (John O'Neal). Roadside Theatre was formed in 1975 as a wing of the media organisation Appalshop established in 1969 in Whitesburg, Kentucky, as a War on Poverty/Office of Economic Opportunity Job Training (filmmaking) programme. Junebug Productions was established in 1980 by John O'Neal as he started on a solo performance project after the closure of the Free Southern Theater (FST), of which O'Neal was a co-founder. Based in the American South, FST (est. 1963) had been at the forefront of the Black Theatre Movement closely aligned to the Civil Rights Movement. At the same time, as the national progressive social movements of the 1960s/1970s waned and fragmented, O'Neal staged a jazz funeral in New Orleans for the FTS (a 'valediction without mourning') simultaneous with a conference to formally recognise the founding of Junebug Productions, whose mission remains "to create and support artistic works that question and confront inequitable conditions that have historically impacted the Black community" (https://www.junebugproductions.org/our-mission). A key challenge issued by O'Neal at the time was to how to regenerate the activist energies of the national progressive movements in local contexts. In giving "local direction to the next phase of arts and activism" (Cohen-Cruz 2005, p. 61), arts activism was simultaneously marked by building regional and national coalitions of localised practices. In 1976, Alternate ROOTS was founded as a regional arts service organisation (Regional Organisation of Theatres of the South) "to support the creation and presentation of original art that is rooted in community, place, tradition or spirit" and "to champion social and economic justice and the work of people in our field" (https://alternateroots.org/about-us/). In the 1980s, following the example of Alt ROOTS, Roadside and Junebug began to develop the blueprint for a national support organisation, the American Festival Project, to promote a platform for exchange between grassroots or community-based theatres through artist residencies and partnerships.

At Cornell in 1993, a range of practitioners came together to review histories and reassert the principles of grassroots theatre, given that:

> as non-grassroots theaters are becoming more threatened economically and more isolated socially, they ... are becoming attracted to the grassroots theater's promise of relevance and connection. Already some basic ideas of grassroots theater, such as empowerment and commitment to community, have found their way into the rest of the theater world, so far as little more than rhetoric. (Cocke et al. 1993, p. 11)

The group produced a book, *From the Ground U Grassroots Theatre in Historical and Contemporary Perspective*, offering "A Matrix Articulating the Principles of Grassroots Theater" to strengthen the practice from encroachment and potential competition from "organisations that have no grassroots history and only a professed commitment to it" (1993, p. 11). They also wanted to assert the terminology of 'grassroots' over 'community-based' due to the latter term's lack of specificity. Retaining the term 'grassroots', the group aimed "to preserve and express the values of those without privilege". It was argued that "to describe that kind of theatre as 'community-based', when the term can just as easily describe a theater with values and goals in opposition to it seems limiting" (1993, p. 13). Grassroots theatre located itself in opposition to a culture which was losing its fixed, locational anchor. In that sense, it was running counter to the general culture of displacement, by propagating bottom-up grassroots cultures, trying to stop the hollowing out of authentic organic cultures by top-down mass, postmodern culture. What was known and defended as grassroots theatre in 1993 was displaced by what became known and contested as community-based theatre and performance (Haedicke and Nellhaus 2001; Kuftinec 2003; Cohen-Cruz 2005). North American theatre professor and practitioner, Bruce McConnachie's (1998) intervention could be considered to have resolved this debate with his thesis that the structure of feeling in grassroots theatre is a sense of community.

McConnachie problematised Kershaw's notion of community-based, grassroots theatre as an "ideological transaction between a company of performers and the community of their audience" (1998, p. 33). Questioning the shared assumption that ideological meaning-making is that which is primarily at stake in community theatre, McConnachie reached instead for Raymond Williams' concept of a 'structure of feeling' as an emergent formation within a dynamic cultural system (dominant, residual and emergent cultural formations). His assertion was that a "structure of feeling" would characterise the central dynamics of this multi-principled kind of theatre, "the processes and products of ...[which] are built on a strong alliance (and, at times, a complete merging) of theatre workers with a local 'community'" (1998, p. 37). His critical intervention came after facilitating a community-based theatre production, assisted by Roadside theatre artists (including Dudley Cocke and Robbie McAuley, an African American artist/co-director), with University theatre students from

William and Mary College, and residents of Williamsburg (living in neighbourhoods local to William and Mary College). *Walk Together Children* (1996), the two-hour production resulting from an intensive process of local history research and community engagement, examined race relations in Williamsburg, Virginia, from the late 1950s through the 1960s as the southern US shifted from legal segregation to desegregation. Central to the production were the oral histories of local residents gathered and presented by students, supported by the theatre/education team. As McConnachie explained, the performance-making process involved intense ideological debate as a result of his decision to employ cross-racial casting. While his decisions were prompted by 'artistic' and 'democratic' demands, McConnachie noted that he was concerned to press an ideological and political point casting across race in order to "complicate the local (and national) understanding of race, to recognise it as lived experience but also as a social construction" (1998, p. 46). McConnachie wanted, as he claimed, to get beyond "identity politics along conventional racial lines by recognising that such social designations were fluid" (1998, p. 46).

Despite ideological debate within the ensemble during the process, as the 'politics of representation' was contested and questioned as a form of cultural 'appropriation', McConnachie found that community reception of and response to the piece glossed over these more ideological and political aspects of the performance. McConnachie argued that ideological meaning-making, the "mutual making of meaning" (1998, p. 34), was secondary to a more "general emotional response" to the predominantly oral narratives ('the well told tale'):

> instead of focusing on the meanings and ideological implications of our show ('the politics of representation or appropriation') most of the community spectators [the primary participants] … spoke of the visual and aural images that had given them pleasure… the talk was of images formed through judgment and feeling, and only secondarily of meanings. (1998, p. 33)

Structure of feeling is a central theoretical concept in Williams' work, and one that evolves with 'cultural materialist' project. McConnachie worked with the earlier versions of the concept describing 'structure of feeling' after Williams as "the emotional bonding generated by values and practices shared by a specific group, class, or culture" (1998, p. 64). The concept included ideology, in the sense of an articulated structure of beliefs, but also ranged beyond it to encompass collective desires and concerns below the conscious level. The term suggested both the rich images that spark immediate 'feelings' from audience members and the underlying 'structures' that generate these images. Structure of feeling is that "most difficult thing to get hold of", insofar as it is "this felt sense of the quality of life at a particular place and time: a sense of the ways in which the particular activities combined into a way of thinking and living", as Milner describes it (2002, p. 72). It is from this totality of whole lived experience that the artist draws: "it is in art, primarily, that the effect of the totality, the dominant structure of feeling is expressed and embodied" (2002, p. 71). In his reflections, McConnachie identified the dominant structure of feeling in grassroots theatre as a desire for community. He emphasised the close relationship of identification between grassroots theatres and community, and how they work together to imagine and construct community. McConnachie stressed orality—the 'well told tale'—in the process of imagining and creating a sense of community. In arguing that the structure of feeling in grassroots theatre is community dynamics, McConnachie took grassroots theatre from a search for indigenous roots to an imagined future projection based on ethical relations:

> Community-based theatre, then, is less about representing the realities of actual or historic communities—although markers of these realities need to be present to 'authenticate' the experience—and more about imagining and constructing the relationships of an ethical community for the future. (1998, pp. 40–41)

Conclusions on Pre-millennial Community Performance

Up to this point in the chapter, I've explored different but at times closely related interpretations of a range of community-based practices advanced in Britain, the US and Australia, and situated these in relation to theories of class-based power and culture, discussing concepts of ideology, hegemony and structure of feeling. While Hawkins restricts community arts to a programme of democratisation of cultural policy, Watt (after Kelly) asserts that community cultural development practices assist in the creation of dynamic communities capable of deepening and extending democratic practices through interactive participation in the production of social meaning and value. For Kershaw, community theatre is brought into being by a theatre company that constructs a community as its audience and engages in an active negotiation of social meaning and cultural participation leading to the generation of popular counterculture. Finally, for McConnachie, dynamic community formation is the dominant structure of feeling in grassroots theatre; this taps into affective and ethical (relational) constructions of imagined community, and is connected to "shaping a more inclusive and equitable democratic process, particularly at the local level" (1998, p. 41). Up to this point in the chapter, it has been argued that by 2000 there were sophisticated theories of community theatre connected to a coherent and consistent theoretical framework of cultural materialism. Well before 2000, theatre academics were already exploring how 'culturalist' and symbolically constructed notions of community were being creatively enacted and how collective cultures could be constructed, or facilitated, beyond (yet not excluding) the confines of class. In the following, final part of the chapter, I briefly outline how theorisations of community performance have developed since 2001.

Postscript 2001: An Ongoing Odyssey

Year 2001 was something of a watershed year insofar as it surfaced publications offering international perspectives on community theatre or community-based performance: Susan Haedicke and Tobin Nellhaus' *Performing Democracy: International Perspectives on Urban Community-based Performance* (2001) and Eugene van Erven's *Community Theatre: Global Perspectives* (2001). Haedicke and Nellhaus' text documented what was clearly an international field of 'local acts' and reproduced McConnachie's article bringing his definition of an affective practice that augments inclusive local democracy forward into the new millennium, prefiguring later critical developments as will be discussed in more detail below. Van Erven explored the international field of community(-based) theatre through six case studies based in the Philippines, the Netherlands, the US, Costa Rica, Kenya and Australia. He documented processes of collaborative devising or improvisation—also on video (with assistance from Rob Prosser)—and analysed each theatrical process in its social and cultural context. Following Said's and Bharucha's criticisms of certain uneven tendencies in postcolonial and intercultural performance studies, Van Erven suggests that community performance analysis focuses on more immediate issues including how community-oriented aesthetic practices struggle to negotiate state (funding) policies aimed at creating social (ethnic) cohesion (see 2001, pp. 246–248). Van Erven identifies Cohen's notion of symbolically constructed community as a key definition of community theatre establishing continuity with Kershaw (1991/1992). Van Erven states that community is concerned with "the way people imagine or psycho-culturally experience and interpret their community" alongside "multiple, constantly changing factors that figure in [that process of] construction" (social differences), including "locality, race formation, class fraction, caste, faith, gender, generation, and nation" (2001, p. 256).

Year 2001 also saw the publication of a number of texts on community cultural development theory and practice articulated independently in Australia and the US: Pitts and Watt's *The Imaginary Conference* (2001), Jon Hawkes' *The Fourth Pillar of Sustainability: Culture's Essential Role in Public Planning* (2001), and Don Adams and Arlene Goldbard's *Creative Community: The Art of Cultural Development* (2001). In Australia, community cultural development (formerly community arts and now community arts and cultural development) has been, and continues to be, continuously supported by Federal government through the Australia Council for the Arts. In the US, Adams and Goldbard (2001, 2002), and now Goldbard (2006), led the development of this practice which Cohen-Cruz (2005) has recognised as critical in the formation of the field of community-based performance practice. CCD practice in Australia and the US parallels development of 'community and participatory arts' (Jeffers and Moriarty 2017) in the UK, which "did much to shape the [cultural] policy agenda that takes access and participation seriously today" (O'Brien 2013, p. 41).

In addition to these local and international studies of community(-based) performance and arts practices, the year 2001 also saw the founding of the International Community Theatre Festival by Rotterdams Wijktheater (RWT) as part of Rotterdam's appointment as 'Cultural Capital of Europe'. In 2010, van Erven assumed the role of artistic director of the International Community Arts Festival (its name changed to this in 2008) after the retirement of Peter van den Hurk as artistic director of RWT, the theatre organisation that continues to curate the festival.[9] *Community, Art, Power* (2013b) presents a range of reflections on work performed and/or workshopped at the 2011 festival, including edited transcripts of seminars discussions facilitated by academic-in-residence, Jan Cohen-Cruz (after Liz Lerman's critical response methodology). The event of founding ICAF in 2001 has established the collection of practices variously known as community-based as a vital international field grounded in local cultural contexts and increasingly globally networked. acta Community Theatre (Chap. 3), Big hART (Chap. 4) and Drama Box (Chap. 6) have all participated in the festival; acta has a close relationship with Wijktheater and ICAF; and, in 2021, Drama Box co-hosted a virtual ICAF festival with RWT. In the following sections, in advance of case study chapters on community theatre (Chap. 3), community (arts and) cultural development (Chap. 4), and community-engaged performance or civic practice (Chaps. 5 and 6), I briefly outline key literatures that inform critical discussions of connected practices. A brief overview of applied theatre, which developed in parallel with community-based performance, is included in this overview.

Community Cultural Development

CCD has developed independently in the US and Australia. In Australia, the term was invented by a Federal (Labour) arts minister in an attempt to curtail the political activities of state-subsidised community artists. He proposed that the Australia Council for the Arts restructure the Community Arts Board into the Community Cultural Development Committee. This he thought would shut down the political radicals within the community arts field. While initially resistant to the term, understandably as it anticipated their demise, community artists eventually took ownership of the term and negotiated a greater level of state support and funding for the practice.

---

[9] Three editions of the International Community Theatre Festival were held in Rotterdam—in 2001, 2003, 2005—before the name changed to the International Community Arts Festival (ICAF) for the 2008 edition. Peter van den Hurk, artistic director of Rotterdam's Wijktheater, directed all four festival editions. Eugene van Erven took up the role of artistic director (working closely with producer, Anamaria Cruz) in 2010 and has produced the 2011, 2014 and 2017 festival editions of ICAF (excluding mini-ICAFs and Summer Schools). The 2020 edition of ICAF was cancelled due to the COVID-19 pandemic. See https://www.icafrotterdam.com/about-icaf/our-story

In the US, the term is connected to consultant/activists Don Adams and Arlene Goldbard, who were employed in 1978 by the Neighbourhood Arts Programme National Organising Committee (NAPNOC), to research the outcomes of the Comprehensive Employment and Training Act (CETA), a federal government programme developed during the economic recession of the 1970s to offer employment and training to artists in exchange for public/community service. Adams and Goldbard took direction of NAPNOC in 1979 and turned it into an Alliance for Cultural Democracy, which they felt was a more powerful concept than neighbourhood arts (see Cohen-Cruz 2005, pp. 55–56). They subsequently gained support from the Rockefeller foundation to support CCD. Adams and Goldbard's book, *Creative Community: The Art of Cultural Development*, outlined the US version of the practice. It offered a comprehensive analysis of a field complete with theoretical and historical underpinnings, unifying principles and a matrix of practice. Their 2002 anthology, *Community Culture and Globalisation*, presented CCD case studies from around the world including Australia which they regarded as having "the best -developed apparatus for support of CCD of any nation on earth" (2002, p. 189). Jon Hawkes (2003), former chair of the Community Arts Board, Australia Council for the Arts, articulates a key difference between American and Australian CCD (based on principles articulated in Adam's and Goldbard's 2001 text). He states that the US version of the practice is couched as a professional artistic practice, whereas the Australian version has tended to see CCD as an ongoing process that may be facilitated by a professional artist, but is not dependent on artist intervention (2003, np.).

Pitts and Watt (2001) broached the stages of development of CCD as it was transformed by practitioners from a concern for 'democratisation of the arts' (access and participation) into a concern for "'cultural democracy', which assumes a plurality of cultures and a democratic right that each should be able to be practiced, enjoyed and even supported by funding" (p. 9). Scott Rankin characterises Big hART's practice in terms of this cultural rights-based approach, as will be discussed in Chap. 4. With this fundamental shift towards cultural rights, Pitts and Watt characterise CCD as a form of 'radical welfare' because the practice was more interested in the dynamic creation of community:

> The central function of community cultural development became less the production of "art" and more the consolidation and development of dynamic "communities" as purposive coalitions able to act in their own best interests [...] Thus the aim of a project became not so much the making of "art" as the making and celebrating of "community" through what increasingly came to be called "cultural action": "community" increasingly became less the *object* of projects and more their *goal*. (2001, p. 9)

At the same time, the sector attempted to further decentralise patronage by embedding cultural action within government social welfare agencies and civil society organisations to create an infrastructure to support community-based arts working (including community-led processes in which artists are engaged to enact their visions, rather than the other way around). This notion of CCD is probably best expressed by Jon Hawkes in *The Fourth Pillar of Sustainability: Culture's Essential Role in Public Planning* (2001). Hawkes argued for 'cultural vitality' to be made the fourth pillar of sustainable development, extending the triple baseline of economic, social and environmental factors essential to the sustainable development framework. Pitts and Watt note that these ideas impacted on the nature of practice, shaping "practices as long-term processes requiring the planning of a sequence of overlapping or interlacing projects with a specific set of social goals" (2001, p. 9). This move away from the political or social issue-based play towards extended, iterative processes, with multiple outputs connected to social or civic goals, overlaps with an argument that is being made in relation to cross-sector (arts and non-arts) collaborations, or civic practice (Cohen-Cruz 2015). Chapter 5 explores civic practice through the work of Anne Basting and Sojourn Theatre in partnership with the mixed economy—public and private organisations—responsible for elder care in the city of Milwaukee.

When Kershaw (2016) addresses the issue of how to compose a historiography of the connected yet discontinuous practices of applied/community theatre (UK) and community performance/grassroots theatre (US), I'd suggest that CCD[10] is a third term in that equation. It is notable that formative grassroots theatre organisation, Roadside Theater, has adopted the discourse of CCD within the US field of community-based performance.[11]

Community Performance

In the US, following Haedicke and Nellhaus (2001), Sonja Kuftinec's *Imagining America* (2003) and Jan Cohen-Cruz's *Local Acts* (2005) address the subject of community-based theatre and community-based performance, respectively. Notably these critical texts adopted the terminology of 'community-based'. Cohen-Cruz asserted that "grassroots" was "too redolent of rural models" and reproduced an urban/rural binary. The term 'grassroots' was also seen as too prescriptive insofar as "what is common to the group is at the source of their identity" (Cohen-Cruz 2005, p. 1). For Cohen-Cruz, this excluded other definitions such as Alternate ROOTS' notion of community built on acknowledgement of in/tangible culture: "communities of place, tradition *or* spirit" (in Cohen-Cruz 2005, p. 1). She also problematised Richard

---

[10] Arlene Goldbard and François Matarasso continue discussion on community/participatory arts and CCD praxis in a podcast, A Culture of Possibility: https://arestlessart.com/2021/04/16/funding-community-arts-a-new-episode-of-a-culture-of-possibility-podcast/

[11] See http://roadside.org/topics/community-cultural-development

Owen Geer's sloganistic moniker for community-based performance as of, by and for 'the people'. She noted that it elided the role of practitioner and their relationship to community, which was also problematically characterised as a homogeneous group ('the people'). Pitts and Watt's (2001) reworking of prepositions—in, for, with, of and by—addressed this aspect of power relations between arts worker and 'community' in terms of a spectrum that included artist/playwright *in* residence schemes through to community-led production (see for instance, the case of Craigmillar in Crummy in Jeffers and Moriarty 2017, pp. 83–97).

Both Kuftinec and Cohen-Cruz lay out historiographical narratives in the evolution of community-based theatre and performance. They identify two points as formative in that process. Firstly, fragmentation and/or incorporation of the national civil rights movement led to a reformulation and dispersal of arts activism towards local cultural contexts. John O'Neal's 1985 'valediction without mourning' for the Free Southern Theatre and his search for a different praxis through the creation of Junebug Productions are emblematic of this shift. Secondly, and relatedly, arts activism was reformulated following a shift from identity politics, which intensified as broad-based social movements fractured, to coalition building. Kuftinec recognised that as ever more specific identity groupings were articulated in and through performance, it came to be seen that identity "is not pre-formed but performed"; it is "essential but not essentialist" (2003, p. 37). Against evidence of increasing specificity and decreasing sociopolitical efficacy, Kuftinec draws on bell hook's notion of 'radical postmodern' activism to articulate the revised approach of community-based performance based less on "the performance of a cohesive social subject position or […] prescribed core group unity" and more on the building of empathy—creating ties that will, according to hooks, "promote recognition of common commitments and serve as a basis for solidarity and coalition" (2003, p. 37). From these dual processes—both local/contextual and coalitional—"a renewed vision of community-based theatre and performance emerged as less grounded in assimilated unity, socialism or identity politics and more in strategic bridge building" (Kuftinec 2003, p. 37). Cohen-Cruz asserts that these developments were reflected at a practical level as well as an organisational one. Community-based performance, according to Cohen-Cruz, is "less about homogeneous communities (of place, identity) and more about different participants exploring a common concern together" and negotiating differences via arts-based civic dialogue (2005, p. 3). She draws on the Animating Democracy Institute's definition of community-based performance as "engender[ing] communication around issues that are complex or multidimensional; cross cutting, that is, of concern to multiple stakeholders; and contested by various stakeholders, eliciting multiple and often conflicting perspectives on the issue" (2005, pp. 3–4).

Kuftinec is less interested in defining community, arguing for community-based theatre as a field of practice, or challenging the hierarchies of cultural taste and discrimination that exclude community theatre from a place in US theatre history. After Cohen, she is more concerned with how community is enacted and negotiated as play of identity and difference in theatre practices. She explores the work of community-based company Cornerstone throughout the US (before they settled down in LA) and offers an analysis of how community-based theatre reimagines national (American) identity through local enactments. Cohen-Cruz was concerned to articulate a field of practice that sat within braided understandings of performance studies as between social efficacy (ritual) and aesthetic entertainment (art), closely aligned with 'popular' culture articulated by Williams and Hall and based on practical principles: collective context, reciprocity, hyphenation, process and active culture. As the field of community-based performance was taking shape in the US through the work of Kuftinec (2003) and Cohen-Cruz (2005) and various organisational bodies (Community Arts Network (CAN), Animating Democracy Institute (ADI)) and practical coalitions (Alternate ROOTS in the American South and American Festival Project nationally), the term applied theatre was gaining currency in the UK (see Thompson 2003; Nicholson 2005). I briefly examine that parallel evolution below.

Applied Theatre

Applied theatre, at least the form developed in the UK in the 1990s, evolved, according to James Thompson, "under the combined effect of a harsh funding climate and the post-cold-war impact of postmodernism ... idealism was tempered with a pragmatic search for sites where theatre practice could gain non-arts financial support" (2003, p. xiii). In many ways, applied theatre provided a holding space (at least in academic terms) in which a collection of previously distinct theatre practices could process the socio-economic transformation that had unfixed them (politically and aesthetically). According to Thompson, the capacious umbrella of applied theatre enabled different practices—such as community theatre and theatre for development—to be brought into dialogue with a focus on the 'act of applying', the "mechanics of the process – and not necessarily the specifics of agency or place" (2003, p. 3).

As noted in the Preface, Sally Mackey's work has focused on problematising the notion of community of location that she asserts has sometimes overdetermined concepts of space/place in applied theatre (Mackey 2006). For Mackey, community remains a central concept but the key problem, or paradox, remains how to articulate a notion of community dissociated from physical locus while avoiding the depoliticisation of community reduced to loose social relations and affiliations (2006, p. 26). Nicholson's *Applied Drama: The Gift of Theatre* addresses this problem. She asserts, after Avtar Brah, that the movement of populations across the globe and developments in communication technologies have given rise to diaspora cultures that have "loosened the idea of community from its idealisation as a local and bounded set of practices" (2005, p. 84) and opened the way for community to be conceptualised as "imagined", after Anderson, in and through the dynamic play of identity and difference (as per Kuftinec, above). At the same time, Nicholson creates space for Vered Amit's critique of the deterministic and painful aspects of social processes of indentification and differentiation, which lead her to propose more mundane ways in which community as a sense of belonging can also be forged in and through informal social associations and networks (in Nicholson 2005, p. 86). Speaking (indirectly) to Mackey's concerns, Nicholson suggests that community can be variously imagined and enacted, not least through processes of making theatre. Moreover, her notion of a 'phenomenology of community' reminds us that these theatre-making practices are *embodied* and, therefore, (inter-)actively re-negotiate the social production of historical and other knowledges in the process of being (and working) together with others.

Although applied theatre may have started in mean times (Thatcher government cuts to arts/cultural subsidy came with an economic imperative for arts to be commercially viable), the field of practice grew after New Labour's post-election injection of funding, as did the form's institutional legitimacy with theatre departments established to train students in critical theory and practice. McAvinchey (2013) points to a worrying development in this period of flourishing. Namely, communities were framed by social policy/funding discourses and increasingly came to be defined by external (professional) agents in terms of certain characteristics of social exclusion. In other words, places and people were singled out as exceptional in terms of multiple (economic, social and cultural) deprivation: the deficit model of cultural participation (see Hawkins 1993; O'Brien 2013). At the same time, artists' projects became increasingly subject to measurement according to the impact of practical outcomes on those socio-economic determinants. McAvinchey's (2013) own approach to community and performance, therefore, tends to steer clear of community as concept while excavating the working processes of performance practices set in community contexts, as defined by engaged and embedded practitioners.

Case Studies

These theoretical approaches and debates inform analysis of the case studies that I am now going to present. Primarily, I take into documentation and analysis of community-based performance processes the dynamic notion of embodied community. The case studies that follow will illuminate just some of the possibilities of enacting community in community performance in a variety of different contexts, and provide a detailed examination of specific and distinct—yet connected—practices. The focus in what follows is on documenting creative methods and practices that re-enact community as processes of 'being-in-common' rather than on empirically demonstrating the social effect/s of participation in arts practice (see Van Erven 2013a, pp. 10–15, for broader discussion of these difference approaches to researching community arts and the impossibility of the latter approach).

The methodological approach is, mainly, ethnographic after the mode of rehearsal process analysis pioneered by Gay McAuley (2012). These were not, however, neat (six-week long) professional rehearsal processes in institutional theatre spaces, but long—in some cases, extended over several years—collective devising, improvising and creative development processes that ranged across community and social spaces—including theatre centres—in remote regional towns, as well as in cities. I tried to spend at least two to three weeks intensively immersed in process. Some processes have become more reflexive ethnography than others. I have maintained a close dialogue with acta (Chap. 3), organising community theatre seminars (2015–2016) and a national festival of community theatre (Theatre from the Heart Festival, 2016),[12] and was subsequently invited onto the company's board of trustees (2017 to the present). Similarly, I have followed Drama Box's (Chap. 6) development of the community methodology approach first put into practice in *Ignorland of Its Time* (Chap. 6; see Schaefer forthcoming in 2022). While not quite reflexive ethnography, the work of Big hART (Chap. 4) has served as a model for my own practice-based explorations. Similarly, while practising CCD in Australia it was historical and theoretical narratives of US community-based performance practice that inspired, and I was extremely fortunate to participate in Michael Rohd's Sojourn devising and civic practice training in Washington in the Summer of 2013 before settling on *Islands of Milwaukee* as a case study (Chap. 5).

Taken overall, the case studies offer insight into processes that were a very small part of companies' histories and programmes, and practitioners' ways of working that were developing, at the time. The case studies should not be read, in any way, as exhaustive. They are not definitive of the field or of a practical methodology. I have been more interested, as stated in the preface, to articulate a dynamic notion of community brought through from community arts discourse into contemporary practice and to examine how community is enacted in community performance practices.

References

Adams, D. and Goldbard, A. (eds) (2001) *Creative Community: The Art of Cultural Development*. New York: Rockefeller Foundation.

Adams, D. and Goldbard, A. (eds.) (2002) *Community, Culture and Globalisation*. New York: Rockefeller Foundation. Available at: https://arlenegoldbard.com/essays/books/ (Accessed: 18 July 2019).

Anderson, B. (1983) *Imagined Communities. Reflections on the Origin and Spread of Nationalism*. London: Verso.

Binns, V. (ed.) (1991) *Community and the Arts*. Sydney: Pluto Press.

Cocke, D., Newman, H. and Salmons-Rue, J. (1993) *From The Ground Up, Grassroots Theater in Historical and Contemporary Perspective*. Cornell University: Community Based Arts Project. Available at: https://roadside.org/asset/book-ground-grassroots-theater-historical-contemporary-perspective (Accessed: July 19, 2019).

---

[12] See acta's 'Theatre from the Heart' Festival supported by an AHRC Follow On For Impact and Engagement grant (PI Schaefer, AH/N001230/1) and Arts Council England: https://www.acta-bristol.com/festival-2/

Cohen, A. P. (1985) *The Symbolic Construction of Community*. Chichester: Ellis Horwood Limited and London and New York: Tavistock Publications Limited.
Cohen-Cruz, J. (2005) *Local Acts. Community-based Performance in the United States*. New Brunswick, N.J. and London: Rutgers University Press.
———. (2015) *Remapping Performance. Common Ground, Uncommon Partners*. Basingstoke: Palgrave Macmillan.
Cohen-Cruz, J. and Van Erven, E. (2013) 'A Field Ready to Leave Home. Notes From The ICAF Seminar' in Van Erven, E. (ed) *Community Art Power. Essays from ICAF 2011*. Rotterdam: Rotterdams Wijktheater, pp. 140–80. Available at: https://www.icafrotterdam.com/user_files/ICAF_2011/ICAF-community-art-power.pdf
Craig, S. (1980) *Dreams and Deconstructions: Alternative Theatre in Britain*. Ambergate: Amber Lane Press.
Crehan, K. (2011) *Community Art: An Anthropological Perspective*. London and New York: Berg.
Crummy, A. (2017) in Jeffers, A. and Moriarty, G. (eds.) *Culture, Democracy and the Right to Make Art. The British Community Arts Movement*. London, Oxford, New York, New Delhi, Sydney: Bloomsbury Methuen Drama, pp. 83–97.
Delanty, G. (2003) *Community*. London and New York: Routledge.
Filewod, A. (2011) *Committing Theatre. Theatre Radicalism and Political Intervention in Canada*. Toronto, Ontario: Between the Lines.
Gibson, L. (2001) *The Uses of Art. Constructing Australian Identities*. St Lucia, QLD: University of Queensland Press.
Goldbard, A. (2006) *New Creative Community: The Art of Cultural Development*. New York: New Village Press.
Haedicke, S. and Nellhaus, T. (eds.) (2001) *Performing Democracy. International Perspectives on Urban Community-based Performance*. Ann Arbor: University of Michigan Press.
Hawkes, J. and the Cultural Development Network (VIC). (2001) *The Fourth Pillar of Sustainability: Culture's Essential Role in Public Planning*. Melbourne, VIC: Common Ground.
———. (2003) 'Community Cultural Development according to Adams & Goldbard', *Artwork*, 56. Available at: https://culturaldevelopment.net.au/community/ccd.html (Accessed: June 17 2019).
Hawkins, G. (1993) *From Nimbin to Mardi Gras. Constructing Community Arts*. Sydney: Allen & Unwin.
Heddon, D. and Milling, J. (2006) *Devising Performance. A Critical History*. Basingstoke: Palgrave Macmillan.
Horkheimer, M. and Adorno, T.W. (2002) 'The Culture Industry: Enlightenment as Mass Deception', in Noeri, G. (ed.) *Dialectic of Enlightenment*. Redwood City: Stanford University Press, pp. 94–136. https://doi.org/10.1515/9780804788090-007
Itzen, C. (1980) *Stages In The Revolution. Political Theatre in Britain Since 1968*. London: Methuen.
Jeffers, A. and Moriarty, G. (eds) (2017) *Culture, Democracy and the Right to Make Art, The British Community Arts Movement*. London, Oxford, New York, New Delhi, Sydney: Bloomsbury Methuen Drama.
Kelly, O. (1984) *Community, Art, and the State: Storming the Citadels*. London: Comedia.
Kershaw, B. (1991) *Theatre and Community. Alternative and Community Theatre In Britain: 1960–1985. An Investigation Into Cultural History and Performance*

Efficacy. PhD thesis. University of Exeter. Available at: https://ethos.bl.uk/OrderDetails.do?uin=uk.bl.ethos.280752 (Accessed: 3 June 2017).

———. (1992) *The Politics of Performance. Radical Theatre as Cultural Intervention.* London; New York: Routledge

———. (2016) 'Toward a historiography of the absent: On the late pasts of applied theatre and community performance', in Hughes, J. and Nicholson, H. (eds.) *Critical Perspectives on Applied Theatre.* Cambridge: Cambridge University Press, pp. 15–39. doi:https://doi.org/10.1017/CBO9781107587977.002

Kuftinec, S. (2003) *Staging America. Cornerstone and Community-based Theatre.* Carbondale: Southern Illinois University Press.

Kuppers, P. (2007) *Community Performance. An Introduction.* London; New York: Routledge.

Mackey, S. (2006) 'Community. Performance Related Fray', *Performance Research,* 11(3), pp. 25–29.

McAuley, G. (2012) *Not Magic but Work. An Ethnographic Account of a Rehearsal Process.* Manchester: Manchester University Press.

McAvinchey, C. (ed.) (2013) *Performance and Community: Commentary and Case Studies.* London: Bloomsbury.

McConachie, B. (1998) 'Approaching the "Structure of Feeling" in Grassroots Theatre', *Theater Topics,* 8(1), pp. 33–53.

Milne G. (2004) *Theatre Australia (Un)limited Australian Theatre Since the 1950s.* Amsterdam: Rodopi.

Milner, A. (2002) *Re-Imagining Cultural Studies. The Promise of Cultural Materialism.* London; Thousand Oaks, California; New Delhi: Sage Publications Ltd.

———. (1999) *Class.* London; Thousand Oaks; Delhi: Sage Publications Ltd.

Nicholson, H. (2005) *Applied Drama and the Gift of Theatre.* Basingstoke: Palgrave Macmillan

O'Brien, D. (2013) *Cultural Policy: Management, Value and Modernity in the Creative Industries.* London and New York: Routledge.

Pitts, G. and Watt, D. (2001) 'The Imaginary Conference', *Artwork Magazine,* 50 (August), pp. 7-14. Available at: http://www.ccd.net/pdf/art50_imaginary_conference.pdf (Accessed: 15 May 2015).

Storey, J. (2012) *Cultural Theory and Popular Culture. An Introduction.* 6th edn. Harlow, Essex: Pearson Education Limited.

The Shelton Trust. (1986) *Culture and Democracy. The Manifesto.* London: Comedia.

Thompson, E.P. (1963/2013) *The Making of the English Working Class.* New Edition. London: Penguin Books.

Thompson, J. (2003) *Applied Theatre: Bewilderment and Beyond.* Peter Lang.

Van Erven, E.A.P.B (2001) *Community Theatre. Global Perspectives.* London: Routledge.

———. (2013a) *Community Arts Dialogues.* Utrecht: Treaty of Utrecht.

———. (ed.) (2013b) *Community, Art, Power. Essays from ICAF 2011.* Rotterdam: Rotterdams Wijktheater. Available at: https://www.icafrotterdam.com/user_files/ICAF_2011/ICAF-community-art-power.pdf

Watt, D. (1991) 'Interrogating 'community': Social welfare versus cultural democracy', in Binns, V. (ed.), *Community and the arts: History, theory, practice: Australian perspectives.* Leichhardt, NSW: Pluto Press, pp. 55–66.

Williams, R. (1958) *Culture and Society.* London: Chatto and Windus.

———. (1961). *The Long Revolution.* London: Chatto and Windus.

CHAPTER 3

acta Community Theatre, the 'Cycle of Engagement' and a 'Community of [Theatre] Practice'

INTRODUCTION

On 12 July 2010, I attended the acta Centre in Bedminster, Bristol, to experience a touring production by Rotterdams Wijktheater (RWT). *Hooyo Ma'aan: De dag dat ik vrouw werd* (*The Day I Became A Woman*) was an original performance created and performed by four Somali Dutch women from Rotterdam, facilitated and directed by RWT's Kaat Zjoontens, about the women's lives in the Netherlands and "about the difference between generations, about making choices, about being in love, about female circumcision" (postcard, RWT, 2010). On this evening, I was witness not only to a theatre performance that explored meaningful female/feminist experience but also to a partnership between two European community theatre companies, in which a performance by RWT served to develop new constituencies for acta theatre in Bristol. Members of Bristol's Somali community were invited to be in the audience for *Hooyo Ma'aan* at the acta Centre, and some were subsequently inspired to make their own piece of community theatre.

Some months later, on 26 March 2012, an intergenerational group of seven Somali British women from Bristol premiered *Tahriib Haajiraad* (*Crossing Borders*) at the acta Centre in Bedminster as part of the *COAST* (*Community Oriented Arts and Social Transformation*) festival. The performance focused on intergenerational relationships as Somali British teenagers (school leavers) born and raised in Bristol sought to determine the next steps in their lives. This prompted their parents and elders to reflect on the cultural dislocations of forced migration and to confront intergenerational differences within the diasporic community. The partnership between RWT and acta has served not only to nurture new Somali British constituencies as theatre audiences and theatremakers; it highlights the cycle of engagement central to these European community theatre practices. The initial visit of RWT to acta led to further exchange and to the development of ongoing strands of work produced with and for

© The Author(s), under exclusive license to Springer Nature Switzerland AG 2022
K. Schaefer, *Communities, Performance and Practice*,
https://doi.org/10.1007/978-3-030-95757-5_3

Bristol's Somali constituents (see, for instance, *Yusuf Can't Talk* and Aabe et al. 2019).

This chapter on acta community theatre company is in two parts. In the first part, I explore the practical history and development of the company from its founding in 1985, in a period of 'retrenchment and reorientation' of the alternative and community theatre movement in the UK (Kershaw 1991, 1992), through to acta's articulation of a model of community theatre in the late 1990s (Beddow 2001). The 1990s was a time in which the question of the fragmentation of the alternative and community theatre movement was posed by Kershaw (1991, 1992) after divisions had opened up within the field during the phase of reorientation in the 1980s, revealing differing notions of community (class-based vs community of location), practical methods (conscientising vs cohering) and politics of cultural action (directly oppositional versus subversive). Kershaw's argument for a more expansive understanding of 1980s practice carried on into a rearticulation of alternative and community theatre in the early 1990s as both cultural democracy and community development (1992, pp. 240–242). This debate was somewhat overtaken by the election of a (New) Labour government in 1997, which drew the subject of cultural participation to the forefront of cultural policy *and* harnessed it to the Labour's government's core political concern to address what it termed 'social exclusion'. I carry through the analysis of acta into the 2000s, after the New Labour injection of conditional funding to constitute the participatory arts sector. My account will include when acta gained its own building in Bedminster, Bristol, and founded a productive partnership (and exchange) with RWT, curator of the (then) International Festival of Community Theatre in Rotterdam. Through partnership with RWT, acta introduced touring community theatre as part of a multilayered system of community engagement, known as the 'cycle of engagement'.

In the second part of this chapter, I examine the devising of two community theatre productions: *Gas Girls*, created and performed by a combination of youth theatre, adult and advanced acta participants, and *Ticky Picky Boom Boom*, devised and performed by the acta satellite company, the Malcolm X Elders Theatre Group. I am focusing on these two productions because they both exemplify acta's 'cycle of engagement' within and across different groups of participants and audiences, and because the making of these two productions provides insight into some of the work acta produced over the space of one year (2013–2014). Through the analysis of these two productions, I aim to illustrate how community theatre engages embodied and emplaced (situated) knowledge and experience in the process of making theatre and, simultaneously, establishes a 'community of practice' for which theatre-making is the point of mutual engagement and joint enterprise. This community of (theatre) practice will be demonstrated to be both dynamic and durable.

Defining Community Theatre

Writing on the work of London Bubble (est. 1969), one of a handful of still operational alternative theatre companies formed in the late 1960s, Louise Owen defines the company's practice as community theatre while acknowledging that

> the contours of this domain have been, and continue to be, far from stable. The multiplicity of art-forms, methodologies and political positions falling under the rubric of 'community', all in dialogue with cultural policy changes, have entailed the field's uneven metamorphosis and expansion in Britain since the 1960s. (2013, p. 156)

Reinforcing Owen's observation, the long-term creative director of London Bubble, Jonathan Petherbridge, prefers the term 'vernacular', rather than 'community', to define the company's theatre practice. He regularly adopts the metaphor of the 'Foraging Process' to articulate London Bubble's five-stage theatre-making methodology: foraging, prepping, recipe design/writing, cooking and feasting (in Alston 2015). In doing so, Petherbridge aligns London Bubble's theatre-making process with more informal, everyday or non-industrial processes of cultural production and consumption. I agree with Owen that a notion of community theatre can probably encompass this articulation of a theatre-making practice. At the same time, in this chapter, I aim to present a case study of a theatre company that self-defines as community theatre: acta Community Theatre. Established in the mid-1980s, acta has developed a particular model of community theatre-making and is a leading organisation in the development of inter-national community theatre networks (including, on several occasions, Petherbridge and London Bubble). The company articulated its definition of community theatre in advance of a meeting of European practitioners (Rotterdams Wijktheater, Theatr Grodzki, Bielsko-Biała, and Expedition Metropolis, Berlin) in Bristol in 2012 as part of a two-year EU-funded project, *Community Oriented Arts and Social Transformation* (COAST):

> Community theatre principles are centred on the idea that everybody has a story to tell; that individual life-experiences have a relevance to the rest of society. The methodology of identifying and releasing these stories [varies] …, but in general it involves the interaction between trained professional Community Theatre practitioners – facilitators, writers, directors – and participants who volunteer their time. … The process is usually protracted over a number of months, with regular meetings through which the play is slowly built from the experiences and creative contributions of participant and practitioner. The resulting play is given professional technical support to create a high-quality product. The play is performed by the participants who created it, giving a direct, authentic and natural quality to the performances, which would be difficult to achieve or replicate with professional performers. (2013, pp. 4–5)

THE ACTA MODEL OF COMMUNITY THEATRE, 1985–1999

Avon Community Theatre Agency (acta) was co-founded in 1985 by a collective, including Neil Beddow, who went on to lead the organisation as its Artistic Director from 1989 until his retirement in March 2021. The company takes its name from the non-metropolitan administrative county in the south-west of England, carved out by the path of the River Avon as it flows through Bath and North East Somerset, and parts of South Gloucestershire and North Somerset on its way into the Severn Estuary at Avonmouth, near Bristol.[1] The devolution of funding for educational and community cultural practices in the early 1980s from the national body, the Arts Council of Great Britain, to Regional Arts Associations (RAAs) and Local Government Authorities (LGAs) cemented community theatre practice as part of local or regional ecologies. According to Beddow, the term 'agency' was meant to loosely characterise acta practitioners as 'agents of change' (https://www.acta-bristol.com/neil-blog/). The terminology reveals something of the negotiation taking place between practitioners self-defined as cultural catalysts of social change and a cultural organisational identity pressed into competition with public services for limited (public and charity sector) funding.

There are a number of practical sources leading into the formation of acta. Foremost amongst these is the tradition of theatre in formal and informal educational contexts (TiE and Youth Theatre) that emerged in the UK in an era of post-war reconstruction (see Nicholson in Cohen Cruz 2015, pp. 22–26). Experiments with the large-scale community play format are indebted to revivals of medieval mystery plays in the 1950s, Arden and D'Arcy's community dramas in the 1960s and the community play model popularised by Ann Jellicoe and the Colway Theatre Trust in the late 1970s and 1980s. Community theatre is also part of the long and uneven history of documentary theatre (see Forsyth and Megson 2009) and more specifically linked to the oral history-based 'verbatim' theatre (Paget 1987) pioneered by Peter Cheeseman in regional documentaries at the Victoria Theatre, Stoke on Trent, in the late 1960s and 1970s (see Watt 2003). These traces converged in Bristol in the 1980s through the persons of acta co-founders, Beddow and Caroline Green. They met, as Beddow explains,

> when I was working for Bush Telegraph on a large-scale community play, 'Bread and Blood' [in 1981]. She joined me to lead a youth theatre 'Kids Theatre', and we developed and performed a range of devised plays, taking some on tour around the West Country. At the time, I was working as a freelance youth arts activity facilitator, (including work for Avon County [a maternity cover role as Youth Arts Officer in Youth and Community Services]) and it was clear that there was a real gap in the market – no one else was doing this sort of work – so setting up a company was a very logical step. (https://www.acta-bristol.com/neil-blog/)

---

[1] When the county of Avon was dissolved in 1996, acta became known by the lower-case acronym alone, and continues to work across the greater Bristol area in the south-west of England.

Beddow credits Bush Telegraph TiE, with whom he worked as assistant administrator before the company lost its funding and folded (2001, pp. 6–7), with introducing him to the whole community theatre movement, and asserts that it was "instrumental in the formation of acta in 1985" (https://www.acta-bristol.com/our-batch-1989/).

Craig notes that professional Theatre-in-Education companies, the first of which—Belgrade Theatre, Coventry—was founded in 1965, and Youth Theatres shared a model of "participatory and 'developmental' drama which sought to strengthen the child's self-expression or to develop his/her critical understanding of the world" (1980, p. 24). The Standing Conference of Young People's Theatre (SCYPT), founded in 1972, embraced TiE companies who worked within the state education system and those who performed theatre in community venues, youth clubs, playgrounds and other accessible sites. The 1974 SCYPT conference, which focused on company organisation, noted that the field was committed to "democratic decision-making" which was also reflected in practice: "it was normal for work to be collectively devised" (1980, p. 79). acta's founding reflected this tradition of democratic collectives and collective devising, and extended it through into the 1980s. This was collective devising drawn primarily from Youth Theatre, theatre-based community arts organisations (such as Telford Community Arts) and the community play movement as it was alternatively articulated by TiE companies (such as Belgrade, Coventry and Bush Telegraph, Bristol).

Some of the first productions by acta with younger people were produced in collaboration with Kids Youth Theatre. By the end of 1986, and facilitated by a trust/foundation grant enabling the purchase of a refurbished minibus, acta had established a network of Youth Theatre groups across the Avon region: in Easton, Knowle West, Kingswood, Central Bristol, Yate, Radstock and Lockleaze, and on the Bournville estate in Weston-Super-Mare. The company brought all these groups together over two weeks in Summer of 1987 to create *Wake Up and Dream Summer* (1987), performed in disused outdoor swimming pool in Eastville Park:

> The project had a massive team of acta workers, freelancers and student volunteers, and every day we picked up young people from their local areas and took them to the Park to devise and rehearse… [over a] fortnight culminating in… performances which mixed theatre, dance, giant puppets, original music and song. (Beddow; https://www.acta-bristol.com/wake-up-and-dream-summer-1987/)

The first community production, *Playground Palaver* (1985), was made after an approach by a group of women from Peasedown St John, a village to the south-west of Bath. The performance initiated the tradition of acta Christmas plays drawing on the popular mode of pantomime, an accessible form of theatre that acta further imbued with original, relevant and devised content. Beddow described the Christmas play as a "punchy mix of agit-prop and slapstick comedy" with "local references", drawing attention to the relevant council's under-resourcing of the village, which lacked a children's playground (https://www.acta-bristol.com/neil-blog/). The Christmas play proved to be "a great way to engage people in making theatre for the first time", and bolstered the development of the South Wansdyke Community Play, *Our Batch*, in 1989 (Beddow; https://www.acta-bristol.com/neil-blog/).

Commissioned by South Wandsdyke Arts Council, the community play was focused on the Somerset towns of Midsomer Norton and Radstock, and the many villages around the area, including the village of Peasedown St John. Beddow states that it was "a vast epic of a play":

> acta developed a 3-year programme, with a series of small outreach projects in the first year, the community play in year 2, and a third year which was to consolidate and create sustainable groups to continue beyond [...] It was an extraordinary and massively ambitious project, with 250 performers, including a community orchestra, primary schools, people of all ages and abilities. We took over an old engine shed in the centre of Radstock for the year of the show, which was big enough for the show, but too big to heat, which was a bit problematical as the performances were in a particularly cold November. (https://www.acta-bristol.com/our-batch-1989/)

At the end of the production, Green moved to another organisation, leaving Beddow as the sole remaining co-founding member. He became artistic director, and formalised the organisation as a company with charitable status. This shift was less a renunciation of democratic principles and more a pragmatic acceptance of the co-constituting role of the state (local/regional government) and the third sector/civil society in community theatre practice. Writing on a similar moment of formalisation of theatre companies, also in the 1980s, in the long history of radical theatre troupes in Canada, Alan Filewod notes that while such a move presented "irreconcilable conflicts between ideological principles and the institutional demands of an increasingly corporatized cultural delivery system", there were some cases in which practitioners were capable of forging an accommodation between self-defined purpose and the demands of institutional survival in the system (2011, pp. 212–213).

Following *Our Batch*, acta's first community play in 1989, the company went on to create community plays in different parts of the county: Kingswood (1993), Southmead (1994) and South Bath (1995). The Kingswood Community Play *We Face The Dawn* (1993) was supported by Avon County Community Leisure, Kingswood Borough Council and (at the last minute) the Foundation for Sports and the Arts. The Southmead Community Play *Lifelines* (1994) started from an enquiry from an Avon County community worker, and continued with funding from SW Arts, Avon County Council and Bristol City Council. The South Bath Community Play, *The South Side Sisters* (1995), was initiated after an invitation from a participant in *Our Batch*, who was also working for a Health organisation, and thought a community play could contribute to the flourishing of local communities. At around this time, Beddow felt the need to articulate the particular characteristics of the community play. He did so with reference to the popular participatory tradition of amateur performance with which acta's work was closely aligned and from which it also differed in specific ways:

> People often ask for a definition of a community play, and why it's so different to say, an amateur production of a musical. The difference, for us, lies in the involvement, in the participation of a community in making the play for themselves. A play that speaks their words, reflects their experiences, honours their memories, celebrates their present, and hopes for their future. A community play is a living thing, a joint creation containing the ideas, imagination and inspiration of many. A community play should seek to involve everyone, and in our play we have made every effort to contact and include people who might normally be excluded from being in a play. There have been no auditions – people fall naturally into parts – most of which they have created for themselves during devising sessions. (https://www.acta-bristol.com/the-south-side-sisters-1995/)

By the mid-1990s, acta had reached an organisational turning point as grassroots demand for community play projects exceeded the company's ability to resource the demand through available funding. With the recent establishment of the National Lottery Charities Board, Beddow planned the execution and evaluation of a large project in response to grassroots requests, and to redress the "lack of understanding by funding bodies about the benefits of the [community theatre] work, and a lack of evidence about its impact" (2001, p. 35). The funding bid was successful, and *Making A Difference*, a three-year, multi-sited community play project, began in Avon county. Funding enabled acta to continue phases of work already begun in Southmead and South Bath and to begin work in two further locations, Stoke Gifford and Bourneville.

Turning Points: The Impact of Participation in Community Theatre (Beddow 2001) documents and evaluates the implementation of the *Making a Difference* project, taking acta's experimentation with regional, community-based theatre-making to the end of the decade (1999). Crucially, this publication specifies the seven-point community play model implemented by acta across multiple sites. According to Beddow, the community play:

1. is primarily concerned with individual and community development
2. determines theme and content through community consultation
3. is devised then scripted; casting takes place without auditions
4. is based on living memory and present issues
5. holds process and product as equally important, and mutually dependent
6. actively promoted access and inclusivity to excluded sections of community, which impacts on production style
7. has a three-year structure—pilot projects, play, consolidation—which works towards long-term sustainability of projects (2001, pp. 12–13).

acta's community play model bridges divisions that came to the fore in the alternative theatre movement in the 1980s, and which threatened to fragment the movement in the 1990s, according to Kershaw (1991, 1992). A key point of debate was whether the notion of community (of location) in the community play displaced the working-class constituencies at the centre of processes of cultural action for social change. In other words, production of the community play appeared to restore (traditional) social relations, or the status quo, rather than facilitate intervention to challenge class-based social inequality. Also in question was the role of professionals in facilitating participation in theatre versus collective collaboration which distributed ownership of the means of cultural production. Kershaw approached this from two angles. Firstly, he argued that the Jellicoe/Colway Theatre Trust (CTT) community play introduced subversion to augment oppositional (countercultural) strategies thereby expanding the potential for social efficacy: "in the sense of adopting subtle, and sometimes heavily disguised strategies of resistance at a localized level" (p. 204) and producing theatre that served to "liberalise attitudes … [and] reinforce local democracy" (p. 205). Secondly, his analysis of Welfare State International (WSI) in Barrow-in-Furness explored how a community theatre organisation might embed itself in a post-industrial town, in which macro-economic changes had fragmented working-class identity both within and without, to promote broad community development. acta's community play model encapsulates some of the bridging of community development and cultural democracy that Kershaw articulated.[2]

Events in 1997, namely the election of a Labour government after 20 years in opposition, overtook this settling of the question of the fragmentation of the alternative and community theatre movement. The new Labour government placed cultural participation at the centre of policy operations harnessing arts/culture to address the problem of social exclusion (see PAT 10 1999). There has been much written concerning New Labour governance and its impact on the arts/cultural sector, re-igniting a long-running debate on the role of art in society (Jeffers and Moriarty 2017, p. 152). Beddow (2001) locates acta's work (including his evaluation study to demonstrate the social impacts of participating in community theatre-making) as part of a turn in cultural policy from a singular focus on the economic case for the arts towards a concern with the social impacts of cultural participation (Matarasso 1997).[3] He located his own work within a "mature and resilient community arts

---

[2] Heddon and Milling (2006) have since described the diversity of community theatre practice in terms of "four spectra along which a company's practice may lie: the level of involvement of theatre professionals; the level of participation of community members; the relative importance of process or product; and the political impetus of the work, from radical to supportive of the status quo" (p. 136).

[3] Matarasso's study, *Use or Ornament*, proved highly influential on Labour cultural policy emerging at the time and has attracted more than its fair share of criticism. See Jeffers and Moriarty (2017, pp. 120–125) for a full discussion.

movement" (2001, p. 61), which had found its practice constrained within very narrow parameters and had been developing a case for broader scope and recognition. With the election of New Labour, there was, at a national policy level, renewed interest in and funding for community theatre as a participatory art form.

Participatory Community Theatre, After 2000

A key change to the way acta worked came in 2002 when the company acquired its own repurposed space in Bedminster, a neighbourhood located just south of Bristol city centre.[4] Having a permanent, physical basis of operation in a local neighbourhood did not bring an end to acta's work across the Greater Bristol area. However, the move to a (black box) theatre building necessitated a change in practice. acta shifted from large-scale, community-based play production focused on specific geographical areas, with hundreds of participants, and thousands of audience, to producing the work of many smaller groups within the centre each year. The acta bus is no more; however, the company supports participants to access opportunities through paying transport costs to the centre. According to Beddow, "in every year acta will work on around 20 projects, many of them ongoing groups which meet weekly through the year, and who create at least one new play, usually with a small number of performances in their local area" (Beddow 2013, pp. 96–97).[5]

Critical to the shift from a peripatetic community theatre company working across a large, regional area to a theatre company operating out of a permanent base in a local neighbourhood, was the opportunity afforded Beddow by South West Arts to visit the International Community Theatre Festival (ICTF) hosted by Rotterdams Wijktheater in 2003. Co-founded by Peter van den Hurk and Annelies Spliethof in 1992, Rotterdams Wijktheater (*wijk* translates into English as neighbourhood or district) has established a reputation for co-creating original theatre productions for, with and by (under-represented) residents of the port city's working-class and immigrant neighbourhoods. It was on this basis that the committee organising Rotterdam's tenure as European Capital of Culture commissioned RWT to programme an international festival placing Rotterdam at the forefront of the emerging map of community and participatory arts practice. Beddow's visit to ICTF had several important outcomes. Beddow established an ongoing relationship with Van den Hurk; acta was introduced to RWT's 'touring' model of community theatre; and acta's

---

[4] acta signed a 30-year rental agreement with Bristol City Council. The company pays a peppercorn rent in exchange for participating in civic community development efforts. After recent investment by Arts Council England, the centre boasts two performance spaces, including a black box theatre (adjoined by props and wardrobe rooms) and a medium-sized foyer and café area.

[5] In 2011–2012, acta worked with nearly 1000 participants, delivered 750 workshops, created 16 shows with a total 38 performances, and attracted 3000 audience members, over 80% of whom were new to theatregoing: https://www.acta-bristol.com/wp-content/uploads/2012/08/New-business-plan-2012-15-september-12_with-images.pdf

network was extended from the national (e.g. the Community Play Network and the National Association for Youth Theatre) to "a global community theatre movement" that "shared acta's particular vision and approach to community theatre" (Beddow 2013, p. 97).

ICTF initiated a key partnership and critical friendship between RWT and acta. acta has been influenced by and experimented with the RWT approach to making community theatre which is largely audience based, working with small groups of participants to create and rehearse a play over a year, and then to tour the play for a further year, with a minimum of 20 performances. RWT's approach is, as Kees Denik (one of RWTs freelance facilitator/directors) states, "rooted in Dutch cultural policy, which is highly performance oriented":

> A government funded company [in the Netherlands] is required to make strict agreements with the funding organisation on matters such as the number of productions you make, the number of times each production will be performed, what audience you are targeting and the size of audience you will attract ... partly for this reason there comes a time in every production process that we expect the performers working in it to have developed a professional attitude and a willingness to collectively focus on a full-fledged work for the stage that we can sell to theatres and performance approximately twenty times. (in COAST 2013, pp. 51–52)

After Van den Hurk visited acta in 2004 (the first of many practitioner exchanges between the two—and other—companies), acta began to create a piece of issue-based theatre, *For Love Nor Money*, with six experienced acta participants, all women, which it toured to community venues across Bristol and to the 2005 ICTF. This exchange led to this strand of work becoming a major part of acta's annual programme. According to Beddow:

> This aspect of our work continues to engage skilled and experienced community performers to devise and tour high quality, original, relevant and affordable theatre to disadvantaged areas where there is no access to, or tradition of, theatregoing. In this way we develop a new audience for theatre. (2013, p. 100)

The exchange also enabled acta to address a perennial issue in community theatre: artistic excellence (or quality). Working with a small group of experienced participants for one year enabled the company to contribute to "the 'quality-debate' within the arts sector, by developing a high-quality product, working with a small number of performers over a long period of time – both devising and through rehearsal – and, crucially, performance" (Beddow 2013, p. 99).

At the same time, Eugene van Erven, has stated a reciprocal relationship between acta and RWT, noting that acta is "one of the oldest partners of ICAF" (2013, p. 11), and that the exchange between acta and RWT has constructively illuminated "differences in approach – such as the stronger emphasis placed on ownership and community collaborations" (p. 17) within the British tradition of community theatre. The partnership and exchange with RWT has led acta to develop audience-focused, touring participatory community theatre as an integral part of the company's programme of work. The organisation has articulated a multilevel (triangular—narrowing from a wide base) system of access and participation called the 'cycle of engagement', comprised of primary contact projects (maximum participation, aimed at being accessible entertainment—'fun, free and local'—and socially bonding), development projects (developing and building on skills in theatre-making) and the advanced touring theatre company (devising and touring community theatre throughout Greater Bristol).[6]

I'm now going to turn to examine *Gas Girls* and *Ticky Picky Boom Boom*. I note that what follows is a slice taken from a cross-section of activities in one year of acta's working life. These two productions—one made by participants drawn from discrete youth theatres, an adult group and the advanced company, and brought together for the purpose of making *Gas Girls*, and the other, made by a satellite company, the Malcolm X Elders—reveal how the company engages embodied experience (practical knowing) to produce relevant and original theatre with an affirmative aesthetic. I'm calling this process a collective 'corporeography' because the term, after feminist post-structuralist theorists, places emphasis on the body as materiality (flesh, matter) re-marking itself. As Threadgold notes, "the subject, the embodied, sexed, raced biology of the subject, the material world, and language are enfolded, folded into one another" (Threadgold 2000, p. 52). The term also places emphasis on performance as practice, a doing (which might involve speaking) distinct from performativity as the practical/material effect of a speech act (doing things with words) (Threadgold 2000, p. 54). According to Threadgold, "the metaphor of performance is more useful than performativity alone because it will not allow the elisions of the body that performativity permits. To perform is to struggle with the substance of the body" (Threadgold 2000, p. 57). The processes examined below enact that 'struggle with the substance of the body' in remembering and re-enacting subjects that matter. As a practice relying on embodied knowledge, I will argue that community performance is a community of practice and explore the implications of conceptualising community performance in this way.

GAS GIRLS AND *TICKY PICKY BOOM BOOM*: COLLECTIVE CORPOREOGRAPHIES OF MEMORY AND IMAGINATION

Gas Girls: The Untold Story of the Women Who Made Mustard Gas (GG) was researched, devised and rehearsed over the course of one year, April 2013–March 2014, by an ensemble of 20 people, varying in age (from 16 to 60), experience and ability, brought together for the first time for the specific

---

[6] For more detail on the cycle of engagement, see acta business plan 2012–15, pp. 7–8: https://www.acta-bristol.com/wp-content/uploads/2012/08/New-business-plan-2012-15-september-12_with-images.pdf]

purpose of making GG. The process was facilitated by Neil Beddow and Associate Director Ingrid Jones; Rosalie Pordes joined the archival research group as an acta Foundation worker and assistant director. Supported by the Heritage Lottery Fund (HLF) and Arts Council England (ACE), the performance premiered at the acta Centre on 19 March 2014 as part of the HLF's centenary of the First World War. The production played for three nights at the acta Centre before touring to local venues in June 2014.[7] In addition to the performance, the company compiled and published a book containing the archival research that underpinned the performance: *Gas Girls: The Untold Story of Avonmouth's Mustard Gas Factories*, researched and written by Neil Beddow, Karen Chodkiewicz, Rebecca Davidson, Tracey Harvey and Rosalie Pordes. GG was revived for a second performance tour in April–June 2017.[8]

Ticky Picky Boom Boom (TPBB) was the sixth production made by the Malcolm X Elders Theatre Group with acta. The Malcolm X Elders came to performance directly from an oral history project after a group of women, mainly from the Elders Forum at the Malcolm X Community Centre in St Pauls, Bristol,[9] collaborated with Professor Madge Dresser from the School of History at the University of the West of England (UWE) and the Bristol Community Education Unit to create an oral history booklet and video, *Many Rivers To Cross* (see Dresser 2004). Once they had completed the book about migrating from the Caribbean to the UK and the early days of their lives as immigrants to Bristol, the Elders decided they wanted to perform their stories. The community development officer based at the Malcolm X Community Centre contacted Neil Beddow at acta. Together, acta and the Elders created the oral history performance, *Time of Our Lives* (2006), inaugurating the Malcolm X Elders Theatre Group (MXETG). At the time of writing, the Elders

---

[7] 2014 Tour dates: Avonmouth Community Centre, 10, 11 & 12 June; Wickham Theatre (UoB) Cantocks Close, Woodland Road 16 June; Withywood Community Centre 21 June; Orchard School, Horfield 24 June.

[8] Return season and tour, April–June 2017: acta Centre, Bedminster 27–9 April; Rondo Theatre, Bath, 5 May; Trinity Centre, Bristol, 19 May; Blakehay Theatre, Weston, 3 June; Stoke Park School, Bristol, 6 June.

[9] The Malcolm X Community Centre was established in the wake of an uprising against discriminatory policing practices targeting African-Caribbean populations in inner-city neighbourhoods, criminalising young men in particular. On 2 April 1980, police raided a black-owned business in St Paul's, the *Black and White Café*, which led to a violent disturbance. It was the first of many uprisings against socio-economic inequality and racial discrimination in British cities in the early 1980s. In the aftermath of the disturbance, the City Council responded by constructing a community centre to facilitate promotion of African Caribbean culture and inter-ethnic relations. Dresser and Fleming note that "[m]embers of the St Paul's Community Association initially boycotted the Centre, although it eventually came into use some years later, pointedly renamed as the Malcolm X Centre" (2007, p. 176). See Ambar (2014) on the significance of the African American civil rights activist's visits to the UK in 1964 (in which he took up an invitation to speak at Oxford University union debate broadcast world-wide by BBC-TV) and 1965 (X visited Smethwick in the West Midlands in solidarity with the black and South Asian constituencies after the election of Conservative MP Peter Griffiths, whose campaign deployed a racist epithet to focus negative attention on issues of race and immigration).

have created at least nine original performances: *Time of Our Lives* (2006), *Lost Connections* (2008), *Use It or Lose It* (2010), *Little Irritations* (2011), *We Have Overcome* (2012; 2019 tour),[10] *Ticky Picky Boom Boom* (2013; 2014 tour to ICAF 2014), *The Now* (MXETG and acta's advanced company, 2015) and *Moonshine Nights* (2016).[11]

TPBB was created specifically to tour to local primary schools for whole school performances in November–December 2013. Based on African Caribbean folk tales (the Anansi trickster stories), the performance was promoted as a Christmas show, or pantomime. *TPBB* was devised and rehearsed by the Elders, a group of seven women, at the Malcolm X Community Centre in St Pauls over an eight-week period. Weekly sessions—Monday 1.30–3.00 pm—began on 27 September 2013; Neil Beddow and Phillipa Smith (now community producer with Strike A Light Festival, Gloucester) facilitated. Two one-day workshops were held, one in October and one in November, at the acta Centre before the final dress rehearsal on the day of the first evening performance, 11 November 2013. Supported by ACE, *TPBB* premiered at the acta Centre for three nights before commencing a tour of Bristol primary schools (14 November–5 December 2013).[12] The Elders re-workshopped *TPBB* for a further eight weeks (3 February–24 March 2014) as part of the two-year EU-funded Grey Matters project. TPBB toured to and was performed at the ICAF in Rotterdam from 26 to 30 March 2014. The Elders were supported on tour by members of acta's 'advanced' company.

Both community performances provide an opportunity to explore the close connection between community performance and popular memory. *GG* dealt with official secrets and sought to excavate the hidden history of the women who worked in local factories producing chemical weapons in the last six months of the First World War. *TPBB* was a performance for primary school children made by Caribbean elders based on memories of stories they were told as children. Whereas the elders drew on embodied experience, the performers making GG had no access to living memory in the form of oral history. In its absence, the group drew largely on imagination to improvise the social world of the munitions factory that their invented characters worked in. This imaginative work was combined with analysis of existing documentary evidence, which was scant, and archival research undertaken by acta workers and group members.

[10] The Elders revived *We Have Overcome* for touring in 2019 after the 'Windrush scandal' broke in 2018.

[11] In *Winter Fires: Art and Agency in Old Age* (2012), François Matarasso notes that the stories the Elders perform are both based in their own experience and varied: "Sometimes they look back at life in the Caribbean or working in the factories, shops and hospitals of Britain. But the women are also keen to get across their ideas about life today, and to help others both through their example and by dramatizing everyday situations" (p. 47).

[12] Monday 11 November 2013, dress rehearsal and first performance, 7.30 pm acta centre, 11 and 12 November (including Compass Point KS1 matinee); St Mary Redcliffe Primary, 14 November; Avonmouth Primary, 19 November; Oasis Bank Leaze Primary, 21 November; Glenfrome Primary, 26 November; St Werburghs Primary, 28 November; St Nicholas of Tolentine, 5 December.

Performing *Ticky Picky Boom Boom* (acta Centre, 12 November 2013)

We (me and my four-year-old daughter) settle into our bench seats in the acta Centre. The transgenerational audience is a mix of family and friends of the performers and quite a few participants I recognise from other acta performances. The painted plywood set is placed on a bright floor carpet that is red with a large green circular spot in the middle criss-crossed by yellow lines. The set consists of two palm trees (blue trunks, each with four big red leaves and yellow coconuts) at either end of a black board background with a rail running between the trees and a bench below which doubles as a seat and box for props. Elements of the animal costumes (coats, masks, ears and hats) and other props hang from the rails. A large cardboard sun painted bright yellow is stuck on the blackout curtain behind the set.

The lights dim and a line of women dressed in black trousers and t-shirt each with a colourful vest enter stage singing and moving rhythmically in time to a song that usually accompanies a children's game, Guh Dung A Manual Road/ Go Down Emmanuel Road.[13] Once all the women are in a line across the front of the stage one women calls to the group who respond in unison:

Caller (Ca): Children! Children!
Chorus (Ch): yes mama
Ca: where have you been –
Ch: to see the queen
Ca: What did she give you?
Ch: Bread and cheese
Ca: Where's my share
Ch: Up in the air
Ca: How do I get there
Ch: Climb the stair
Ca: What if I fall
Ch: We don't care
Ca: Who taught you that?
Ch: Anansi! (*Ticky Picky Boom Boom* 2013)

This introduction to the figure of Anansi, who plays at undermining adult authority and disrupting respect for elders, has clearly animated the younger audience members. The caller then presents front stage. She is dressed as Anansi with a black coat of eight hairy aims and furry black earmuffs:

Some say he's a spider
They all say he's a trickster
…

---

[13] 'Emmanuel Road' is a Jamaican folk song sung in accompaniment to a children's game typically played by a group seated in a circle moving stones around in time with the rhythm/beat of the song. It can be varied by increasing the number of stones and the speed of the song: see Miss Lou/National Library of Jamaica: https://www.youtube.com/watch?v=Yzg4-Ajf8Kc

When we were little girls, our grandparents used to tell us stories about Anansi and all the tricks he played on the other animals in the forest.
We're going to tell you some of the stories. (*Ticky Picky Boom Boom* 2013)

One of the women from the chorus steps forward level with the Caller and announces loudly to the audience that the story we are about to hear is *TPBB*. The chorus behind shake their collective heads and say, "no, not yet". This refrain takes place each time a new story is about to be introduced, provoking laughter while also keeping the audience in suspense waiting for the (final) eponymous story.

The performance ensemble mostly enacts the Anansi stories with some narration undertaken by different members of the group. The repertoire of stories enacted [Tiger and Anansi; Fowl and Cockroach; Dog and Pony; Monkey and Anansi; Tiger and Turtle; and Ticky Picky Boom Boom] shows Anansi playing tricks on animals in the forest proving his superior ingenuity and skill. The change between scenes is fluid with costume and props drawn from the railing or box onstage and the elders stepping into various roles (performing, narrating, assisting on costume changes and operating props). The engaging performance invites participation from children at one point. Several rush down onto the floor to help Anansi create a pen to capture pig to entice and catch snake. Anansi has to catch snake to prove he's the biggest, strongest and cleverest animal in the forest (more than the tiger). After several failed attempts—including the attempt to pen the pig—snake confronts Anansi and asks why the spider is trying to catch him. Anansi says he's been trying to catch him to measure him. He says that he has been telling the animals that snake is the tallest animal in the forest, but they don't believe him. This way Anansi cunningly convinces snake to allow the spider to tie him to a long measuring stick before delivering the bound snake to the animals, reasserting his superiority over the jungle animals.

Devising *Ticky Picky Boom Boom*

The devising process for *TPBB* takes place at the Malcolm X Community Centre in a smaller side room that comes straight off the large, main hall. The room, with posters of Harriet Tubman and Malcolm X on opposite walls, contains several filing cabinets and storage cupboards. Sessions are frequently (and politely) interrupted by people entering to deposit or remove items. Quite often the devising process competes with sounds—songs amplified on CD player and accompanied by singing and percussion—from the main hall. Some of these songs make their way into the final performance. Beddow coins the term 'adaptive devising' to refer to the process of working in social spaces not primarily dedicated to theatre-making and to adapting the process around the busy lives of the Elders (eight weeks of devising takes place over several months to allow summer holidays). The space is usually arranged as a large circle of nine to ten chairs (seven Elders, two acta facilitators and me). The process begins with the elders' recalling Anansi stories from (embodied) memory. The performers then begin to enact the stories working out who's going to play which animal, improvising speech and dialogue, and roughly blocking position and movements in the space. Decisions about the set, costume, sound and lighting are worked on at the same time by relevant acta team members with the elders. Once the eight-week devising period is complete, the performers move over to the acta Centre for an intensive dress rehearsal period in the theatre a few days before opening.

The process of remembering the stories is slow and somewhat painstaking. The stories are not simply available to be recalled on demand in the small room between the hours of approximately 1.00–3.00 pm on a Monday afternoon. The facilitators (Neil and Philippa) take note of the Elders' fragmented reminiscences and are also adamant that, outside workshop hours, the elders should continue the process to remember stories told to them as children, and bring their memories into the room throughout the following weeks. It was in one of these very early sessions that Neil felt the need to recall the task for the group. He reminds the group that towards the end of the performance tour of *We Have Overcome*, the Elders took the performance into local schools. The group note that the performance was well received by the school children, and the Elders affirm that they were moved by the enthusiastic response of the younger audience. In the final evaluation of the project by the Elders and acta, it was decided to make a touring performance exclusively for primary school age children. Neil said that the performance is to be based on stories that the Elders were told when they were children: "What were the stories you were told as children? We're going to perform them to the children." Given that the performance tour would take place in November and early December, that is, in pantomime season, Neil said that the idea had been for the Elders to create a play in line with acta's tradition of making original Christmas plays. Rather than perform traditional pantomime plays, such as *Puss in Boots* or *Cinderella*, the Elders would perform stories from their own cultural heritage, imbuing pantomime with African Caribbean oral storytelling (or orature after wa Thiong'o 2007). Mentioning the Anansi (spider) stories, Neil said he could go online and find plenty of stories, but he wanted to know the ones the Elders were told as children. He wanted the stories to be, he said, 'authentic'.

Authenticity is a point of debate in community performance. Gay Hawkins (1993) has located an 'aesthetics of affirmation' as a critical plank to community arts practice (pp. 133–155) whose "commitment to affirm" is "also, at the same time, a confrontation of marginality" (p. 137). She is, however, critical of the "representation of community as the source of authenticity" (p. 138) that tends to underpin the dominant mode of documentary realist representation in community arts practice. She asserts that the reflex to locate the "community as a source of authenticity" (p. 162) understood as "knowledge, skill and unmediated experience" (p. 138) tends to reinforce cultural difference as exotic and/or worthy 'other-ness' (p. 162). It tends to fix collective identity of cultural otherness as (safely) in the past, brought back only in a nostalgic (uncritical) form. Eugene van Erven counters Hawkins' critique arguing that community theatre deploys a wide range of aesthetic styles not limited to documentary (with its confessional mode of address), and that authenticity, while a critical source of much community theatre, is mediated by processes of devising, improvising and rehearsing, thereby introducing repetition into the locus of actual experience. In other words, experience is well and truly mediated by the time it makes the stage. He asserts that the "aesthetic of affirmation" typical of community theatre engages a "politics of representation" that produces positive images of others typically under-represented or negatively represented in public culture (van Erven 2001, p. 137). This commitment to affirm [difference] enacts a confrontation of marginality (p. 137) and a contestation of discourses of domination (p. 155).

When Neil says, he wants the stories the Elders recall to be authentic, he is facilitating dual social and aesthetic processes. In terms of the performance aesthetic, privileging embodied experience and insisting on remembering stories (and the social context of the telling) laid down the performers' memory recall. The remembered stories were written down by the facilitators who began to build a (loose) performance script. The Elders, however, moved from remembering to enacting the stories. Though there was a script, they tended not to refer to it. At one point in the process, the elders had scripts in hand but reading from a script interrupted the flow: one read stage directions, while another stood becoming visibly frustrated at the lack of response to her lines, and shouted 'improvise'! The facilitators used the scripts to follow the performance making that was happening as oral and physical storytelling on the floor. The text provided an outline of the performance and was used in rehearsal to focus in on scenes that needed work (repeating or adjusting and resetting), and sometimes the facilitators used the script to prompt the performers on the order of scenes. The performance of the Anansi stories maintained a close connection to oral storytelling because it was based on the performers remembering and enacting stories they were told as children. Thus, the young children received the stories as oral and improvisational storytelling (as the Elders had as children from their Elders). This unfolding of time was also a spatial interlinking of Britain and the Caribbean (at least since the opening of the 'middle passage'). The performance enacted this enfolding of time and space, affirming inclusion of *anansesem* within the pantomime repertoire of popular British performance culture.

The Anansi stories are already a part, if little or under-known in terms of performance repertoire, of British popular culture through the bodies of African-Caribbean Elders who immigrated to Britain post–Second World War and are recognised, in their own right, "as performers, people with stories to tell: agents of change" (Matarasso 2012, p. 47). These stories have already undergone geographical and historical adaptation since Anansi, the spider trickster, travelled from west Africa to the Caribbean with "the Akan group of Twi-speaking people of whom the Ashanti are best known [and who] [f]or a significant part of the eighteenth century, from 1730 to 1790, ... were in the majority of those imported as slaves to Jamaica" (Austin-Broos and Smith 1997, p. 46).[14] In the Caribbean, in the context of plantation slavery, Anansi transformed from deity in Ashanti cosmology—a godlike liminal figure going between earth and sky—to a more earthly character engaging with other mundane animal figures such as dog, rat, and so on, although Anansi retained boundary-breaking qualities at least in terms of everyday, social relations (Austin-Broos and Smith 1997, pp. 46–47). In the process, according to British scholar Emily Zobel Marshall, Anansi became a "folk hero of Jamaican slaves who took to stories of the trickster extraordinaire as a figure of resistance" and whose "escapades filled with inherent humour played a vital role in the face of great difficulties encountered by slave populations in the Caribbean" (2012, pp. 89–91). Onuora agrees that "in the context of plantation slavery, the folk icon Anancy (and the stories named after him) became a vehicle for cultural, psychological and physical resistance and survival" (2015, p. 199).

In the journey from the Caribbean to Britain, Anansi is still undertaking humour-filled escapades to forge resistance and accommodation to given situations. In TPBB, the Malcolm X Elders bring Caribbean folklore into dialogue with the British popular tradition of pantomime. Recent criticism has questioned the British tradition of pantomime performance arguing that its playfulness tends to rest on lazy stereotypes of race, sex/gender and sexuality.[15] In the Epilogue to his study, *Representing China on the Historical London Stage*, Dongshin Chang analyses multiple performances of *Aladdin* leading him to question claims that uphold pantomime as "Saturnalian [at its best], [...] the most joyous and democratic form of theatre, the last miraculously surviving relic of traditional variety, in which everyone in the audience is both welcome and generously catered for" (2015, p. 188). He notes that the representation of China and the Chinese central to the story of *Aladdin*, often justified in terms of artifice, contain direct reference to British Chinese community through the figure of Widow Twankey. Her name maintains reference to the laundry trade which, "due to a combination of factors (discrimination, low capital requirements, minimal contact with customers), was the main business of the British Chinese in the early twentieth century" (p. 186). Chang asserts

---

[14] Emily Zobel Marshall (2001) notes that the Anansi/trickster folk cultural tradition remains in process and multivalent in present-day Caribbean contexts. She notes that, in Jamaica the early 2000s, Anansi was at the centre of moral panic initiated by educational leaders concerned about endemic levels of corruption and violent crime—dubbed "the Anansi syndrome"—in the modern postcolonial nation. A national debate followed a suggestion to discontinue teaching of Anansi stories to Jamaican children. Anansi was therefore revealed to be a symbolic figure very much at the centre of ongoing complex negotiations of African heritage and tradition, resistance to imperialism (in the form of plantation slavery) and the value system of the modern postcolonial nation as it navigates neoliberal globalisation.

[15] See https://www.bbc.co.uk/programmes/articles/1kP4W7p26QfHHb070ZsKhHs/is-there-still-a-place-for-panto-in-the-21st-century

that Widow Twankey is evidence of cultural incorporation of British Chinese identity in the pantomime tradition but that this inter-culturation process is an exclusive one that remains in Yellow Face mode (p. 187). Chang recognises the critical importance of inclusion of authentic markers of culture in modern Pantomime (he gives as an example the inclusion of a dragon performance troupe in the Hackney Empire production of Aladdin), and calls for more fruitful collaboration with "the local Chinese community" with hope that "future Aladdin pantos may welcome the Chinese themselves to participate in the interculturation process, and not only to enhance their artificial Chinaface look" (p. 188).

Acta's experiment in bringing Caribbean storytelling into dialogue with British pantomime affirms the possibility of producing inclusively, rather than exclusively, 'joyful and democratic' forms of popular performance. The MXETG production of TPBB went beyond participation in performance (initiating a process of inter-culturation as per Chang, above); it introduced new repertoires (bodies and oral storytelling) to pantomime. The MXETG production of TPBB introduced children who don't usually go to the theatre as a rich dialogue between different adapted popular performance traditions: pantomime and *anansesem*. The pleasure of experiencing popular performance extended to appreciation of skilful performances of mischievous humour by the children's elders. I'm now going to turn my attention to acta's production of *Gas Girls: The Untold Story of the Women Who Made Mustard Gas*. The process of making GG was different to TPBB as the story of GG was not to be found within (remembered) lived experience or even living memory. The process involved imagining an absence and drawing on emotional sensibilities to create characters against bare outlines. It involved inventing language (monologue) and dialogue, putting words into mouths that had been made silent through an act of official secrecy. It also meant bodies accessing archives and bringing different systems of knowledge (official and unofficial) together in performance. This is how acta excavated and enacted a little known, all but untold episode from Bristol's (and the nation's) past.

'DIG WHERE YOU STAND' (LINDQVIST 1979)

In *Digging Up Stories: Applied Theatre, Performance and War*, James Thompson, cautions that while "story creation and story narration are vital parts of creative work within communities [...] the exhibition or valorisation of a story has no automatic connection to the liberation of the teller" (2005, p. 5). His own richly storied reflection on applying theatre/performance in a conflict zone hovers between a critique of the prospector [resource extraction] and admiration for the archaeologist [excavation] (p. 238). I mention Thompson's text in order to reintroduce a methodological approach to storytelling central to community performance (throughout most of the examples in this book), that sets it apart from extractive practices. Shannon Jackson has noted that "oral histories have … become another type of resonant document in service of [socially committed theatre practitioners'] goals" which she states as to make "use of documentary texts to create a theatre of public dialogue" (2005, p. 52). Oral history was one of the innovative techniques pioneered by the History Workshop Movement, a new social movement, that appeared in the UK in the mid-1960s (after the work of Raphael Samuel at Ruskin College, Oxford), simultaneous with developments in France, Sweden and Germany in the 1970s and 1980s. The History Workshop movement famously invented the term 'history from below' to refer to the collaborative workshop-based enterprise of making history from formerly overlooked or excluded (e.g. working class, female) perspectives. Swede, Sven Lindqvist's, *Dig Where you Stand* (1979),[16] issued a "call to unearth the past in your own location – whether geographical or social – and to uncover the wealth of experiences and resources available in order to understand how current circumstances came about" (Wüstenberg 2017, p. 154). Lindqvist's nomenclature seems an apt articulation of community performance practice concerned with "theatres of memory" (Samuel 1994).

Watt makes explicit connections between oral history practice and documentary and community theatre. He asserts that community theatre is a development of documentary theatre, although it adopts "a less strict embrace of the techniques associated with verbatim theatre", placing oral history at the centre of an "unbroken and vital tradition" (2009, p. 197) of documentary theatre practice:

> [Community-based theatre] has habitually used stories collected via the developing techniques of the oral historian, transmuting them into 'local acts', to use Jan Cohen Cruz's term (Cohen-Cruz 2005), through varying processes of collaboration with their sources. It is marked by a substantially more enlightened, and ethically sound, understanding of the roles and techniques of the oral historian than that indicated by the quarrying of communities for "source material" implicit in some of the examples of verbatim theatre which have become fashionable, and has also found other ways of being "political" than in the manner of Piscator or Weiss ("world-historical", "explanatory" model of documentary theatre). (p. 196)

acta's work can be viewed in this broad tradition of documentary community theatre, and has most in common with Cheeseman's associational mode of documentary which interweaves different perspectives on relevant social happenings. At the same time, acta could not adhere to Cheeseman's strict verbatim method as the performers were busy imagining and improvising the past, and it was this process that stood in for history re-created in (enforced) silence. This is an account of community theatre practice 'digging where it stands' and what it does when it comes up against a wall of official secrecy.

---

[16] Lindqvist "demonstrated how to research personal and occupational history, using the example of the Swedish cement industry" (in Wüstenberg 2017, 153).

Gas Girls: Following the Story, Finding the Money, Assembling the Cast

In early 2012, work on a building site in Avonmouth was halted (temporarily) after construction workers experienced nosebleeds. Concerns were raised as the building site had apparently been a site for the production of chemical (mustard gas) weapons during the First World War. It was queried whether there was a link between the workers' physical symptoms and an escape of the noxious gas, as the ground in which it was buried was disturbed by excavations. Soil samples were taken and sent to a top-secret government facility for testing. The story was picked up by a local newspaper serving Bristol (*The Post*), and then appeared in the BBC local news website.[17] The inter-animation of an assemblage of construction workers, ground excavations, liquid/gas sediment and bloodied bodies (noses) indicated that the past was acting in the present, unearthing a myriad of questions concerning the production of gas/chemical weapons in local munition factories, government secrecy, women munitions workers, worker safety and environmental hazards: all questions that acta as a community theatre company wanted to explore. *Gas Girls* continued the excavation started by the machines and workers, bringing together archival research and 'acts of substitution' (raising the dead) (Roach 1996), revealing history making to be a process of imagination and improvisation. This performance was about what one does when there is little remaining oral history and living memory, or the role of creative reinvention in popular memory.

Beddow began to trace the story pointing to Avonmouth as a centre of chemical warfare manufacturing in 1917. He started to research in archives and to follow up expert and local knowledge of the munitions factories in the time of the First World War. In the initial phase of the project, Beddow visited the Bristol Record Office and consulted historical and archaeological experts working in the city's archive. He attended meetings of the Avonmouth Genealogy group and local history groups, putting to them ideas for projects, seeking feedback and appealing for local knowledge and memory. He consulted biomedical and chemical experts at local universities (Bristol, and the West of England). From this initial research and consultation, he began to develop proposals for funding. One possible project was focused on the bio-medical effects of mustard gas on the human body, and the connection between war and medical technologies. Chemical compounds in the weapons had been subsequently used in cancer treatments, due to their liquifying effect on human tissue. Another possible project formed from a conversation with an officer in the Bristol Records Office. The man recalled his grandmother telling him as a boy about her work in the munitions factory, when prompted by him asking about the suppurating wound on her leg that had been dressed weekly by

---

[17] 'Bristol Chemical experts check "contaminated" land at Avonmouth', report 15 May 2012; 'Avonmouth site tests negative for mustard gas', report 25 June 2012; 'World War One: Avonmouth gas factory safety "secondary"', report 24 February 2014.

community nurses. This memory illuminated the dangerous working conditions of the women in the munitions factories, filling shells with poisonous gas.

This was an atypical way of working for acta. Normally, acta groups generate their own topics or themes for performance themselves. However, in Summer 2012 acta's funding from Big Lottery Young People's Fund, which supported a youth theatre network in north Bristol, came to an end. acta needed to generate funding to continue the youth theatre groups, an adult group and the advanced group. After he came across the story about the gas munitions factories in Avonmouth and Chittening, Beddow had the idea to bring together the different groups and to make a large funding bid to support theatre-making on this subject. Beddow aimed to secure a level of funding that would support a cast of about 20 over the time needed (12 months) to bring together an intergenerational group of people as a bonded entity: to research a subject on which there was little archival or local knowledge, due to official secrecy at the time with regard to the British production of chemical weapons, and to devise a performance.

While waiting on news of funding applications, the company worked with 20 local children in the Spring Term of 2013 to create a short piece of theatre on the impact of the First World War on the people of Avonmouth. Their performance at Avonmouth Community Centre was attended by 50 local people, who were also informally consulted about the pending project. At the same time, acta began to merge groups together towards working on the larger project. In March 2013, acta premiered 1963, which was made in response to the 50-year anniversary of the Bristol Bus Boycott.[18] Seven youth theatre members who had remained together through several iterations of youth theatres (Bedminster Youth Theatre, Vibe and Emergency Exit) came together with an adult theatre group of five to produce the 'verbatim' performance created entirely from interviews with local people asked to recall that eventful year.

In the Summer of 2013, acta had news that their bid to the Heritage Lottery Fund and Arts Council England for Gas Girls was successful. Five (originally six, although one dropped out, her due date being during the run) members of acta's 'advanced' touring community theatre group joined the 1963 cast, along with a friend of one of the youth theatre members and a new adult member, to make up the cast of 20 that went forward to work on *Gas Girls*. Grants from the Heritage Lottery Fund (HLF) and Arts Council England (ACE) made *Gas Girls* firmly a 'heritage' theatre project,

---

[18] The 1963 boycott of the Bristol Omnibus Company occurred due to the company's racially discriminatory employment policy. Organisation against the bus company was led by a group of African Caribbean men, who came together to form what came to be called the West Indian Development Council. News of the success of the boycott and the company's change in policy came on the same day that Martin Luther King made his famous "I Have a Dream" speech at the March on Washington (28 August 1963). Influenced, in part, by the bus boycott, legislation was subsequently introduced to combat racial discrimination in the form of the 1965 Race Relations Act.

commemorating the Centenary of the First World War. The Deputy Director of HLF, Karen Brookfield, notes that the Fund took a distinctive approach to heritage by leaving it to those who applied for funding to define it in their own terms, and to determine "'what they valued as heritage and the outcomes for heritage, people and communities" (2018, p. 119). Deferring definition, the organisation sidestepped the contestation of heritage and focused its attention instead on enabling a 'bottom-up approach' to the Centenary of the First World War, in the process opening up an unprecedented scale of funding support: £94.2 million was distributed to almost 2000 projects across the UK with at least one award in 93% of local authority areas. Through this open exercise, the HLF aimed to "reflect not only on the First World War and its legacy, but also on the nature of the Centenary itself" (Brookfield 2018, p. 122). While the HLF avoids debates around heritage by deferring definition, community theatre has been criticised as the "'performance of nostalgia', where the struggles of the past are sanitised into a commodified heritage" (Nicholson 2005, p. 92). This analysis follows Kershaw, who has, in fact, argued that what may be "apparently and reassuringly" recognisable as "heritage industry theatre: the performance of nostalgia" (1999, p. 160) masks a subtle, creative play with "doubled memory" (p. 164). He characterises community theatre—EMMA Theatre Company (by example of *The Poacher*), Peter Cheeseman's Stoke documentaries and Anne Jellicoe's community plays—as at the forefront of popular re-enactments whose examination, he asserts, may reveal not only "how history might be authored through performance by *almost anybody* at any time" (p. 162) but also the (post-modern) hybridity of historiography and aesthetics (1999, p. 177).

ACTS OF EXHUMATION, IMAGINATION AND ARCHIVAL RETRIEVAL: THE DEVISING PROCESS

acta's *Gas Girls* came in between two history/heritage theatre projects, *1963* and *Lost Not Forgotten (LNF)*, by acta's young adults' company, Phoenix Theatre, at Arnos Vale Cemetery. While the team utilised verbatim theatre techniques to produce *1963*, *LNF* engaged with the heritage site's professional historians to create a promenade performance through Arnos Vale cemetery, drawing on the biographies of its inhabitants. In making *Gas Girls*, the company quickly came up against an absence, a lack of historical record about the women who worked in the munitions factories near Bristol during the First World War. Ingrid, who was just starting work on the Arnos Vale project, spoke of her frustration at how little information they had on the GG project because the women had all signed the official secrets act and because, given the amount of time that had elapsed, it was unlikely the company would be able to access living memory (first-hand accounts). They knew very little about the 'gas girls'. There was a grandson's recollection of a story told to him as a boy by his 'gas girl' grandmother (the character Maud is based on the grandmother). There was also a photo of a Gas Girls' football team (Chittening Football Team) which had played returned soldiers. It was offered by family members of one of the women pictured in the image, but they had no further knowledge to depart. Apart from this second-hand memory and photographic image, particulars about the women or their work at the factory (and contribution to the war effort) were shrouded in mystery, buried under a veil of secrecy and silence. In the absence of memory and material remains, the living stand in for the dead, a process which Rebecca Schneider, after Joseph Roach's writings on performance as substitution, has referred to as "inter(in)animation" (2011, pp. 160–164).

There were two aligned processes to bring the women back to life: devising theatre and archival research. All ensemble members were involved in the theatre-making process. To begin with, the devising process drew heavily on historical documents sourced by the facilitators/directors, Neil and Ingrid. Using newspaper clippings, archival films, diary entries and photographs, the group imagined what it might be like to inhabit Bristol in 1917/1918. Central to this 'stripping back' process (peeling back layers of modern life) was a thought experiment the facilitators gave the performers: "Who might I – a working class person living in Bristol – have been 100-odd years ago? Why take up such dangerous work? Why carry on when it was known that the work was dangerous?" The performers began to build their character based on a sense of their own identity as they immersed themselves in the past through group analysis and discussion of the historical documentation. In this way, the cast began to detail the women and men who worked in the chemical weapons munitions factories. Rebecca developed an interest in the Suffragette movement and decided that her character (Polly) was influenced by the movement and therefore would have fully supported the war effort by working in the munitions factory. Katie, through the development of her character, explored the high death toll of war and the impact on women of the loss of a fiancé or husband. Her character's, Emily's, husband is missing in action. She works to support herself, in the absence of the family breadwinner, but also partly for the camaraderie, enjoying new-found friendships and freedoms (such as drinking with other gas girls in a public house). While, externally, the character of Emily enacts the construct of the female munitions factory worker enjoying social freedoms that come with working life, she is also seen to be navigating the dangerous nature of the work, the moral judgements of others concerning her more 'liberated' behaviours and her own mental anguish over the presumed 'loss' of her husband. The male characters were worked out in a similar way. Jack's character, Bernard, is based on a conscientious objector serving out a national service order. The character of Henry, invented by Jake, is based on a returned soldier discharged through injury. He takes up work in the factory (as foreman) to continue his contribution to the war effort, but also to revenge the death-in-action of his father, as well as his own injury.

The cast invented characters in keeping with historical and social (external) structures. At the same time, they built the internal (emotional) world of their characters. In the process, the performers wrote, edited and rewrote their character narrative as text. Some of this writing remained in monologue form and was performed as direct address (Mrs Brown, Emily and Jake). Other times, it informed spoken dialogue between characters as performers improvised scenes. Performers improvised interactive scenes in character, inventing action and dialogue. Neil and Ingrid often filmed improvisations on mobile phones so that they could then transcribe the scenes (words and actions). These transcripts were introduced back into the process as an emerging performance script. It was as if the characters created by the performers were 'real' people, and their words and actions were being recorded 'verbatim' as a basis for documentary theatre-making in the style of Cheeseman's more 'associational' style of documentary. Of course, these people were not 'real', but characters created by performers through (psychologically motivated) naturalistic theatre techniques. In other words, simulation was at the centre of this 'theatre of the real'.

At the same time as the devising process was simulating reality, a smaller group of participants elected to join Neil and Rosalie in the archives (in particular, the National Archives) to find information about the mustard gas factories in Avonmouth and Chittening (a village just to the north of Avonmouth), and the people who worked in them. There was such a wealth of information gained from bodies going into archives that the group co-authored a sold-out publication released with the performance: *Gas Girls: The Untold Story of Avonmouth's Mustard Gas Factories*, researched and written by Neil Beddow, Karen Chodkiewicz (Mrs Brown, factory cook), Rebecca Davidson (Eleanor, nurse's help), Tracey Harvey (Nurse Harrison) and Rosalie Pordes. The archival research process flowed into the theatre devising/writing process. Snippets of information gleaned from the archives were placed into the process in such a way so as not to dominate or overwhelm the simulation of reality, but to enhance it. Thus, the process was a hybrid of narrative and documentary (verbatim) techniques based on hybridised systems of knowledge, both official and unofficial.

Re-enacting the Factory: *Gas Girls*, acta Centre, Bedminster, 21 March 2014.

The set in the black box theatre space is a simple installation of angled flats, one back left and the other back right. The angled flat, stage left, indicates medical hut. A chair and table are placed in front of the flat when the medical team (doctor, nurse and nurse's help) is in. The angled flat, stage right, defines a change/washroom. Entrances/exits to the performance space are behind each flat. The back wall is a projection screen for film/video, compiled by Ingrid Jones, from the selection of archival footage on Bristol during the war, trench warfare, and munitions factories. The team also shot a 'historical' (sepia-toned), comdedic short film/video of a football game between gas girls and returned soldiers. At the beginning of the piece, a factory floor plan is projected on the wall (the buildings were hastily erected—the mechanical processes of liquid/gas delivery were constantly developing through trial and error, and the medical facilities remained under construction). All the walls—flats, side and back—are painted in a rough whitewash. The floor, a vinyl carpet, is a mottled light grey in colour, like concrete. A wooden box of shells on a hand/sack truck is stage right. The characters are the gas girls (shell filling) including the factory cook (Mrs Brown), the factory workers (fitters and general factory workers), including the superintendent (Whitelaw) who liaises with MoM to fulfil production orders, the medical staff (doctor, nurse and nursing assistant) and returned soldier, Robert, blinded after German gas attack in the Battle of Passchendaele 1917. Robert and Lizzie, a maid who signs on to work in the factory, are engaged, although the state of the relationship is unknown as Robert recuperates from his injury at a local infirmary, St Dunstans.

The two-hour long play is in two acts. In the opening scene, the cast assembles on stage one after the other. Each performs a repetitive movement that captures their character in a single gesture. A spoken phrase is overlaid with the physical gesture, and once all the performers are on stage, the assemblage increases in speed and sound to a crescendo before it slows and fades. The last words are those of the doctor, in a white coat and with a stethoscope around his neck, miming the action of looking down a patient's throat: "the whole system is completely unsafe." The action then turns to examine character motivations for working in the factory.

There are two scenes before we come to the factory: two maids at work (Lizzie and Maud) and a Bristol street scene (overlaid by a segment from an archival film showing a Bristol street circa 1918 with trams stopping and going again). The scenes dig into why/how the characters came to work in the factory. In the first scene, Lizzie comes across Maud, both dressed in black, full-skirt/blouse uniforms with white frill trim, folding a basket of washing. She adopts a proper voice and asks why Maud hasn't finished the folding. Maud doesn't realise that it's Lizzie until she has started answering and turns to address her questioner. Laughing, Lizzie informs Maud that she is leaving to work in the factory. The pay is better, and she won't have to empty madam's dirty chamber pots. In the following scene, a discussion is had at a tram stop where a group of men and women wait. Mrs Brown, the factory cook, greets an acquaintance (Kathleen). Mrs Brown remarks on how good her friend smells (she works in Frys, a large, well-known confectionary store in the city). Kathleen then tells her that she won't smell nice in future as she has signed up to work in the factory. Mrs Brown suggests that she might not want to leave her retail job. Kathleen mentions that the work is paid three times more than at Frys. This provokes a lot of interest, particularly from the other women in the group, including Bernie, whose husband was killed in action (the women offer condolences when they meet). It is confirmed that the factory is hiring. One of the men suggests that there is a high turnover of women workers because they are incompetent at operating the filling machines. He is given short shrift by Mrs Brown but before she can explain the dangers, another man reminds the group that they signed a secrecy act, cutting short the conversation.

Better pay is presented as the main reason why (working class) women took up work in the factories alongside men who were returned, discharged (after injury) soldiers, conscientious objectors undertaking national service, medically unfit or awaiting conscription orders. Even so, there are an array of viewpoints presented. Lizzie and Maud also desire to escape domestic servitude ("emptying madam's dirty chamber pots"). The work presents an opportunity for war widows (Bernie) or those whose husbands are missing in action (Emily) to earn a wage. Inspired by and following the direction of the suffragette movement (which turned from protest to support), Polly went to work in the munitions factory to support the war effort. Mrs Brown's work as a cook means she has access to provisions in extremely short supply and is using her access to foodstuffs to support vulnerable people in her community who might otherwise starve to death (her character is based on an archival document of a cook charged with stealing food). This is revealed in Mrs Brown's monologue, spoken directly to the audience, at the end of the tram stop scene. In other words, there are a range of motivations and perspectives presented, and in this sense acta's simulated 'theatre of the real' (Martin 2013) is closer to Cheeseman's associational (multi-perspectival) documentaries than the more didactic model developed by Littlewood from the European theatre tradition of Piscator, Brecht and so on.

Monologue is a device used early in the play to express characters' inner feelings (Henry, for instance, reveals that his motivation for working in the factory is revenge. This feeling intensified with the delivery of his dead father's pocket watch in the mail, the only keepsake of his father sent back from the front), communicate essential information (Mrs Brown's monologue indicates severe food shortages are due to U-boat attacks on merchant shipping around Britain and that the population, at this stage in the protracted conflict, is in a perilous state), and to sketch conflicts between key characters in the play (these conflicts structure the dramatic narrative). Gas girl, Lizzie (played by Kirsty Ireland), and injured (blinded) soldier, Robert (played by Cassius Ghandi Livingstone), take to the stage simultaneously and speak separately. Robert recalls the gas attack on the trenches at the Battle of Passchendaele that left him blind (film footage shows images of wounded soldiers with heavy bandages around their eyes walking in a line formation with men behind holding the shoulders of the man in front so that they can slowly feel their way forward). Lizzie doesn't know if their relationship has a future. Their tentative attempts to reconcile uneven, and even opposed, experiences of the same conflagration offer a concrete presentation of a larger problem: how to reconcile British use of chemical weapons—outlawed in international treaties at the time—given damage on all fronts—foreign and at home. The other main conflict in the play is between Whitelaw, factory superintendent (played by Laurence Daly), and Captain Harry Roberts (played by Gary McAlister). Whitelaw carries out the directions of the Ministry of Munitions (then led by Winston Churchill), implementing ever increasing production targets as demanded. His willingness to sacrifice regulations to meet targets set by the war government puts him at odds with Roberts whose concern is the women's health.

After these introductory scenes and monologues, the action moves to the factory site. First, we are introduced to the medical team. At the point at which the play begins, there has been a high casualty rate, hence the factory being in the position of hiring and taking on a group of new recruits including Maud, Bernie, Kathleen and others. Gearing up to prepare for the new cohort, Nurse Harrison expresses her unfailing sense of purpose and her conviction that the cause they are working towards is just. At the beginning and end of each shift, the women present to Roberts and Nurse Harrison. One by one, the women present to medical staff and in a gestural ballet show the white of their eyes, poke out their tongues to show their throats and present the front (palms) and backs of their hands. After health checks, the women change for their shift into their work uniforms. Here the experienced female munitions workers informally induct a new group.

Lizzie: Good job you're here. We had 20 girls laid off last week
Maud: What happened to them?
Lizzie: Big accident in hut 3. They were filling the tank in the roof with HS [Hun's stuff] and it spilled everywhere. Lucky not to be killed.
Maud: killed?
Phyllis: Here you go, put these on quick [hands her a uniform bundle]. Shift starts in one minute.
Polly to Maud: You're not wearing a corset are you? Better take it off.
Maud: I can't do that
Polly: Well you can't work with one on…
Mary: [holding up clothing item handed to her] Trousers? I can't wear trousers. It's not decent.
Phyllis: It won't be decent if you don't. The HS vapour gets everywhere and everywhere it gets it gives you a rash.
Emily: Or worse. So make sure you tie the bottoms of the legs when you've got them on. It goes straight up otherwise
Mary: I've never heard anything like it
Kathleen: Make sure your hair is tied back. If you get HS on it, it'll go yellow and burn your face
Emily: If any goes on your skin, you make sure you scrub it off straight away with bleach powder
Bernie: But it'll ruin my skin
Emily: Not as much as the HS will
Polly: Come on girls, time to go!
Mary: What about the face mask? Doctor said we had to wear them
Emily: No point wearing them. The HS just soaks into them and burns your face. Don't want blisters around your mouth do you?
Mary: Googles?
Phyllis: Can't see out of them and when you take them off you get HS all over your face…
Mary: But the doctor said we had to
Polly: Doctor? what does he know? He's only a man. (*Gas Girls* 2014)

The scene demonstrates how the women have become used to dealing with the dangerous liquid/gas and have gained knowledge in how best to equip themselves to deal with the risks, knowledge they share with their peers. This is (unofficial) knowledge the doctor doesn't have, as Polly points out, because he isn't working directly with the gas. Having changed into their uniforms the gas girls take to the floor (stage) for their shift. Spaced out in a long line across the floor, the performers mime the repetitive action of taking a shell off a conveyer belt, positioning it under a machine, attaching the filling machine to the shell, filling the shell, tapping it off, placing the full shell onto another conveyor belt before taking an empty shell and so on. The action follows this group through to the end of the play as they eat and chat in shift breaks in the canteen, play a football match against a team of returned soldiers (organised by Whitehall to boost flagging morale) and navigate relationships (with a focus on the engagement between Lizzie and Robert). At the end of Act One, there is a serious accident, foreshadowed by several small mishaps, in the form of a major spill from the overhead pipes. Lizzie hears the hiss of escaped liquid and steps away from the production line, looking up to the ceiling confirming her worst fears. She cries out, but it is too late. Bernie is placed directly under the spill, and her blood curdling screams end the first act.

When the performance resumes for Act Two, the health check line-up logs injuries from the accident. Maud presents her foot to Captain Roberts while Nurse Harrison helps a whimpering Bernie remove her coat, revealing huge blisters on her upper body. Bernie is immediately ushered off stage and transferred to hospital. She later dies of her injuries, and a funeral is held. At Bernie's funeral, Nurse Harrison, who steadfastly expressed her belief in the just cause, wonders if she can go on: "I've seen too much suffering to believe in a kind god... if I don't have my faith what else is there?" Meanwhile, Whitelaw increasingly ramps up production of shells in line with MoM numbers. One of the final scenes is the choreography of the women on the production line filling shells at speed to the point of utter exhaustion (they are literally gasping for breath at the end) juxtaposed against a sped-up film showing soldiers going over the top of trenches and running into gunfire, again and again. With supplies of gas exhausted, Whitelaw writes to the MoM to request instructions. Before he receives an answer, the armistice is signed. His final scene is congratulating the workers on the factory floor. He shakes the men's hands and exits. The women are left wondering whether they will be recognised for their work. Most think it unlikely, and, Emily, ever the quick-witted one, quips that any medal should be called the "medal of the blistered bum".

A Community of Practice: Practising Community Theatre

GG was not a performance uncritically celebrating women's hidden contribution to the Great War. In telling the story of the women and men who worked in the mustard gas factories in Avonmouth and Chittening in the last six months of the First World War, GG illustrates the sacrifice of those who worked to support the war effort on the home front, but it does not condone their suffering. As heritage theatre, and as an act of remembrance, the performance is not a strategic practice reinforcing the status quo but, rather, stages a difficult return to the past (see Thompson et al. 2009, p. 214). The play returns to the contentious (and current) topic of chemical weapons examining how the British government justified its production/use of these munitions based on German use, their apparent efficiency and the (misplaced) hope that these weapons would bring the entrenched war to a close. The play questions whether the manufacture of mustard gas shells was the decisive element in ending the war (they got to the front in September 2018), exploring instead the terrible and overlooked impact of production of chemical weapons on the home front.

In the final scene of the performance, Maud leads the ensemble in collective reflection. The performers speak of feeling broken by the experience (Captain Roberts), question whether their efforts were worth it (Henry) and note that life hadn't changed in ways they'd expected or hoped (Polly). The reflections of the ensemble cast doubt on the value and integrity of the dangerous effort that was undertaken. The sacrifices of the munitions factory workers (women, men, health staff) didn't build a sense of community, but destroyed it leaving feelings of shame and guilt:

> **Maud**: When it all ended, we didn't keep in touch. ... We sometimes passed on Castle Street, never stopped to speak, just a glance and look between us. We knew what it meant. Recognition. Guilt? As if, somehow, we knew what we had done was wrong, but what was done to us was worse. *(Gas Girls 2014)*

Overwhelmingly, the final scene of the play communicates a deep sense of suspicion towards a traditional notion of community based on sacrifice of self to a higher cause (King, Country, God, a Just Cause). It ends by recounting the early deaths of the workers whose health was severely affected (weakened respiratory systems laid bare to the gathering Spanish flu pandemic). Only Maud lives a long life, and finally breaks her silence in older age. The silence at the end of this 'head count' marks an injustice, and is a silence that is not empty but pregnant with embodied, affective knowing.

In her exploration of forms of political theatre, Erica Fischer-Lichte (2005) notes that theatre after the 1970s staged a critique of a traditional notion of community based on sacrifice of the individual self to a single unity or a common ideology or belief. According to Fischer-Lichte, theatre in post-industrial society established new modes of gathering that "do not require sacrifice" (2005, p. 257). Instead, it "allows…temporary ephemeral communities that do not ask for any longer-lasting commitment nor for a collective identity to emerge… [and] provides a 'viable dialectic between solitude and being with others' for members of post-industrial societies" (p. 258). While Fisher-Lichte focuses on cultural performance as a model for a new type of community, one that is temporary and self-organising, I want to extend the search for a new model of community after the example of GG, which staged a critique of community and demonstrated (celebrated) that facilitated community theatre practice can generate new social knowledge. In other words, I want to examine the idea of community performance in the case of acta as a "community of practice", understood as a "social learning system" (Wenger 2010). The notion of 'community of practice' comes out of academic studies of organisational management, although it is a concept also used in feminist sociolinguistics and studies of professional workplace communities. It is grounded in social learning theory that views learning not as a process of formal instruction but as "an essential part of everyday life and thus a capability inherent in social systems" (Wenger 2010, p. 2). The key point here is that a community of practice is a different construct to the traditional community because it is defined primarily by social engagement, that is, "it is defined simultaneously by its membership and by the practice in which that membership engages… membership and practices grow out of mutual engagement" (Eckert and McConnell-Ginet 1992, p. 464). It is, in other words, self-organising (membership is self-selecting) but unlike Fischer-Lichte's community modelled on performance, an experience [economy] of coming together and breaking apart, the community of practice is a social learning system, and it generates knowledge—social and cultural—for those who actively and mutually engage in the practice of, in this case, making and audiencing community theatre.

acta's 'cycle of engagement' means that its 'practice community' is dynamic and interactive. It remains open to new and diverse membership invited to audience and/or to make theatre, and all members, regardless of social differences, share an understanding of the process of collectively devising theatre. Each group goes through the same process of making theatre and cross-audiences each other's work, thus building communities of (theatre) practice. A sense of mutual appreciation and co-regard emerges through building a common practice rather than denying or obliterating social differences in forced social cohesion.

Wenger notes that "knowledge is not a separate object from the people who produced it or even the process of producing it" (2010, p. 10). So it is that knowledge generated in practice tends to go back into practice, sustaining it beyond the temporary relations of Fischer-Lichte's performance community. Built on the inexhaustible resources of memory, imagination and improvisation this community of practice endures as (in)tangible sets of practices, beliefs, values and aesthetics of affirmation. After TPBB, and specifically the tour to ICAF supported by acta participants, the Elders and acta advanced members collaborated to create *The Now* (2015). At the same time, it seems that TPBB inspired the Elders to further explore oral storytelling traditions, this time with a focus on adult storytelling, and so they devised *Moonshine Nights* (2016). Meanwhile, the focus on women working in non-traditional industries during the First World War, along with changing social attitudes and social mores towards women in general in the early part of the twentieth century, led directly from *Gas Girls* into *Clippies*. *Clippies* examines conflict between men returning from battle in the First World War and women working on the tramways who refused to give up their livelihoods. This conflict spilled over into a large social disturbance in 1920s Bristol, an important aspect of local social/civic history. *Clippies* opened at the acta Centre in July 2021, after the relaxation of pandemic restrictions.

References

Aabe, N. O., Fox, F., Rai, D. and Redwood, S. (2019) 'Inside, outside and in-between: The process and impact of co-producing knowledge about autism in a UK Somali community', *Health Expectations*, 22(4), pp. 752–760. doi: https://doi.org/10.1111/hex.12939

acta Community Theatre Company. (2014) *Gas Girls,* dir. Neil Beddow and Ingrid Jones. acta Community Theatre Centre, Bedminster, Bristol. First performance 19. May 2014.

Ginko-Humphries, A. and Schejbal, M. (eds.) (2013) *COAST. Crossing Borders in Community Theatre*. Bielsko-Biala: Grodzki Theatre Association.

Alston, A. (2015) 'Parallel Interview with Jonathan Petherbridge from London Bubble and Tom Bowtell from Coney Contemporary Theatre Review', *Interventions*, 25(2). Available at: https://www.contemporarytheatrereview.org/2015/interventions-25-2/ (Accessed: 18 January 2018).

Ambar, S. (2014) *Malcolm X at Oxford Union: Racial Politics in a Global Era*. Oxford: Oxford University Press.

Austin-Broos, D.J. and Smith, R.T. (1997) *Jamaica Genesis: Religion and the Politics of Moral Orders*. Chicago: University of Chicago Press.

Beddow, N. (2001) *Turning Points. The Impact of Participation in Community Theatre*. Dartington: South West Arts in conjunction with the Centre for Research in Contemporary Performance Arts, Dartington College of Arts.

———. (2013) 'Same Difference: Learning Through international Partnerships', in Van Erven, E.A.P.B. (ed.) *Community Art Power. Essays from ICAF 2011*. Rotterdam: Rotterdams Wijktheater, pp. 94–106.

Brookfield, K. (2018) 'The People's Centenary: a perspective from the Heritage Lottery Fund', *Cultural Trends*, 27(2), pp. 119–124. doi: https://doi.org/10.1080/09548963.2018.1453455

Chang, D. (2015) *Representing China on the Historical London Stage: From Orientalism to Intercultural Performance,* London and New York: Routledge. doi: https://doi-org.uoelibrary.idm.oclc.org/10.4324/9780203734940

Craig, S. (1980) *Dreams and Deconstructions: Alternative Theatre in Britain*. Ambergate: Amber Lane Press.

Dresser, M. (2004) 'Bristol's Black History Month', *The Regional Historian*, Issue No. 11, pp. 24–27. Available at: https://www.uwe.ac.uk/research/centres-and-groups/regional-history/the-regional-historian [Accessed: 15 March 2016].

Dresser, M. and Fleming, P. (2007) *Bristol: Ethnic Minorities and the City, 1000–2001*. Chichester: Phillimore, 2007.

Eckert, P. and McConnell-Ginet, S. (1992) 'Think Practically and Look Locally: Language and Gender as Community-Based Practice', *Annual Review of Anthropology*, 21(1), pp. 461–488. doi: http//doi.org/10.1146/annurev.an.21.100192.002333

Filewod, A. (2011) *Committing Theatre. Theatre Radicalism and Political Intervention in Canada*. Toronto, Ontario: Between the Lines.
Fischer-Lichte, E. (2005) *Theatre, Sacrifice, Ritual. Exploring Forms of Political Theatre*. London and New York: Routledge.
Forsyth, A. and Megson, C. (2009) *Get Real: Documentary Theatre Past and Present*. Basingstoke: Palgrave Macmillan.
Hawkins, G. (1993) *From Nimbin to Mardi Gras. Constructing Community Arts*. Sydney: Allen & Unwin.
Heddon, D. and Milling, J. (2006) *Devising Performance. A Critical History*. Basingstoke: Palgrave Macmillan.
Jackson, S. (2005) 'Touchable Stories and the Performance of Infrastructural Memory', in Pollock, D. (ed.) *Remembering. Oral History Performance*. Basingstoke: Palgrave Macmillan, pp. 45–66.
Jeffers, A. and Moriarty, G. (eds.) (2017) *Culture, Democracy and the Right to Make Art. The British Community Arts Movement*. London, Oxford, New York, New Delhi, Sydney: Bloomsbury Methuen Drama.
Kershaw, B. (1991) *Theatre and Community. Alternative and Community Theatre in Britain: 1960–1985. An Investigation into Cultural History and Performance Efficacy*. PhD thesis. University of Exeter. Available at: https://ethos.bl.uk/OrderDetails.do?uin=uk.bl.ethos.280752 (Accessed: 3 June 2017).
———. (1992) *The Politics of Performance. Radical Theatre as Cultural Intervention*. London; New York: Routledge
———. (1999) *The Radical in Performance: Between Brecht and Baudrillard*. London and New York: Routledge.
Lindqvist, S. (1979) 'Dig Where You Stand', *Oral History*, 7(2), pp. 24–30.
Malcolm X Elders Theatre Group. (2013) *Ticky Picky Boom Boom, dir. Neil Beddow and Philippa Smith*. acta Community Theatre Centre, Bedminster, Bristol. First performance 11. November 2013.
Marshall, E.Z. (2001) '"The Anansi syndrome": A debate concerning Anansi's influence on Jamaican culture', *World Literature Written in English*, 39(1), pp. 127–136. doi: https://doi.org/10.1080/17449850108589351
———. (2012) *Anansi's Journey: A Story of Jamaican Cultural Resistance*. Kingston: University of the West Indies Press.
Matarasso, F. (1997) *Use or Ornament. The Social Impact of Participation in the Arts*. Bournes Green, Stroud: Comedia.
———. (2012) *Winter Fires. Art and Agency in Old Age*. London: Baring Foundation, Available at: https://parliamentofdreams.files.wordpress.com/2016/12/2012-winter-fires.pdf (Accessed: 15 March 2017).
Martin, C. (2013) *Theatre of the Real*. Basingstoke: Palgrave Macmillan.
Nicholson, H. (2005) *Applied Drama and the Gift of Theatre*. Basingstoke: Palgrave Macmillan
———. (2015) 'The Silence within the Noise: Reflections from the UK on "A Vibrant Hybridity"' in Cohen-Cruz, J. *Remapping Performance. Common Ground, Uncommon Partners*. London and New York: Routledge, pp. 22–26.
Onuora, A. N. (2015) *Anansesem: Telling Stories and Storytelling African Maternal Pedagogies*. Bradford, Ontario, CA: Demeter Press.
Owen, L. (2013) 'The witness and the replay: London Bubble' in McAvinchey, C. (ed.) *Performance and Community Commentary and Case Studies*. London, New Delhi, New York, Sydney: Bloomsbury, pp. 155–188.

Paget, D. (1987) "Verbatim Theatre': Oral History and Documentary Techniques', *New Theatre Quarterly*, 3(12), pp. 317–36.

Policy Action Team 10. (1999) *National Strategy for Neighbourhood Renewal: Policy Action Audit: Report of the Policy Action Team 10: The Contribution of Sport and the Arts*. London: DCMS.

Roach, J. (1996) *Cities of the Dead. Circum-Atlantic Performance*. New York: Colombia University Press.

Samuel, R. (1994) *Theatres of Memory. Past and Present in Contemporary Culture*. London and New York: Verso.

Schneider, R. (2011) *Performing Remains. Art and War in Times of Theatrical Reenactment*. London; New York: Routledge.

Thompson, J. (2005) *Digging up Stories. Applied Theatre, Performance and War*. Manchester: Manchester University Press.

Thompson, J., Hughes, J. and Balfour, M. (2009) *Performance in Place of War*. Calcutta: Seagull Books.

Threadgold, T. (2000) 'Poststructuralism and discourse analysis', in Lee, A. and Poynton, C. (eds.) *Culture and Text. Discourse and Methodology in Social Research and Cultural Studies*. St Leonards, NSW: Allen and Unwin, pp. 40–58.

Van Erven, E.A.P.B. (2001) *Community Theatre. Global Perspectives*. London and New York: Routledge.

———. (ed.) (2013) *Community Art Power. Essays from ICAF 2011*. Rotterdam: Rotterdams Wijktheater.

Watt, D. (2003) "The Maker and the Tool': Charles Parker, documentary performance, and the search for a popular culture', *New Theatre Quarterly*, 19(1), pp. 41–66.

———. (2009) 'Local Knowledges, Memories, and Community: From Oral History to Performance', in Haedicke, S., Heddon, D., Oz, A. and Westlake, E.J. (eds.) *Political Performances. Theory and Practice*. Amsterdam and New York: Rodopi, pp. 189–212.

wa Thiong'o, N. (2007) 'Notes towards a Performance Theory of Orature', *Performance Research*, 12(3), pp. 4–7. doi: https://doi.org/10.1080/13528160701771253

Wenger E. (2010) 'Communities of Practice and Social Learning Systems: the Career of a Concept', in Blackmore, C. (ed.) *Social Learning Systems and Communities of Practice*. London: Springer, pp. 179–198. doi: https://doi.org/10.1007/978-1-84996-133-2_11

Wüstenberg, J. (2017) *Civil Society and Memory in Postwar Germany*. Cambridge: Cambridge University Press.

CHAPTER 4

Yijala Yala: Big hART Creative Producing Cultural Livelihoods in the Pilbara

INTRODUCTION: FROM THE MARGINS TO THE MAINSTREAM

Big hART is an arts and social change company established in Tasmania, Australia, in the early 1990s. Co-founder and CEO, Scott Rankin, is playwright and director of mainstage theatre productions that emerge from long-term (minimum three-years duration), community-based, interdisciplinary arts projects co-ordinated by creative producers. Big hART engages professional theatre practitioners (directors. performers, writers, set and costume designers) in creative processes and performances which bring the narrative experiences of marginalised individuals and communities to the nation's mainstages, often in capital, arts festival cities such as Sydney, Melbourne, Perth and Adelaide. Performing the stories of excluded individuals and communities on the nation's mainstages—from the margins to the mainstream—unsettles the schema of 'containment' typically associated with community-based theatre as an affective practice geared to the local level (McConachie 1998). Big hART's practice utilises the status of mainstage performance to drive policy change at a national level. A multilayered approach holding in tension individual experiences of exclusion, assets-based community development, the creation of 'exquisite' art and national policy change animates Big hART's dynamic and iterative practice.

This chapter and case study focuses on the *Yijala Yala* project created by Big hART for and with the people of Roebourne, a town of approximately 1000 inhabitants in north-west Western Australia. The population of Roebourne (*Ieramugadu*) is mainly Indigenous. The project title points to the major Ngarluma and Yindjibarndi language groups of the area: *Yijala* means 'now' in Ngarluma, and *Yala* means 'now' in Yindjibarndi. The *Yijala Yala* project commenced in approximately 2010, and is ongoing in the form of the legacy project, *New Roebourne*.[1] I first heard about the *Yijala Yala* project at

---

[1] See https://yijalayala.bighart.org/about/ and https://newroebourne.bighart.org/

the 2011 International Community Arts Festival (ICAF) in Rotterdam, where Big hART presented a version of *Ngapartji Ngapartji* (NN) compatible with international touring. Senior Roebourne women formed a chorus accompanying lead performer, Trevor Jamieson, onstage. By this point, the Roebourne women were in the early stages of working with Big hART on their own project to tell the story of Roebourne anew, as part of a wider process of civic and cultural renewal in a post–Native Title era. Taking part in an international touring production offered insight into processes of production and reception of community performance (see Schaefer 2013). In May 2013, I travelled to the Pilbara region to follow two weeks of a creative development process geared towards production of the major theatre piece, *Hipbone Sticking Out*, as a professional theatre cast and crew joined a core creative team based in Roebourne, led by Creative Producer Debra Myers. The process I observed[2] was the final creative development process *in* Roebourne before *Hipbone Sticking Out* subsequently moved to Sydney for a three-week intensive creative development and rehearsal before opening in Canberra, Australia's national capital city, in July 2013.

Yijala Yala comes in a sequence of performances made by Big hART with and for Indigenous language groups, including *Ngapartji Ngapartji* and *Namatjira*. Both those productions have been strenuously critiqued in line with debates around Indigenous Theatre. Maryrose Casey notes that questions concerning the contested contours of Indigenous theatre turn on "the level of Indigenous control of creative processes, theatrical form, the context of production and the inclusion of tangible markers of Indigenous culture" (2009, p. 122). She is critical of *Ngapartji Ngapartji* for its framing of "Indigenous stories as testimony of Indigenous oppression for political agendas" (2009, p. 137), and argues that this is part of a pathological dynamic in which the oppressed seek recognition from the oppressor and the oppressor (in this case, non-Indigenous Australians who make up majority of audience members) "recuperates virtue through witnessing the testimonies of oppression" (2009, p. 136). Thurow has recently highlighted the recurring issue of Indigenous control over artistic products, which particularly applies to Big hART's work given that Rankin, a non-Indigenous Australian, maintains creative control as writer and director. According to Thurow, "it can be debated whether Big hART's work – despite its culturally sensitive working model – should be labelled fully 'decolonising'" (2019, pp. 93–95).

In these critiques, Big hART's work has been examined more as Indigenous theatre and less as 'community arts and cultural development', although this is how Rankin has recently identified the work (2018). Rankin's use of terms such as 'cultural rights' locates Big hART's work in relation to Article 27 of the United Nations' Universal Declaration of Human Rights, which overlaps with

---

[2] Big hART required that I undertake Cultural Awareness training, which I did with other members of the team and FIFO mining workers. The training was led by Clinton Walker, at Gurrgura Cultural Organisation, in Karratha on 17 May 2013.

later manifestations of community cultural development practice, as Pitts and Watt (2001) note when they assert that an early formulation of community arts in terms of "access and participation" was transformed by practitioners into a concern for "cultural democracy", which assumes "a plurality of cultures and a democratic right that each should be able to be practiced, enjoyed and even supported by funding" (2001, p. 9). The chapter focuses on the articulation of big hART's cultural rights-based approach within what anthropologist, Mary Edmunds, refers to as "the hard demands of an overwhelming Pilbara development trajectory [in which] both government and resource companies are essential players in determining what the extent, and the limits, of [Indigenous] self-determination might be" (2012, p. 51).

Before I come to this detailed case study of the *Yijala Yala* project within the broader frame of 'negotiated engagement' (Edmunds 2012, pp. 49–51), the chapter sets out the place of Big hART in the contemporary Australian neoliberal state. Big hART was formed in a time of socio-economic and cultural transition. I examine how this set of factors influenced the company's core values and principles ('it's harder to hurt someone if you know their story'), its multilayered approach (methodology) and its emphasis on virtuosity (practical skill and technical expertise) over standards of 'artistic excellence'. Then I turn to examine the process of making *Hipbone Sticking Out* in Roebourne as part of a creative development process within the larger *Yijala Yala* project. I aim to provide detailed examples of a way of working that enables individuals and communities that have experienced exclusion and marginalisation to stake a claim in mainstream spaces, to call for a response to systematic injustice and to enact cultural livelihoods.

MADE IN TASMANIA, STAGING AUSTRALIA, VIRTUOSICALLY

Big hART was founded in 1992 by Scott Rankin and John Bakes (d. 2014) in Burnie, Tasmania's fourth largest city (pop. approx. 23,000) located on the north-west coastline of the island state separated from the Australian mainland by the Bass Strait. In the same year (March–June), a divisive and protracted industrial dispute at the Associated Pulp and Paper Mill (APPM) propelled the small regional city to the forefront of national politics. Burnie's modest civic growth was intimately connected to the manufacturing industry (established 1936) that came to dominate the city. The first mill in the world to produce fine paper from Eucalypt trees, unsustainably sourced from nearby old growth forests, 'The Pulp', as it was locally known, was viewed as a 'benevolent' employer "vital to the city's economy" (Baker 2001, p. 9). In 1992, it was the district's largest employer with "third generation members of local families" counted amongst the 1100-strong workforce (Baker 2001, p. 9). That workforce was engaged, via its representative unions, in negotiations with management—since 1984, Broken Hill Holdings Ltd (NBH), a mining corporation headquartered in Melbourne—to reform the workplace, a process that was taking place across industrial workplaces throughout Australia as part of a programme of economic reform undertaken by the Hawke/Keating Labour government (1983–1996). Industrial/labour relations scholar, Thompson, notes: "workers saw award restructuring, reskilling, retraining, increasing efficiency and productivity, and the acceptance of voluntary redundancy as their way of assisting management to keep the plant operational" based on a keen awareness of the "dependence of the community on the plant" (1992, p. 152).

The 1992 APPM dispute was triggered by management decision to end joint negotiation with relevant unions over workplace reforms and, instead, to unilaterally alter traditional award payments and conditions. The Burnie dispute, according to Thompson, was "another act in an on-going drama set up to construct a new edifice of industrial relations in Australia" (1992, p. 161). The first act of that drama took place in 1986 with the Pilbara iron ore Robe River dispute (between mining unions and Broken Hill Holdings Ltd.). For the Burnie workforce, it represented a shocking and sudden introduction to an "aggressive and competitive corporate [mining] culture" (Thompson 1992, p. 162) in which the corporate enterprise's "right to manage" (1992, p. 149) was ruthlessly pursued.

Big hART was established in this crucible of crisis: the second act in the drama of corporation-led industrial relations reform as part of the process of 'economic rationalism', or neoliberalisation of the nation state economy. At the same time, there was a realignment of national cultural policy to conservative management of the so-called flagships theatres according to restrictive values of 'professionalism' and 'excellence' (see Milne 2004). Keenly aware of "changing economic and social conditions" (Rankin 2018, p. 12), Big hART's co-founders began to pragmatically build an arts organisation through a process of "trial and error" (p. 10). There were, however, several directions taken during this time when Big hART was "not an entity so much as a tenuously linked series of poorly funded projects" (Rankin 2018, p. 14) that determined the future shape of the organisation.

First, Rankin and Bakes partnered with local government and social service organisations to address the hidden side effects of industrial decline and regional underemployment. Big hART took a "non-welfare, task-focused approach" (2018, p. 12) which found accommodation within social services undergoing a fundamental restructuring of arrangements for social welfare, as part of the government-led economic reform process. Rankin himself describes this period as akin to 'riding a wave' of federal government support for "unusual strategies that could be proved to be working" (in Waites 2008, p. 53). Interest in Big hART's work continued into the term of a new federal government, a Liberal/National coalition, particularly in the wake of Australia's deadliest mass shooting at Port Arthur, a heritage tourism site in south-west Tasmania, committed by a 28-year-old Tasmanian man in 1996. Big hART's ongoing work was called to Parliament House, Canberra, to demonstrate innovative arts and social change projects that were proving to be successful in violence prevention. In addition to the performance, "we also wrote a manual and [made a] video about how you do this kind of work" (Rankin in Waites 2008,

p. 54). The event with the prime minister (John Howard) in Parliament House, Canberra, launched the newly incorporated charity, and it also established a status for the company and connections between Big hART and federal government ministries that the company has maintained to the present day. Securing federal government support, that is non-arts, social policy-based funding at a time of crisis in arts funding, especially for work with a 'social aesthetic' (Burvill 1986, p. 80) and located in regional or remote parts of Australia, has been vital to the continuing evolution of the company. As Rankin explained in relation to the discrete funding pots (regional, CCD) available via the main arts funding body in Australia:

> if we tried to do all of this on $25,000 Australia Council grants we'd be nowhere. If we were trying to move through the regional arts network we'd be nowhere. […] mov[ing] through the Department of Prime Minister and Cabinet […] opens up a whole lot of things. (In Waites 2008, p. 54)

In addition to accessing mainline sources of government support, and this is the second directional point, Big hART gained a national, mainstage platform for performance via an invitation to the arts festival circuit. The company's distinctive 'very visual' (Rankin in Waites 2008, p. 46) aesthetic drew the attention of Robyn Archer, renowned cabaret artist and then director of the National Festival of Australian Theatre, Canberra. She invited Big hART's work to Canberra and then to the 2000 Adelaide Festival when she was the festival's artistic director. The company took a performance piece entitled, *Big hArt Works*, which was "a very big piece with a big cast…made [out of] everything we'd done for the last six years" (Rankin in Waites 2008, p. 55). It was well received and established Big hART's profile on the arts festival circuit.

From this point, Big hART's self-definition appears to flex between art-making—'making art that is big' (Rankin 2018, p. 22)—and community development, depending on the audience. Sophia Marinos notes that art and community mean "different things to different people" and that, in relation to the term "community",

> often to arts or non-CCD arts crowds you try your hardest not to use the word because it's a dirty word and it means substandard art, whereas if you're talking to a funder you'll overuse it because that's what they want to hear: that you're working with the community, for the community, by the community. (9 January 2013)

Marinos states that while "we're probably in some ways a bit savvy with the use of the word 'community'" (9 January 2013), the company need not engage in defensive argument because Big hART's practice operates according to an approach that upholds art and community (and more) in productive tension. Rankin articulates Big hART's practice in terms of a layered approach:

Individual: building social and economic participation;
Community: building connections and capacity for change;
Nation: contributing to social policy change;
Art: creating exquisite, high-calibre art outcomes for national and international festivals. (In Wright et al. 2016, pp. 42–44)

The articulation of a multilayered method consisting of four equally weighted domains sidesteps interminable debates concerning art and aesthetic affect, community development and social (policy) change. Tensions are encapsulated within an assets-based community development approach. Focus on individual experiences of social exclusion or marginalisation speaks to the rise of neoliberalism, and how the economic-led social framework stresses individual risk, or precarity. In an oral history interview with Rankin by James Waites, the discussion touches on the centrality of aesthetic practice in creating slow, iterative change across many levels:

> **Rankin:** […] what happens in our work is that we make something beautiful, […] there's a successful, exquisite […] moment. And everybody around the [person/people at the centre of that beautiful moment], 'cause you've set it up in the right way, goes, 'I … cannot believe that that was you doing that.' […] I can guarantee that within two days of that, that that young person will have destroyed that because it's so threatening to their identity. […] and you need to […] embrace that […] work with that […] and already have planned the next phase that you're going to take them into which will create a moment […] that shakes their identity again. […] The good growth happens in three years by putting enough of those things in a sequence that that there is a shift […].
> **Waites:** 'a slow accumulation of a broader sense of identity'. (Waites 2008, pp. 26–27)

Rankin views a multilayered methodology as not simply extending representation, or visibility, to the marginalised, but as actively reimagining the nation state from its so-called margins, or aporias. This aligns the practice with US community-based theatre, which Sonja Kuftinec asserts is an "interrogation in and through performance, of the constituent values that constitute that aggregate entity of the nation-state" (Kuftinec 2003, p. 19).

Stressing the complexity of method and approach over definitive definition as community-based and/or art, Rankin introduces the notion of virtuosity as essential to the practice. Rankin's call for "a renewed 'commitment to virtuosity'" in the cultural field foregrounds the technical expertise of the creative practitioner in operating the multilayered methodology and in dealing skilfully with the demands and tensions inherent in managing the many layers of practice. Through this commitment to virtuosity, practitioners hone skills in 'wrestling with the many layers of practice', as part of a process of developing expertise in 'experimenting with community dramaturgies' (Rankin in Wright et al. 2016, pp. 21–22).

Practical Principles: 'It's Harder to Hurt Someone If You Know Their Story'

Core principles underpin a practice whose definition flexes to encompass tensions between the many constituent layers. Sophia Marinos, states: "It isn't that one size fits all, but things like 'positive regard' and 'it's harder to hurt someone if you know their story' ... those principles guide the conversations we have" (9 January 2013). Big hART's socially active work gets in front of policymakers in a way that is different to the familiar story of lining up anecdotes to personalise stories of deficit. Their work does not see a story as utilitarian, or taken from the teller, but as an asset, and it does not see service workers and policymakers as in opposition, but presumes a desire to achieve good outcomes for, and collaboration with, the story sharers. So, although the mechanism of telling stories—personalising the problem—might look familiar, the way it is done it is different. Marinos expresses this as follows:

> [we're] not asking people to get up and tell their story ... you won't just invite people to a workshop and say ok we're creating a safe space [in which to tell your story] ... it'll be more like what's your natural comfortable space and we will enter that if it's ok with you... It is strengths focused, it is homing in on who our community is and them then teaching us ... They are co-creators. Even when you're bringing them into the theatre world, which is foreign to them, the relationship you've developed ensures that they feel safe and comfortable, and that they remain experts of their culture. (9 January 2013)

Big hART starts from community strengths, building projects slowly, with communities imagined not as just participants but as experts. Rather than extract stories from individuals and communities to stage in the belief that the public act of truth-telling leads to liberation, Big hART enters into social spaces to understand the experience of exclusion, to identify strengths and capacities, and to build up to expression from a basis in the experience of social systems.

This asset-based community development (ABCD) approach has been developed by Big hART with community development scholars, most notably Peter Wright and David Palmer (see Wright and Palmer 2007, Palmer 2010 and Wright et al. 2016). Developed originally by Kretzmann and McKnight (1993) in inner-city neighbourhoods in North America, ABCD has gained purchase in community performance practice through Jan Cohen Cruz's writing about her practice in post-Katrina New Orleans: *HOME, New Orleans?* (2009, pp. 115–116). Cohen Cruz asserts, after Borrup, an equivalence between ABCD and performance practice insofar as creativity plays a key role in identifying capacities and catalysing local cultural assets, "building on strengths to overcome weaknesses" (2009, p. 116). Australian feminist economic geographers, Gibson-Graham (2006), argue that narrative storytelling is a critical method of ABCD as "a simple and incredibly powerful tool for invoking a reframing of community members and a re-narrativising of community-development trajectories" (p. 145). Distinct from the normative "needs-based" approach which "invites solutions from the outside" in the form of "grants and assistance from government and non-government agencies", thereby perpetuating a "dependence on needs profiling to continue aid", ABCD emphasises the "assets and capacities of community members, associations, institutions and infrastructure" (p. 145) and "invites communities to begin thinking about what they can do to mobilise what they already have" (p. 146). An asset-based approach such as this, as Gibson-Graham assert, "invites people to document their personal gifts and capacities" (p. 145), thereby introducing "a new fullness into the representation of identity": "no longer were subjects defined as lacking or victimised; instead they were invited to see themselves as skilful and competent" (p. 145). Narrative storytelling in this context draws focus onto "the meanings people attach to experience and the effect of these meanings on behaviour", and these alternative stories, "outside of the dominant story", generate new representations of people and places (p. 146). I'll return to this argument linking Big hART's practice and development theory in the conclusion, where I will develop it further.

Big hART's approach views story (the lived experience of exclusion) as a form of knowledge, and collaborates with knowledge experts to "place [their stories] with the right audiences in order to illuminate the things we need to know about ourselves and things we need to shift as a society" (Rankin in Van Erven 2013, p. 208). As well as a narrative approach, it is dialogic, since stories are prompts for reflective, real-world action based on "knowing that within government there are many people who are desperately trying to do things like us and are dedicating their life to it in a way that we are – that is the generosity of spirit and not the adversarial nature of it" (Rankin in Van Erven 2013, p. 210). Big hART works with participants to express experience as part of a process of articulating an alternative story, putting these narratives through production into dialogue with those in positions of power, those who deliver social services or those who make social policy. The assumption is that the harm done to socially excluded individuals is inadvertent and accidental, the product of a system that operates automatically, unconsciously or bureaucratically. The expression of experiential knowledge in/through creative practices has the power to transform unintentional harm into intentional or conscious care. This 'political ethic of care' (after Tronto 1993) is based in a relational ontology which locates care as a collective response-ability (Barnes et al. 2015, p. 10) and as personal and policy/political renewal (p. 12): "the critical feminist political position in which care ethics is based makes it more than a set of characteristics for the pursuit of good: it is a broad set of theories for the pursuit of justice that require action within political and institutional systems as well as within interpersonal caring relationships" (p. 12). This framework encompasses Big hART's aim to create a more caring social policy and social services community through directly taking into account the personal narratives of those excluded from social systems. This will hopefully become clear in the following example taken from performance.

Hipbone Sticking Out: Remembering John Pat in Canberra

Hipbone Sticking Out (*Hipbone*) is a touring theatre production made by Big hART with and for the people of Roebourne. Performed by theatre professionals and members of the Roebourne community, the production is one of several co-produced creative outputs of the *Yijala Yala* Project, an interdisciplinary arts, media and social/policy change programme, based in Roebourne in north-west Western Australia, since 2010. *Hipbone* premiered at the Playhouse Theatre, Canberra Theatre Centre, as part of the Centenary of Canberra celebrations, from 3 to 6 July 2013. This theatrical encounter between a remote Indigenous community and the national capital city audience is examined as a fundamental part of the long-term *Yijala Yala* project. I will focus on the performance and a two-week Creative Development process in Roebourne in May 2013. My discussion begins with an examination of the opening scenes of the performance.

As the theatre house lights fade to black out, the image of Jan Brueghel the Elder's *Orpheus in the Underworld* (1594) is projected across the flat front of the curtained proscenium arch stage. A female soprano introduces a melodic riff before she is joined by a harmonic chorus of voices singing (in an original composition) the first words of the 'Orphic Hymm to Pluto', a poetic celebration of the Roman god and ruler of the underworld. With the audience initiated, visually and aurally, into the mysteries of the ancients, the main blackout curtain lifts revealing a stage screened by several strategically placed scrims that carry the projection image of Brueghel's underworld deep into the space. Behind the forward scrim, stage right, stands a boy (played by Nelson Coppin or Maverick Eaton)[3] dressed in black shorts, white shirt, and white socks and sneakers. The boy is performing, on one spot, a slow-motion sequence of body pops and freestyle moves. Across from the boy, stage left, stands Pluto (Lex Marinos), in a long-hooded cloak, head bowed towards a globe of light he is holding in his hands. Behind a second scrim towards the rear of the stage space, far behind the forward line of man and boy, a congregation of hymnal singers, each carrying a small glowing orb of light, slowly process across the back of the stage space (left to right), singing:

> Pluto Magnanimous, whose realms profound
> Are fix'd beneath the firm and solid ground,
> In the Tartarian plains remote from sight,
> And wrapt forever in the depths of night

The moving play of light and shadow animates the landscape of the image of the underworld into which enters a man (Trevor Jamieson) in the same

---

[3] Nelson was one of two community cast members who learnt and alternatively performed the role of the young John Pat. Maverick was the other.

clothing as the boy. He looks at the boy, then back at himself, patting himself down and checking that he is, in fact, materially present. He speaks:

> The Man [looking at the boy]: In two hours, I'll be dead.
>
> Pluto [lifts his head from the ball of light to directly address the audience]: Don't want to ruin your night,
> Thought you should know
> Seeing we're in this together…
>
> The Man: John. John Pat
> 'Murrdu' – nickname,
> Mum's heart will break, and,
> They'll call me 'The Boy'
>
> A loud staccato drum track plays over the musical chorus, and 'the boy', stage right, falls to the ground. The man turns and points to the boy collapsed on the floor.
>
> The Man: Me there see, in my cell, brain swelling … it's true,
> Everything flashes before your eyes […] (*Hipbone Sticking Out*)

The protagonist of the play, John Pat, died, aged sixteen, in police custody on 28 September 1983. This premier of *Hipbone* in a theatre in Australia's national capital city in 2013 is the thirty-year anniversary of Pat's death in custody. The Yindjibarndi man's death placed further pressure on the Australian government to investigate an issue of national import. In 1987, the federal government established a Royal Commission into Aboriginal and Torres Strait Islander Deaths in Custody (RCADC). Pat's was one of 99 deaths over the period of a decade (the 1980s) investigated by the Commission. Along with 339 specific criminal justice recommendations, the 1991 Commission report recommended that "Reconciliation of Aboriginal and non-Aboriginal communities must be an essential commitment on all sides if change is to be genuine and long term" (Commonwealth of Australia 1991). Shortly after, legislation was introduced to establish a statutory authority, the Council for Aboriginal Reconciliation (*Council for Aboriginal Reconciliation Act 1991*), to begin a formal process to advance reconciliation between Indigenous and non-Indigenous Australians. In returning to Pat's death in Roebourne in 1983 in a Canberran theatre in 2013, *Hipbone* establishes a narrative and performative encounter between a cosmopolitan theatre audience in the nation's political, policymaking capital and a remote, Indigenous community. This encounter between the national capital city audience and the kin and community of John Pat stages a care-filled reckoning with the (the rights-based) policy of reconciliation which portended major changes in racialised relations between Indigenous and non-Indigenous Australians.

The beat of clap sticks accompanied by traditional (male) song (played/sung offstage by Ngarluma man, Patrick Churnside) clears the stage. The scrims and the illusion of a shadowy underworld retreat, revealing a picture frame stage. Pluto and the older Pat remain on what is now visible as a raised and (flexible) tilted wooden platform, protruding forward of the neoclassically adorned flats framing the picture frame stage with a stage (the back surface of this stage doubles as a projection screen or is curtained off). Younger Pat is lying on the stage floor in front of this platform. A group of people, led by singer/percussionist, Churnside, alongside Violet Samson (Ngarluma), Allery Sandy (Yindjibarndi) and Josie Samson (Ngarluma) enter from the wings and take up positions in front and to either side of the picture frame stage. The senior men and women sit on either side of the stage observing and performing witness to the action, offering the soundtrack to it, while members of the ensemble—the professional and community cast—stand to the side watching and waiting to perform. The Man approaches the Boy, and lifts his prone body, carrying him back to the performance platform and placing him upright on his feet. The underworld is now embodied in the figure of Pluto. In the following scene, Pluto faces the audience with his back to the boy/man while clever shadow play projects his overblown shadowy figure somewhat menacingly over the boy/man:

> Boy: So what now?
> Man: I don't know.
> Boy: You dyin inni?
> Man: You are, we are, maybe.
> Boy: Who is we?
> Man: Not sure ... the boy I think.
> Pluto: Hold on...young fella. Not yet you're not.
> Boy: Who that is?
> Man: Aks him aks him what he's here for [man pushing boy forwards to Pluto].
> Boy: What's up?
> Pluto: What's up? Who are you, Snoop Dogg?
> Boy: Yeah. Na. Who you?
> Pluto: No respect... Pluto.
> Boy: Like the dog with floppy ears?
> Pluto (sarcastically): Yeah, just like the dog with floppy ears.
> Boy: What you here for?
> Pluto: Oh well, let's see... you're lying smashed up on the floor of your police cell, your brain swelling, der...
> Man: [to boy] Hey, how does he know?
> Boy: [to Pluto] Hey, you don't know me.
> Pluto: Yes I do... [Pluto goes on to identify Pat by name, nickname, favourite animal and favourite song] In two hours you'll become a symbol in the fight for justice.
> Man: Hey, I don't wanna be no symbol [to the Boy]: tell him.
> Pluto: Archie[4] will write a song about you, there'll be a Royal Commission, and you'll end up being a metaphor in a theatrical production celebrating the centenary of the capital of the country that stole your land, displaced your people, and threw you in prison. (*Hipbone Sticking Out*)

---

[4] Archie Roach is a famous Indigenous Australian musician (singer, songwriter, guitarist) and activist.

The opening scenes of the performance represent 'the boy' dying of a traumatic brain injury on the floor of the police lock-up in Roebourne. In the theatre, the boy is accompanied by his older self, recalled from the world of the dead by Pluto 'the magnanimous', and members of his family (Pat's mum makes an appearance in Act Two) and the community. Pluto and John, man and boy, remain on stage throughout the performance narrating the story of the people of Roebourne and commenting on the (historical) action they set in play. Pat's doubled persona is a key device in presenting Roebourne's hidden history, confronting negative representations and stereotypes and creating a counter-narrative. When Pluto says: "You've got two hours to live what's flashing before your eyes?", The Man, confused, states: "Everything's all mixed up in here (gesturing head)… Who's this me that I am? What's this past that I was?" When the confusion passes, he realises with certainty: "We have to go back, back to when the world was soft." Thus, the rich and resonant story of the people of Roebourne unfolds from creation story, through European contact and colonisation, to the mining boom of the 1960s and beyond, through the persona/e of 'the boy' as he lies dying, his life story flashing before his eyes. In the return to this traumatic event, with its local and national reverberations, the particular enactment created by Big hART with and for Roebourne kin and community enables a cultural or ceremonial re-marking of 'the boy's' passing. The performance ensemble perform witness to the action on-stage *and* establish the ceremonial space of marking another's passing. The bodies between stage and auditorium partly break the illusory frame, and serve as a bridge (a ceremonial circle) to link the audience physically and experientially in this near-ritual enactment of custodianship. The community recovers the death story of 'the boy' represented in national media headlines, Royal Commission reports and regional/state court proceedings, and sets it back within the living continuity of the Ngarluma and Yindjibarndi custodians of the land, language and culture of the Roebourne region long before it became a town established by an officer of a colonial government (Mr Sholl), and long before cultural (song) lines leading from ancient mysteries embodied in the figure of Pluto were dreamt up. The transformation of the theatre into a space in which an alternative (gently ironic, ruthlessly humorous) mode of custodianship is palpable only highlights the abrogation of care that contributed to Pat's death in police custody. This disjunction is meant to engage thinking about alternative modes of custody (protection within a political ethics of care). It is about renewing an affective response to caring about and reckoning with rights, equality and justice, starting in a theatre in the capital city of Australian nation. This is how the opening scenes of the performance open a space/time continuum in which to set the Indigenous history of the people of Roebourne and the wider Pilbara region. I will not come back to the play again until I have unpacked the context and process, focusing on a two-week Creative Development, the third of three such processes in the making of *Hipbone*. In order to do this, I need to travel approximately 4000 km north-west from Canberra to Roebourne, and back to

2010 (and earlier) to explore how Big hART came to be in the Pilbara making a performance for and with the people of Roebourne: a performance in part about the Burrup Peninsula—part of the Dampier Archipelago, named after the English 'pirate' (as he's referred to in *Hipbone*), William Dampier (HMS Roebuck, 1699)—that juts into the Indian Ocean like a hipbone sticking out.

'Don't Go Where You're Not Invited But It Is Possible to Foment an Invitation' (Pauline Peel in Pitts and Watt 2001): Big hART in Roebourne/*Ieramugadu*

How projects start is often overlooked in analysis, although, as Pauline Peel notes above, it is better if practitioners follow an invitation, or at least foment one. The following chapter explores how beginnings (artist-led or cross-sector partnership collaborations) might distinguish one kind of practice from another. According to Big hART:

> [a]n artist and community partnership can begin in many different ways e.g.: a community inviting an artist to work with participants as a new approach. Or an artist recognizing an issue and seeing how their skills could create a new engagement. 1. R&D: Community Consultation. (Big hART *Lucky Learnings Manual*)

Sophia Marinos adds that Big hART projects start from "a combination of an artistic vision, a community invitation and the money being there somehow or being raised" (9 January 2013). The project she produced, the *Namatjira* project, "had no money to begin with, but we did have an initial relationship with the community that was able to then be translated into funding slowly but surely" (9 January 2013). The *Yijala Yala* project came about after Woodside Energy Ltd, an Australian resource extraction company, signed a Conservation Agreement (2007) with the Commonwealth of Australia permitting expansion of the corporation's operations on the Burrup Peninsula at the same time as committing the corporation to conserve and protect the "National Heritage Values of the National Heritage Place Dampier Archipelago (including Burrup Peninsula)" (2007, p. 1). Woodside engaged Big hART to work with the people of Roebourne (*Ieramugadu*) to achieve what it had been tasked by federal government, that is, heritage conservation in exchange for land use for industrial development. Creative Producer Debra Myers, who came into role in May 2010, was clear that

> [Big hART] come into the promoting and transmitting of cultural heritage values… our project is working on community capacity building. We're hoping to bring through a generation of young people so that in 5–10 years' time they'll be the community spokespeople, the cultural spokespeople, the rangers, the ones sitting on boards, the decisions makers, and they'll be better placed to do so. (18 May 2013)

I will outline a very brief history of Roebourne in order to explain how it is a centre of Indigenous cultural organisation and why groups from Roebourne figure as custodians of the Burrup Peninsula's extraordinary collection of rock art. Woodside figures in this narrative from the 1980s onwards.

The town of Roebourne was established on Ngarluma country by a government officer (Scholl) in 1866, following colonial-settlers (the Withnell family) who founded Mount Welcome pastoral station on the Harding River (*Ngurin*), a secure source of freshwater, in the early 1860s. The town was created to support expansion of the pastoral industry in the north west, although its growth and prosperity was supplemented by the pearling industry at nearby Cossack and the discovery of gold, copper and tin. Despite the existence of other industries, the pastoral industry was dominant determining the contours of regional economic and social development. According to anthropologist Sarah Holcombe (2005), the (then) Department of Native Affairs deferred to "pastoralists as the major regional economic stakeholders" (p. 110): "[t]here was no representative body, or mediating organisation, between Aboriginal people and developmental interests related to exploitation of the land. Relations between Aboriginal and non-Aboriginal people initially occurred through the pastoral industry" (Holcombe 2005, p. 110). According to anthropologist Mary Edmunds, this period of pastoral industry dominance is viewed nostalgically by Aboriginal people as a (relatively) 'harmonious' period (1989, p. 21). *Hipbone* contradicts this view as we shall see, and is more in line with Holcombe's summation that "while this view [of a harmonious past] does not accord with the realities of the harsh indenture system that led to the strike action of the 1940s [organised by Aboriginal stockmen], it contrasts with the subsequent negative relations with the mining industry from the 1960s" (2005, p. 110).

In 1961, the federal government removed regulation banning the export of iron ore sparking a mining boom in the mineral rich Pilbara region. According to Edmunds, "the beginning of iron ore mining in the 1960s marked the most serious disruption to [people of Roebourne's] processes of social reproduction as embedded in kinship relations and introduced modernity in its most destructive form" (2012, p. 49). The development of the iron ore mining industry involved the building of several large, open-cut mines and supporting infrastructure such as roads, railways, an airport, port facilities and accommodations across the Pilbara region. Rather than develop the town of Roebourne, the decision was taken to build a number of new 'open' and 'closed' mining company towns. It followed that administration, services and (human) resources were moved to these new towns. Karratha (established 1968) became the new administrative centre of the region[5] "crystallis[ing] the economic and social marginalisation of the Aboriginal population" remaining in Roebourne (Holcombe 2005, p. 112). Government planning decisions reinforced separa-

---

[5] In 2012/2013, the Shire of Roebourne became the City of Karratha.

tion and marginalisation, as Holcombe notes: "[t]he then Department of Native Affairs concluded that there were no employment opportunities for Aboriginal people, despite the fact that the iron ore industry [...] was heavily reliant on non-skilled labour and despite Aboriginal people's early experience with mining" (2005, p. 113). Within a decade, Roebourne was transformed from a prosperous regional administrative and service centre to a marginalised town whose majority Indigenous population was excluded from participation in the mainstream economy. In the documentary, *Exile in the Kingdom* (Parts 1 and 2), Roger Solomon (co-writer with Frank Rijavek) states that this period in Roebourne's history is referred to as an "infamous" one, a time when "everything fell apart" (1993). Edmunds notes that even in this difficult period, "there was another story" (2012, p. 48). Roebourne people were actively practising law ceremonies, creating alternative (spiritual-based and alcohol-free) settlements (Cheeditha), and establishing new indigenous organisations (Ieramugadu Group Inc. in 1974) to negotiate partnerships with mining corporations and to pursue commercial/business enterprises (such as pastoral companies) (Edmunds 2012, p. 48).

This activism gained a boost after the 1992 Mabo decision of the High Court of Australia destroyed the fiction of *terra nullius*. The Native Title Act (1993) subsequently introduced legislative frameworks enabling Indigenous groups to legally establish continuous connection to land and, if successful, to pursue rights as native title holders to negotiate land use agreements with resource companies. A joint native title claim was submitted by Ngarluma and Yindjibarndi[6] in 1996 and awarded in 2005. In this post-native title era, regional Indigenous groups have begun to assert custodial rights and responsibilities over the Burrup Peninsula, or *Murujuga* (which translates to 'hip bone sticking out'), to the south-west of Roebourne. Murujuga is a significant site as an open repository of rock art held to be one of the oldest and largest concentrations of rock art in the world: the art complex is estimated to contain over one million petroglyphs. The traditional owners of the land, the Yaburara, were subject to a systematic, sustained and murderous campaign now known as the Flying Foam Massacre (February–May 1868). Neighbouring Indigenous groups have stepped in to take up custodial duties for the area, including Ngarluma, Yindjibarndi, Mardudhunera and Wong-Goo-Tt-Oo. The urgency of the situation was underlined when the National Trust (NT) of Australia (WA) nominated the Burrup Peninsula to the NT Endangered Places List in 2002.

Woodside Energy Ltd. established a presence on the Burrup Peninsula in the 1980s after exploration off the north-west coast of the state of Western Australia (WA) in the 1970s led to the discovery of vast quantities of (liquid) natural gas. Woodside's (AU$19 billion) North West Shelf project, the largest resource project of its time, constructed onshore facilities at Karratha (Karratha

---

[6] It was a joint claim but there are separate organisations to represent each language group: Ngarluma Aboriginal Corporation (NAC) and Yindjibarndi Aboriginal Corporation (YAC).

Gas Plant) with support infrastructure on the Burrup Peninsula. At this time, the WA government, through the WA Museum, managed the heritage assessment of the site on behalf of the North West Shelf Project, and relocated (without consultation) approximately 1800 of the most endangered pieces of rock art to a temporary holding area, known as the Hearson Cove Compound. In the early years of the new century, Woodside sought to expand its operations on the Burrup after discovery of additional offshore gas fields. It founded the corporate sub-entity, Pluto LNG, to exploit the resource, and plans were developed to establish a processing plant on the Burrup. In a shift of approach, Woodside placed Traditional Custodians in a central role in relation to the heritage management process. Woodside entered into a conservation agreement with traditional custodians to preserve the heritage values of the area: the Burrup and Maitland Industrial Estate Agreement (BMIEA) 2003. The Murujuga Aboriginal Corporation (MAC) 2006 was formed in response to signing of the BMIEA, and includes Ngarluma, Yaburara, Yindjibarndi, Mardudhunera and Wong-Goo-Tt-Oo. In 2009, Woodside (Pluto LNG) became part of Reconciliation Australia's (RA) Reconciliation Action Plan (RAP), which has seen the company support the founding of Murujuga National Park (2013) and undertake a restoration project with Elders to resituate rocks removed from site (2014). In 2016, Woodside achieved the highest (Elevate) status from RA for RAP outcomes. In 2020, Woodside supported an application for World Heritage Listing of Murujuga (2020) based on (the not uncontroversial) belief that industrial development and cultural heritage can co-exist.

Big hART was engaged by Woodside in early 2010. To begin with the corporation facilitated meetings between Scott Rankin (Big hART CEO) and Trevor Jamieson (Big hART cultural consultant and performer) and the Roebourne community as Burrup custodians. Rankin explains that these early meetings were "conversations with community elders, mainly women" (24 May 2013). Conversational meetings developed into sharing Big hART work: a production of *Namatjira* was staged in the community hall in Roebourne, and the Roebourne women travelled with *Ngapartji Ngapartji* to ICAF Rotterdam, 2011. When Debra Myers joined the project as creative producer (based in Roebourne) in May 2010, already the feedback from the community was

> that they wanted a show like NN. They saw the power in that kind of storytelling ... for their story. And they wanted to get people thinking differently about Roebourne. I think they even coined the phrase 'the new Roebourne' or 'the real Roebourne'. I remember early on in meeting the community someone said, 'people read the Newspapers and watch the news and they think they know us', and so they want people to know the real story because the story that is out there is only negative or largely negative. (18 May 2013)

The Art of Creative Producing the 'New Roebourne': 'Don't Do One Thing When You Can Do Several' (Pauline Peel in Pitts and Watt 2001)

As has already been discussed, Big hART have devised an approach to project working that is multilayered, with acknowledged tensions between the elements of individual change, community development, national-level social policy change and high-quality art production. In this respect, their working methods, set within a minimum three-year project framework, are far from the singular one-off, 'parachute in and out' model that the statement by Peel above alludes to. Here I want to examine that approach before looking at the process in more detail.

The creative producers I spoke to (Debra, Sophia and Cecily) followed the *Lucky Learnings Manual*, a breakdown of Big hART's approach set out across over 40 (playing card-sized) cards in a cardboard box produced as part of the Lucky Learnings project based in Tasmania. I was sent the pack of cards which outlines the structure of the process thus:

> Research and Development: community consultation (1), creative concept (2); project plan and budget (3), stakeholders (4), in-kind support (5), funding (6); Engagement: creative team (7), six degrees of celebrity (8), participant referrals (9), engagement workshops (10), reporting (11); Promotion: marketing (12), media (13), a launch (14); Production: participants' journey (15), stakeholders' journey (16), creative team journey (17), art outcome (18); Closure: participants (19); Legacy: community (20); Reporting and Acquittals (21); Evaluation and Policy (22); and, Making (23–42): workshops, creating art, games, group games, devising games, writing games, performance, voice, movement, visual art, visual art games, digital media pre-production, digital media games, digital media post production.

While the LL 'manual' offers a detailed breakdown of process, Sophia Marinos indicates that it is difficult to give specific timings to particular activity domains:

> there's [not] a specific time period. Again, it's just juggling the things. It depends on …when the relationships [are] there enough that I can then apply for funding to get some artists onboard to then work towards a collaboration that gets a festival involved and investing. …it's not a specific time period. You're doing it throughout the whole life of the project. Because it shifts as the project grows and where it goes and there'll be relationships that are solid that you're nurturing throughout and there'll be always new ones that you're cultivating as well. (9 January 2013)

Debra Myers spoke of a 'project arc' (Myers May 18, 2013) in relation to *Yijala Yala*: engagement and relationship building in year one, content creation and continued engagement in year two, and performance making and touring in year three. The YY project is probably unique compared to most other Big hART projects because it began with 'secure financial support' (Myers, 18 May 2013) from Woodside. This meant that there was perhaps one less ball to 'juggle'. I utilise the LL cards and Myers' YY project arc to offer a brief outline of the project leading into the creative development process I joined in May 2013.

Community Consultation

Myers states that after arriving in Roebourne in July 2010 she "just started getting to know people really. By that stage I knew about 6 people in the community and then those 6 people took me around and introduced me to other people" (18 May 2013). Cecily Hardt, creative producer (mentored by Sophia Marinos) on *Blue Angel*, a project about the global shipping industry, seafaring and sustainability, explained that she was having a "whole lot of conversations":

> It's me ... asking: 'what conversations should I be having, can I be having?', and just trying to throw that net as wide as possible [...] I know [Scott's] interested in ... bigger ideas ... as well as engaging with individuals and hearing individual stories. ... that turns my conversation possibilities into a huge array so you know I'm talking to the unions, I'm talking to the shipping companies, I'm talking to seafarers and their support orgs [...] and also there is that element of me starting to learn all that as well so that I have a foundation of understanding of how to interweave all these different elements. [...] It is about slowly, slowly developing relationships and ... I'm lucky because I've had a few good initial conversations [...] but then I have to, because of resource and because of time, try and open up other avenues all at the same time. [...] already you start to put the pieces together in terms of what is going to be suitable in terms of putting people into a project together [...] and it is constantly something that you are [questioning]: 'how do I respond to this and who [do/don't] I put together?' (9 January 2013)

The *Lucky Learnings Manual* touches on difficulties that may be experienced in the process of community consultation. While encouraging wide consultation with "organisations and individuals across the community, as well as potential participants and stakeholders" in order to gather "a wide variety of opinions and ideas" and to gain a "good sense of what the community sees as its needs", it is suggested that creative producers "be respectful to the ownership a community has over its issues especially when others (particularly from the outside) try to address them" , and "be prepared for cynical or negative feedback, sometimes amongst professionals currently addressing the issue. Often they are overstretched, underfunded and devalued and don't see the relevance of art in the issue context" (card 1). Myers (18 May 2013) states that she found the initial consultation process "unsettling" because she did not then have answers to questions asked or comments made in context of conversations being attempted: "what are you doing here?" "you don't need to be here" "we've got youth workers, we've got arts projects, we don't need you" and "what exactly are you doing?" She also had to be careful to respect the existing cultural ecosystem, which was in the fields of performance and film, areas that Big hART normally work in. She says she worked slowly taking the necessary time (two years) to build collaborative relationships with relevant Indigenous arts organisations.

Cecily Hardt also spoke about being questioned: "Who are you?", "what are you?", "what are you talking about?", "why are you talking to me?", "I've never had this conversation before", "I've never had someone try and ask me these questions before". Her response was to "take it one step at a time" and to "try and build trust [...] about something that is not necessarily unwanted but completely foreign" (9 January 2013). Sophia Marinos puts this down to "the fact that we are an unusual organization...our purpose is to us very clear but to others ... not". She explained:

> there's always a management of people perceiving Big hART's entry into these territories as a threat: 'who are you and what are you doing here?' We're constantly ... negotiating relationships and building trust and assuring people that it is good will and it is about telling an important story and it's not about treading on toes. (9 January 2013)

Myers states that in experiencing "discomfort in those early stages", she "chose to take some of the requests from the community quite literally ... and then it was very easy to frame some objectives that everyone could understand while we got to work on bigger picture of the project" (18 May 2013).

Engagement and Relationship Building—'Quick Wins'

Two of the three main art programmes (digital, music and performance) that constitute the YY project came from Myers responding to direct requests from the community. A direct request from the community "to not forget about the prison" (Roebourne Regional Prison) (Myers, 28 May 2013) led to the establishment of a music programme centred on writing/composing workshops with prison inmates. The women in the community also "wanted a programme of activities for young people". This quickly grew into the digital media programme (the Neomad digital and hard copy comic series and interactive app). Myers notes that not all community requests became ongoing arts programmes. A women's choir was started and ran for approximately six months. However, the participants struggled against the demands of everyday life to maintain the necessary level of commitment to develop the choir into an art project strand. Nevertheless, Myers regards the women's choir as an important relationship-building tool and therefore an important part of the project (18 May 2013).

Three ongoing art programmes were established in the first year: a music programme, a digital media programme and a performance programme. While

Myers has oversight of the programmes, the programmes themselves employ artists based long-term in Roebourne (and surrounds) and freelancers who travel to Roebourne for intensive periods (weeks) of work. Building the team of artist/practitioners was an important part of this stage of the process. This included hiring art programme leaders to live and work in the community (subsidised by Woodside, since rents are expensive because of the high mining salaries), supported by freelance artists visiting for short and intensive periods. Alongside Myers, Dudley Billing (music coordinator) and Cho Cleary (music mentor) headed up the prison music sessions and music production programme; Stu Campbell (digital media coordinator, artist and mentor) and Wah Cheung (digital media assistant, graphic designer and mentor) coordinated the digital media programme; Chynna Campbell (filmmaker and community liaison) recorded short films (for the website and the digital programme) and engaged in community liaison; and Elspeth Blunt supported Myers as associate producer and directed the community performance cast.

It is often the case in Big hART projects that the performance-making programme draws on other arts programmes to create a whole more than the sum of its parts. Rankin, talking about the making of *Stickybricks*, the performance outcome of the *Northcott Narratives* project set in a public housing estate in inner-city Sydney, described the community (residents') engagement in practices of storytelling across different media (photography, short film making, prose/poetry writing, music composition and everyday performance) as creating a resource bank that Big hART then tried to condense the essence of in making a large piece of performance (*900 Neighbours* 2006). The performance programme, Myers explained, happened in blocks. It involved:

> sussing out what kids were into and seeing where things were at really [...] Maria [Randall] and Derek [Lynch] were here for a four-week block at the end of 2010. Then Maria and Suzy [Skinner] ran a programme in the school for the first half of 2011 [which Trevor and Derek came into]. Then we did a small performance for project stakeholders, for community and for Woodside a year in, in July 2011. After that the performance programme switched to 'creative development intensives. (18 May 2013)

Myers regards getting programmes and practitioners into place in the first year and the high level of engagement in art programmes (especially of young people in the digital media programme) as 'quick wins' (18 May 2013). Getting creative production underway quickly, and in a way that is visible to community participants and project stakeholders, promotes community engagement and develops participants' familiarity with public-facing production processes. Quickly establishing programmes that engage participants and produce quality artistic outputs early in the process is essential while working, in the long term, towards a major festival performance connected to social policy objectives.

Content Creation and Engagement

The second year of the *Yijala Yala* project was "all about content creation and (continued) engagement" (Myers, 18 May 2013). The digital media programme became the main focus as the younger people were highly engaged in developing characters (love punks and satellite sisters), dialogue, scenarios and cutting out frames and creating animations. The content being produced was directly related to the Burrup Peninsula/Murujuga's millions of ancient petroglyphs, thus promoting the area's cultural heritage values albeit via a contemporary art form (interactive iPad app) and futuristic quest narratives (see Myers and Palmer 2015).[7] The Neomad app and comic books incorporated cultural learning in the content produced as well as via the process of creation. The music programme turned towards professional production of commercial music CDs featuring performances by the inmates together with high-profile music artists, who had facilitated the writing of or had co-written music with prison inmates. Myers notes that the collaboration of high-profile musicians with inmates "led to opportunities to speak to the Department of Corrective Services about issues facing the community" (18 May 2013). This phase of the process also saw three creative development processes for *Hipbone*: in April, June and October 2012.

Hipbone in Creative Development in Roebourne/*Ieramugadu*

The creative development is an intensive two-week process taking place in and across various venues in the Roebourne area: Point Samson community hall (a 15-minute drive from Roebourne); Big hART offices (Roebourne); the Roebourne community hall (also called the 50 cent hall because it is octagonal shaped like the Australian 50 cent coin), and Yaandina, an Indigenous community services organisation with a purpose-built conference and meeting venue comprising a large hall for approximately 60 people, with large glass doors along one side which can be opened to access a walled outdoor space (Roebourne). A community performance was held on the penultimate evening of the creative development process (Thursday evening, 23 May 2013) in this space at Yaandina, and the audience spilled out of the hall and filled most of the outside courtyard space as well. The creative team—Scott Rankin (writer/director), Luke Kernaghan (assistant director/performer), Neil Fisher (production manager), John Rogers (musical director), Stuart Thorne (sound designer), David Hewitt (performer/live effects artist), Tess Schofield (costume designer), Sarah Stait (stage management), Sera Davies (filmmaker) and Yumi Umiumare (choreographer/performer)—and professional cast—Josie Alec, Jada Alberts, Simon Gleeson (also assistant music director), Trevor Jamieson, Derik Lynch, Lex Marinos and Natalie O'Donnell,—flew in on the

---

[7] See: https://yijalayala.bighart.org/neomad/

Sunday (12 May 2013) preceding and out on the Saturday following the end of the two-week process (on Friday 24 May 2013), mimicking the typical 'Fly In, Fly Out' pattern of work in the dominant mining industry in regional Australia.[8] This was the final creative development process before the production moved to Sydney, for a three-week rehearsal with full creative team, joined in the final week by the Roebourne community cast, before *Hipbone* opened in Canberra in July 2013.

The creative development process began at the Point Samson community hall, at the end of town opposite small sand dunes cut by a path leading directly to the beach. In the distance, a massive jetty (Rio Tinto Cape Lambert) snakes out to sea, flanked by bulk carriers being loaded with mineral wealth deposits extracted from deep, open holes in the ground nearby. The palm-tree fringed, louvre-windowed community hall in this tropical resort in the belly of a twenty-first-century mining industry behemoth is a square, single-storey, concrete block building. A large wooden verandah running along the building's front and side is solidly tied into concrete foundations to withstand cyclonic storm forces. On the first morning, the team sat in a large circle around several tables pulled together in the middle of the space to read the playscript.

Playscript: Written 'With and For'

Myers said that the script was written (by Rankin) over a couple of years, 2011 and 2012. She states that "it is acknowledged that it is written with and for" the people of Roebourne, and is based on a lot of research:

> mainly myself and Scott were doing that, and through my early consultation lots of stories emerged that I was feeding back to Scott and he was gathering a lot whenever he visited and that was starting to inform his narrative. (18 May 2013)

The three creative development processes in 2012 were significant in terms of informing the development of the playscript, with the script-in-process becoming part of a constant performance/feedback/rewriting loop. According to Myers, the creative development processes became "very, very key because we have to be able to check on so many of the scenes" (Myer 18 May 2013). This involved performing scenes to the community: "we can't give a script to someone and say here's the script, read it, because so much is not on the page and so ... when the cast are here doing creative development we use that as an opportunity—it has to be performed" (Myers May 18, 2013). Asked about the difficult subject material in many of the scenes, Myers explains:

> The John Pat scenes have been shown to his mum and his aunts in an intimate performance [...] there weren't that many people in the room [...] it was

---

[8] Not everyone was present for the entire two weeks but most of the named cast were.

difficult [...] we asked them to feed back to us whether we needed to change anything and there were a couple of things that weren't quite right which were corrected. Some of the other scenes were first shown back in April to the group of women we first started working with who said that they wanted this project and we showed them some quite intense scenes like the Flying Foam massacre and some of the John Pat stuff and they – that was incredible – they were in tears and ... they couldn't believe that their story could be told in that way ... they were really overwhelmed. (18 May 2013)

There was minimal time given in the creative development/rehearsal process to reading the text. The main aim seemed to be to get scenes on the floor rather than to analyse narrative meaning, subtext or character motivation and intention. On the final day of the creative development, in a discussion the day after the community performance, an actor asked:

the first few days in Sydney, can we not just talk about what it means [and] what we're trying to play in the scenes so we can take ownership of our roles, especially some of these whitefella roles, which are so awful. (Field notes, 24 May 2013)

The actor was concerned that the roles he was playing were "technically demanding", and that he had to "switch roles" frequently, for example from pastoral settler to member of a massacre party to Captain of a Dutch East Indies ship. In order to be "believable by an audience", he would have to understand the characters and their motivations. In response, Rankin indicated that the script was not finalised, and that as well as inserting transitions in some places to aid the shifting of gears between these technically difficult roles, the mood of the first half of the play will need more lightness and uplift to contrast with the heavier (historical-based) scenes (field notes, 24 May 2013).

By the afternoon of the first day of the creative development, chairs and tables had been pushed back to the wall to create space for getting scenes on the floor. There is a white blackboard with the programme of scene work and timetable set out for the day. At the start of the second day of the creative development, the production manager, Neil, showed the cast images of the stage set in a 3D design programme on computer. The floor of the hall was marked up accordingly with tape to reflect the dimensions of the playing space. Meanwhile, all available wall space is covered in A4 paper-sized drawings of costumes by Tess. The costume designer regularly disappeared with cast members into a small storeroom at the end of the hall to take measurements. This space doubled up as a second practice space where the cast learned songs in language that will overlay the scenes being developed on the floor. Big hART is renowned for a strong visual and musical aesthetic. This was evident in these gestures to theatricality appearing in the space of creative development as the performers took to the floor to embody scenes from the playtext.

'Sketching Scenes'

A scene begins with David (Hewitt) setting up a percussive beat with his body. Once he has a rhythm going, actors join in following the sound and movement he is making to reinforce the beat. Into the rhythm, the performers begin dropping in lines from the script[9]:

> "it was we who did the dispossessing".
> "We took the traditional lands and smashed the traditional way of life".
> "We brought the diseases. The alcohol".
> "We committed the murders".

This text is taken verbatim from a speech given by former Australian prime minister, Paul Keating, in Redfern, Sydney, in December 1992, to launch the International Year of the World's Indigenous People (1993). After Keating's 1996 defeat by the Liberal/National (conservative) government, Indigenous policy moved away from rights-based reconciliation towards a 'mainstreaming' approach focused on narrowing the statistical gap between Indigenous and non-Indigenous Australians in areas of, for instance, health, education and employment. The rejection of symbolic or rights-based reconciliation for pragmatism led to the dismantling of Indigenous-led governance negatively impacting Indigenous self-determination. Here in this room the performers are speaking the text in time with the beat, slowing or quickening phrasing and placing unexpected emphasis on particular words. Luke (assistant director) steps in and directs the performers to sense the impulse in the words spoken so that when a performer drops a line, the others physically react according to the force of the words or phrasing dynamically delivered.

Big hART team member, Elspeth Blunt (with Chynna Campbell), enters into this physical devising process with the members of the younger community performance cast. There are introductions before Luke integrates the casts pairing adult and younger performers together. He explains what they are working on and organises the performers into two lines standing across from each other. The performers set the rhythm going again. They drop lines from the Keating speech to the beat and wait for their partner to respond. This turns into a game where the paraphrased phrase, "we did the killing", flies like a bullet with the performer opposite reacting instantaneously, as if shot. The reactions become increasingly slow motion and exaggerated leading Rankin to comment that there is a bit of 'The Matrix' going on. He also acknowledges to the younger participants that there are sad stories in the play. Rankin decides the scene has had enough time and that they can move on. He says that "the scene might change but we know we've got something". There is a short break before the group reconvene to start animating the next scene. Simon starts

---

[9] Prime Minister Paul Keating delivered the Redfern Speech (in the Year for the World's Indigenous People) in Redfern Park (Redfern, an inner-city suburb of Sydney, is a centre of Indigenous political activism) on 10 December 1992.

singing "I fought the law and the law won", David develops a rhythm track and the performers begin dropping lines from the text into the song/movement sequence (field notes, 13 May 2013).

At the end of a session of work on the first day of the creative development, Rankin described the process as "sketching a scene in the Big hART book" (13 May 2013). Scene development work takes place each day much along these lines. The professional cast work during the day until the younger community cast arrive in the afternoon after school. They might have a swim in the sea and eat muesli bars and orange quarters before joining rehearsal and/or play drama games with the professional cast to build the ensemble before joining in the scene work. They tend to manage about 60 to 90 minutes of intensive scene work each afternoon. The young people not in the scenes are expected to sit quietly and to support their peers. The professional cast, still in the process of learning lines, is required to support the younger cast members by delivering lines on time. The younger cast members look up to the professional cast members. The scene work focuses on achieving a high standard of performance—correct language pronunciation (whether English or Ngarluma or Yindjibarndi, as appropriate), clear speech and precise movement.

Rankin often verbalised the Big hART process. This mode of direction, with action and process underlined by explanation, served to reiterate the particular process to a group of professional theatre workers more used, perhaps, to taking a (written) text into 'rehearsal'. The broad aim of the creative development was to embody and enact scenes to the Roebourne community for their feedback to incorporate into the performance-in-process. Rankin's verbalising of Big hART's methodology and comment on scenes—mainly in terms of how a scene might look/feel in performance with sound and visual effects added—was also for members of the Roebourne community, who were actively present in the creative space.

Community Engagement

There were community members (individuals or family groups) in the creative development process most days. Some observed the process and offered feedback (usually privately to Rankin/Jamieson), while others played an active role. In other words, there were different intensities of active engagement in the project across the Roebourne community. Central to and most visible in the process are the younger members of the intergenerational community performance cast: Max Coppin, Nelson Coppin, Alison Lockyer. Shaeola Toby and Maverick Easton (Easton, who shares the role of the Boy, John Pat, with Nelson Coppin, is in school in Perth and joins the team in the second week). Big hART team member, Elspeth Blunt (with Chynna Campbell), brings the younger cast members (and the odd friend and/or sibling) to the creative development process each afternoon after school. They play drama games with the professional cast, observe and participate in the scene development work and devise and rehearse scenes.

Elspeth, a recent graduate from the Communications and Creative Industries programme at Charles Sturt University in Bathurst, which has a specialism in community cultural development, became involved with Big hART's *Namatjira* project in Alice Springs, first in a voluntary and then in a professional role. This led into a full-time position assisting Myers. Elspeth relocated to the Roebourne area in February 2012. Over time, she increasingly took responsibility for the theatre-making process with a loose ensemble of young people (roughly four to six 11–13-year-olds):

> I run rehearsals with the kids 4 times a week and check in with the adult cast and support them in what they need to be here and also make sure that […] everyone knows what's in the show and is happy with it and has an opportunity to be in it if they want and provide stories and feedback … We have been getting feedback for a long time. We need to keep creating opportunities for people to feed back on it now that its more formed. (21 May 2013)

At the end of the last creative development (October 2012), there was a showing in the amphitheatre (an outdoor community performance space) which was a relaxed performance in the round. While that performance "drew a lot of people together who don't normally come together", the aim for this creative development was to "create focus and concentration", and "to give some sense of the professionalism of this show and what it might sound like and look like and feel like" with "a little bit of the magic of theatre" applied (Blunt, 21 May 2013). The aim of the creative development is for the company to get a sense of what the community response to the piece is as it moves towards becoming a professional performance product.

In terms of her work with the young people, Elspeth explains that she started rehearsing with the young people after the end of the last *Hipbone* creative development (October 2012). The group of four to six she's working closely with now have been largely self-selecting:

> they've got to be interested in it and interested enough to maintain engagement. There are kids who are interested but they come once and then they'll find something else to do, but if they are really keen they'll keep coming. (21 May 2013)

In addition to a level of interest that maintains active engagement, Elspeth says, "they've got to have some talent for either singing, dancing, moving, acting or storytelling" (21 May 2013). It's also important that there is a good group dynamic and a mix of Ngarluma and Yindjibarndi representation, so that characters are played by young people from the appropriate language group. According to Elspeth, "everything that Big hART has been doing for the last two years has prepared them for this" (21 May 2013). Programmes in dance and movement, performance, filmmaking, and digital media production, now embedded in school learning programmes, teach transferable skills and the discipline of creating short films, digital games, comic books and performance.

There are two main speaking roles, and the young people are doubling or tripling up on the roles "in case something happens in someone's family and they need to come back or… there are so many variables" (Blunt, 21 May 2013). At the same time, Elspeth notes that *Hipbone* has been written as an ensemble piece rather than as a two-hander like *Namatjira*, so the young people will have roles in the performance: non-speaking parts within scenes, in large movement/dance pieces, or as part of the community chorus (performing witness). Normally,

> when it's just them and me in the 50-capacity hall I can't replicate a professional process so we drill stuff. We drill choreography, we drill lines and we do a lot of ensemble building to build confidence. (Blunt, 21 May 2013)

Over the two-week creative process, Elspeth states,

> expectations are high and the kids have to maintain a professional level […] they're looking at a bunch of professionals doing what they do which they are part of and expected to act up to. (21 May 2013)

The adult cast seems fluid at this point in the process, although Josie Samson and Allery Sandy (performer and Yindjibarndi cultural advisor and translator) are regularly in sessions supporting the younger performers and taking up various roles. There are a number of senior women who provide constant support to the process by teaching the ensemble the Ngarluma or Yindjibarndi languages that they have translated songs into, as well as advising on aspects of culture and (hi)story: Violet Samson (performer and Ngarluma cultural advisor and translator); the Cheedy sisters, Jane and Marion (Yindjibarndi cultural advisors), Pansy Sambo (Yindjibarndi cultural adviser) and Pansy Hicks (Ngarluma cultural advisor).

Pansy Hicks, a senior Ngarluma woman, is in the room. She is here to observe the process and to help the cast learn the Ngarluma language that songs have been translated into. Later in the day she will work intensively with the cast in a circle around her to practice correct pronunciation of the Ngarluma words. She will also, asked by Scott, speak about the Flying Foam massacre, which relates to the 'killing scene' the ensemble were devising earlier in the creative process. I shall hear (and read) more about the massacre in the Cultural Awareness training I attend, on 14 May 2013, at the direction of Big hART, led by Clinton Walker for the Gurrgura organisation in Karratha.

Pansy is observing the process as performers 'sketch a scene'. As tends to happen, a performer (David) sets up a percussive background beat by striking his heel and sliding his foot across the wooden floor. He's joined by other performers, and they improvise a range of percussive sounds that feet can make on the wooden floor and try to develop a rhythm. Once the rhythm settles, the performers overlay the song, "I fought the law", to the backing beat created by their bodies on the floor. Then they begin dropping lines from the script into the scene (Mavis is pleading with John not to go down there (to the Victoria Hotel the night of his death) and the scene is detailing different stories of what happened that night – from official testimony given by police officers in a later inquiry into the incident, and from witnesses who looked from their houses across the street). Pansy sits watching the ensemble sketch the scene. Then in the middle of the work, she makes a (random) request: Can they do Jailhouse Rock? The performers pause, then slowly, altogether and without speaking, begin to change the beat they're making with feet on floor. They set up a new rhythm and work up into a rousing rendition of Jailhouse Rock. Pansy applauds at the end of the song.

Rankin comments that "there is a lot of the process in that moment" (I think he means the responsive nature of the cast to community members). He goes on to explain that performances of *Hipbone* aim to raise money from the audience for the creation of a memorial to John Pat in Roebourne. There is already a public memorial to Pat, featuring a poem by renowned Indigenous poet and playwright Jack Davis, in Freemantle Prison, a World Heritage site, but that is some 1500 km away. The community has requested a local memorial to Pat, and Big hART plan to deliver on that request. Rankin also takes the opportunity of having Pansy in the space to invite her to speak about the Flying Foam massacre. It is important for the ensemble to hear the account of the massacre, which they are performing, first-hand so to speak. Pansy's oral history explains why Murujuga is a contested site. The traditional owners of the land, the Yaburara, were massacred by colonial-settlers, and the land is now the responsibility of surrounding language groups. Rankin notes that the determination of custodianship is not straightforward and that there are still people who identify as Yaburara. The Indigenous 'community' in the larger Roebourne region, he notes, is comprised of at least five different language groups. There are, at times, disputes between groups and ongoing tensions. He states that Big hART have had to find a way to deal with the tensions, which involves taking a step back when it comes to disputes between the groups, and working inclusively at all times. He notes that being clear about what Big hART's business is, and how it differs from community business, is important. Big hART has worked out a way to work with community as inclusively as possible without taking sides, or exacerbating tensions that have arisen from invasion, massacre or other trauma (field notes, 15 May 2013).

BBQ Dramaturgy

In the middle of the first week of the creative development, there is an evening community event in the Big hART offices in Roebourne. The Big hART office is in a prefab shed with a tin roof on the main road. There are several rooms running off a large central space. There is a computer room full of screens and Wacom tablets. Two rooms are set up for playing and recording music. Another room serves as an office/meeting space. And there is a large kitchen. The event is set up to show work in production across the digital media, music and performance programmes, to practise songs in language led by the senior women (Ngarluma in one room and Yindjibarndi in another), and to get together socially around a barbeque. The evening begins with the showing of a documentary of the making of *Neomad Love Punks* (Part 2) presented by Chynna Campbell, who made the documentary with the 'Love Punks'; Stu Campbell showed some excerpts from the production of the next part of the digital comic, *Neomad Love Punks* (Part 3); Dudley Billing played live music demonstrating the songs written by inmates participating in the prison programme. After showing work, the aunties were in separate rooms teaching songs to the rotating ensemble. In one room, they were teaching Tracey Chapman's *Talkin' About A Revolution* in Yindjibarndi, and in the other Alison Krauss's *Down To The River To Pray* in Ngarluma. The performance cast circulated between the rooms practising singing the songs in language while the space slowly filled with people who moved around the space catching up on work in progress. The gathering was all ages, mostly family groups. A delicious spread of food was produced—barbeque meats, salads and breads. After eating, the performance ensemble sang the songs to the gathering including some pieces not in language such as *The Hymn to Orpheus*, which introduces into the performance the character of Pluto who holds open the liminal space between life and death in which John Pat—Man and Boy—appears. This informal showing and celebration of work in progress appeared to be extremely successful. There was a high community turnout, and people seemed to socialise in high spirits.

Later, in the post-performance wrap on the final day of the creative development, a Roebourne-based member of Big hART said of the event that it was a highlight of the creative development process, and that "it was really significant to have all those senior ladies in the same space teaching different languages sometimes separately and sometimes together". She described the feedback as positive, and overall engagement as a "blessing for the show". She said this to indicate "some of the little community things happening in the background" (field notes, Friday 24 May 2013). The feedback from community members related to the Big hART team member based in Roebourne seemed to confirm the company's way of working inclusively while being respectful of differences between people and ongoing group tensions. The collective cultural space created by Big hART appeared to offer a point of being-together-with-others based on collaborative storytelling: "the process of telling these stories in this way ...has become very important" (field notes, 24 May 2103).

'It's Our Story, It's Important to Us'

There is a community performance in the Yaandina venue this evening, Thursday, 23 May 2013. As the choice of performance space suggests, this is meant to be a more formal presentation to the Roebourne community than the informal presentation in the amphitheatre at end of last creative development, and the mood in room reflects that. The ensemble is dressed in matching dark blue T-shirts which have had a bleach stencil applied at the hipline, turning the material brown-red, with the word 'hipbone.' These have been made by costume designer Tess Schofield with local artists Tootsie Daniel and Laurissa Bobby—Laurissa will travel to Sydney and Canberra to work in wardrobe on the performance. The ensemble is gathered in a circle in the space (the 50 cent hall in Roebourne) with Rankin explaining how he is going to determine the final running order of scenes for the evening performance. He states that they're going to run the scenes, and if the standard of the scene "is not good enough it goes…". He leaves that statement hanging in the air while making eye contact with each performer in the circle, checking that this is understood. Shaeola, who is cast in role of the Ngarluma girl, responds positively: "because it's important to people, it means a lot to people". Maverick, cast in the role of 'the boy' states, "it means a lot to us". Rankin asks, "Do you want to make the show better?" Everyone responds affirmatively. Rankin reiterates that if the standard of the scene "is not good enough it goes… I'll cut anything that's not good enough now because it matters, it all matters" (field notes, 23 May 2013).

The ensemble run the scenes, scripts still in hand. Derik drops a line, while trying to bring words and action together. One of the young people says, "Ha, you got it wrong." Rankin interrupts, and says, "When someone makes a mistake we say thanks for trying rather than you got it wrong." After running another scene, Scott says, "We're going to cut that scene." He turns to Maverick and says, "Maverick, we've given you a lot of support in this process, but you were the one letting that scene down. You need to concentrate and perform the movements sharper." At this point, Aunt Josie reminds the young people that "this is out story … this isn't someone else's story, it's our story". A short time later, Scott pulls someone up for screwing up their nose at the end of a scene: "Don't screw your face up like that, that's not ok." He reiterates the phrase, "This means something to us, it's our story", and it becomes the refrain as they work to build a professional performance ensemble, and a set of scenes that convey a strong sense of the final performance. Rankin states that his process highlights Big hART's 'task based non-welfare' insofar as the focus and expectation is making a professional standard performance (field notes, 23 May 2013).

The performance in the Yaandina venue took place in a large rectangular room, more a conference space, for approximately 60 people. The concertina glass doors between conference room and garden were open, and the whole space was filled with people. After Welcome to Country and introductions, the performance began as described above, and then moved onto showing the scenes enacting the "stories that people wanted told from the very first time we came here" (field notes, 23 May 2013). I'll move onto a discussion of *Hipbone* from where I left off earlier, shortly.

As the ensemble met the following day to debrief the creative development process and look forward to the rehearsal process, comments from some of the cast praised the younger performers: they were at school, so I presume that Elspeth and Chynna related the feedback to them. Simon stated that the audience was "no amphitheatre audience" (everyone laughs at his pinpointing the more formal and focused attending to the performance at Yaandina compared to the outdoor, family-friendly or relaxed mode of performance in the amphitheatre). He says, "there is nothing worse than performing to family and friends...they did an amazing job. Credit to Elspeth and Chynna and everyone up here" (field notes, 24 May 2013). Natalie reinforces these comments, stating, "the focus the performers maintained throughout was extraordinary. They hadn't had that experience of performing in front of people and their peers were there as well... the level at which they maintained focus and concentration was exciting" (field notes, 24 May 2103). Simon says that the Yaandina performance "was important for learning the power of performance, that's it not for you (performers) but for those people sitting there (audience)". He along with Josie Samson felt that the young people had successfully assumed "authority over that powerful story" (field notes, May 24 2013).

With the integration of the younger community cast into the professional ensemble, the creative development process seemed to have achieved one of its key aims. There were also other outcomes such as the inclusivity in difference community-building noted earlier. For one of the performers, the run of scenes the evening before enabled her to begin to make meaningful connections between scenes. Elspeth noted that the performance produced new participation in the project: "there were people in the room who'd never seen stuff before", including a Yaburara women, who responded positively, "[she] didn't have any concerns and was really overcome by the connection [of the Flying Foam massacre scene] with the John Pat story" (field notes, 24 May 2013). The performance also encouraged others who have "just started becoming involved" in parts of the programme to engage with the project (field notes, 24 May 2013).

The final summing up turned towards the forthcoming process in Sydney (June) before the opening run in Canberra (in July 2013).

Hipbone Sticking Out (Part Two): Pat's/Roebourne's Story Calling Out Ongoing Colonisation

Here I pick up the performance from the point at which I left it earlier. The opening scenes of Act One set the scene for the performance that follows as images of a man's life (his life story) flash before his eyes as he lays dying in a police cell. Pat's story is told *as if* in a state of delirium, or a state of suspended animation between life and death, defying linear history or rational thought. Big hART draw on this suspension of disbelief to introduce Indigenous (Ngarluma/Yindjibarndi) ontology that envelops different or differentiated histories of colonisation, from the 1860s to the present day, performed onstage.

A performer (Derik), in black leather jeans and a large shell necklace, takes to the performance platform to the sound of clapsticks as he sings three long, loud, resonant notes that ascend in tone. As he stands on the platform, the screen behind him projects the hand-drawn image of an animated snake weaving across the space and curling into concentric circles. Before the animated imagery, Derik forcefully incants the story of Baramindi Water Snake, the ancestral being who created land and law. The spirit rests in a deep pool it made in the Ngurin River, radiating forceful energies across the land.

With Derik's performance of the creation dreaming, Pat's story is enfolded within an Indigenous ontology based in "deep time" (or 'long history'), which stresses the "interconnectivity of people and sentient land" and is transmitted intergenerationally through performance (storytelling, song, dance and painting/drawing) (James 2015, p. 35). *Hipbone* underlines the fact that different systems of power/knowledge are in play in the theatre space as Indigenous story meets the colonial-settler history of the (largely) non-Indigenous theatre-going audience. In other words, presented on stage are not truth claims whose veracity or factual objectivity is to be critiqued or debated as in the culture wars of the 1990s (in which 'whitewash' and 'black arm band' views of history were debated). Oral storytelling brings into view an alternative system of knowledge (epistemology), and its performance.

The 'stage within a stage' staging telescopes the audience beyond the frame of theatrical illusion into an inverse or imaginary space. The made-up-ness of this space is underscored by references in the script (spoken by Trevor/John Pat, mainly) to a popular 1930s Broadway jazz standard "It's only a paper moon; sailing over a sea of cardboard; but it wouldn't be make-believe; if you believed in me." What the combined effect of story and staging tackles is the subject of contested history, which as Linda Tuhiwai Smith reminds us, is not the invention of post-modern subjects but, rather, "the idea of contested stories and multiple discourses about the past, by different communities, is closely linked to the politics of everyday contemporary indigenous life. It is very much a part of the fabric of communities that value oral ways of knowing" (1999, p. 33). Smith points out the power disparities that make it difficult for Indigenous peoples to "transform history (as true/factual discourse) into justice" (p. 34). Oral storytelling traditions are connected to alternative systems of knowledge, and it is possible to draw on "the pedagogical implications" of "access to alternative knowledge" as the "basis of alternative ways of doing things" (Smith 1999, p. 34). I am arguing that *Hipbone* enables 'access to alternative knowledge', thereby opening a pedagogical (learning) space that could form the basis of alternative ways of doing things.

In *Hipbone*, access to Indigenous story is mediated by the community, itself, positioned in the space between performance frames variously participating in the performance and/or performing witness to testimonies of past injustices. In addition to collective ownership of the story demonstrated by community presence before it, the action is narrated by Trevor and Maverick/Nelson (the John Pat's), with Pluto the magnanimous navigating time/space and also arbitrating in the prosecution of justice that unfolds through the presentation of Ngarluma/Yindjibarndi story and perspective.

From deep within time, the action unfolds coming to rest on the doubled vision of Amsterdam and Ngarluma country circa 1860. The reference to the Dutch capital is noteworthy. It was ships of the Dutch East India Company (VOC) in exploration of new commodity trade routes between Europe and the 'Spice Islands' that first navigated and mapped the west coast of Australia (Nieuw-Holland). The Pats and Pluto remind the audience of this 'pre-history', a time before Australia existed. They stand on Yaburara country observing the ships sailing along the coast. This is the same shoreline where Yaburara etched images of sailing ships into the red rocks.

From this point on, intersecting (sometimes simultaneous and overlapping) scenes contrast the experiences of a little Dutch girl (Jada) living in a European cultural capital and a little Ngarluma girl (Shaeola) living on her *ngurra* (country). European colonisation is performed through juxtaposition of the experiences of the two girls. The scenes with the little Dutch girl move between her schooling and conversations with her father, a shipping merchant, in between voyages of exploration to the *niewe wereld*. To the tune of 'Three Little Maids From School Are We' (from Gilbert and Sullivan's orientalist comic opera, *The Mikado*, 1885), the little Dutch girl, in chorus with two other performers (Josie Alec and Yumi Umiumare) also dressed in 'traditional' Dutch costume, learn about the Dutch Golden Age, that period of unparalleled cultural development powered by the exploits of European Empire. The girls are taken by Vermeer's 'Girl With A Pearl Earing'. They are titillated by stories of the English pirate William Dampier, who wrote a popular book about his expeditions to the new world and the ugly and indolent savages he found there. Their teacher tells them that the world is their oyster. The little Dutch girl puts everything together and asks her father to bring her pearl earrings from 'new world' full of raw beauty and 'savagery'. *Hipbone* exposes the enculturation process by which European civilisation is constructed in relation to new world 'savagery'.

Worlds collide after ship's passage brings the father and girl to the new world. Only now they are pastoral settlers newly arrived in the Pilbara (dressed in the uniform of FIFO mine workers—denim overalls with fluorescent yellow stripes). The arrival of the newcomers is observed by the little Ngarluma girl and her kin. Comment is made on the bedraggled and scrawny (starving) appearance of the group. A welcoming party is organised to offer food (kangaroo tail) and water. At the meeting, the newcomers offer blankets and an invitation to church in exchange. But the material fibres or dust in the blankets causes a 'settler' to sneeze. The sneeze is prolonged, and it can be seen to physically impact the welcoming party. They reel backwards in slow motion, and as they fall their costumes are shed revealing skeletal body suits with bones etched in fluorescent paint. Over the rhythm of clapstick and song, a beat boxer steps up while an ensemble of young singer/dancers rises like zombies performing a body-popping/breaking rendition of 'Dem Bones'. At the end of the scene, Yindjibarndi elder, Allery Sandy, walks onstage with a wooden bowl full of water. She swallows a mouthful of water from the bowl and then sprays a very fine mist of water through her pursed lips to ritually cleanse the space.

The action then focuses on a run of events that leads to what is known as the Flying Foam Massacre, a long-term campaign in which Yaburara men, women and children were systematically hunted down and killed by a group of pastoral settlers led by Government Resident R. J. Sholl. Sholl, played by Luke Kernaghan, and pastoralists (represented by Simon) are reconstructed from official reports (from a subsequent inquiry/commission into the killings). The Pats narrate the run of scenes enacted (rape of a woman by a police officer; Coolyerberri seeks lawful restitution; Coolyerberri is captured; Coolyerberri is freed by Yaburara men who spear the police officer and kill two others in the ensuing struggle; gathering the 'search' party; executing the massacre),[10] filling in the official story with oral history and the perspectives of those who understand land/law. The little Ngarluma girl is present throughout just at the base of the performance platform. She crouches in the shadows calling 'wimbamma mama' (run daddy run).

The little Ngarluma girl's experience of European civilisation as viral disease, rape and violence (genocide) is distinct from the little Dutch girl's gifts of pearl, opera, art and the world as her oyster. Act One shows how European civilisation was experienced by the 'new world' 'savages' and introduces how Indigenous groups were basically left to ravage by disease and the murderous impulses of settlers, unprotected by the state. The performance introduces new story (song/dance) and starts to build new knowledge through juxtaposition of official record and storytelling. Formal hybridisation is used to powerful effect again in Act Two.

Act Two opens with Derik solo, again (after his powerful performance of Baramindi water snake). He is dressed in orange lycra shorts and a black cape and is camping it up for the audience in a stand-up routine. He calls out spectators who are into 'Indigi porn', as in those who derive pleasure or purpose through consuming stories of Indigenous poverty portrayed in mainstream (Murdoch-owned) media. He wants to know if there are any 'ambulance chasers' in the audience. In camp crusader mode, he disabuses spectators of any saviour complex they might have brought to the theatre. Then he turns to don a circus ringmaster's jacket as he is joined by the rest of the ensemble for a postmodern pastiche of a song and dance opening number. While the young ensemble decked out in cheerleader uniforms and pom poms performs a dance routine to Britney Spears' "Oops!... I did it again", sung in Ngarluma, to the beat provided by the young Pat, Derik and Pluto (Lex) commence a roll call of colonial circuses (Batavia etc.) against merchant/settler Simon's civilised protestations in the form of a Smetana opera sung at full volume. Overburdened by the spectacle, the spectator is prepared for the enactment of colonisation mark 2.

In this act, *Hipbone* takes a closer focus on Ngarluma/Yindjibarndi country circa 1860s as the pearling industry starts up along the coast near Roebourne (before it became established in Broome). Although Amsterdam is in the

---

[10] Flying Foam massacre has been written up by Robert G. Bednarik (2002) (his account was given to me in a file of papers from the Gurrgura Cultural Awareness training).

background, associations with the little Dutch girl and her pearl earrings continue to resonate. Like most colonial endeavours, pearling depended on the (indentured) labour of Indigenous men, women and children, and it became increasingly dangerous work. As shells were exhausted close to the shoreline, the collection of pearl shell moved into deeper water and the practice of 'free diving' (diving into deep waters without breathing apparatus) became common practice. Many divers drowned. To replace the workforce, pearlers sent 'blackbirders' inland, into Yindjibarndi country, to secure (steal) labour to replace the drowned divers. Trevor/Pat recounts a particular encounter in which Yindjibarndi led a prolific 'blackbirder' into a trap and killed him according to ritual custom. The man was flayed and his kidneys removed. Trevor/Pat explains that kidney fat is "the power of any man" and the warriors took the victim's kidneys to their senior knowledge men "to use against these slave hunters taking our people in this war". As Trevor notes, the killing was the enactment of law deliberated upon by Yindjibarni warriors responding to multiple unlawful (on both sides) incursions into country and against the enslavement of the group's (younger, fitter) people.

The ensemble start up a barn dance around the platform, which mingles with the underlying sound track throughout most of the act, "I fought the law and the law won" (in language). The scene is based on transcripts presented in the WA Parliament in an enquiry into the labour practices of pastoral and pearling industries. At the end of each 'heel and toe' round, a colonial-settler presents a view defending the labour practices of the industries. After a few rounds of this, performers take to the platform to present dissenting views. A gunshot rings out loudly before each dissenter finishes their line, and they fall to the floor, before the dance goes into another round. With a group of four or five dissenters huddled in a circle on the floor of the platform, Pluto, who has been watching from the centre backstage, pronounces judgement on the proceedings:

> You were all prominent people, and you were the law
> Pastoralists, pearlers, all white
> You may have done much to prevent abuse
> But, instead, in your desperate need for labour
> You legalised slavery
> Chorus [sung in English]: robbin' people with six gun, I fought the law and the law won, I fought the law and the law won. (Hipbone 2013)

A sequence of scenes follow on from this one to present a devastating analysis of the dominant colonial-settler industries—pastoralism and pearling—and their impact on local Indigenous populations. The analysis makes clear that the industrialists who stood to gain most from the exploitation of Aboriginal labour developed an ad hoc system of law (from indentured 'employment' contracts to penal punishment) and applied it indiscriminately in order to secure unequal gain. This is a critical point in the performance because it clearly connects Indigenous resistance to the egregiously provocative actions of colonial-settlers, which initiated frontier violence (war), and the criminalisation of Indigenous nations. In other words, *Hipbone* links colonisation and the racialised legal and criminal justice systems in Australia. It turns the theatre into a tribunal in order to critique these imposed legal and penal systems. And it is this analysis that has been built over two acts that leads back into Pat's story.

After this run of scenes, there is a noticeable shift in the look and feel of the performance as the past gives way to events in living memory. Artifice is shed, and the bare space is illuminated by the projected image of a red/brown rock, a petroglyph, across the entire back wall of the theatre space. A metal scaffold is installed in front of the image (symbolising an industrial infrastructure installed on Murujuga) and before the bare performance platform which also provides seating for the entire ensemble, along with some wooden stools. Derik, walks across the metal scaffold to the performance platform, directly addressing the audience. He speaks about Roebourne prison linking past criminalisation and present incarceration: "all our lives lived through that place… John Pat, hero, fallen soldier brought in that Royal Commission thing to stop us dying from our white fella rite of passage. Still dying…do you feel sad? Sorry, but not our story. Your story. This prison thing." Derik then introduces a song written by 'some of our uncles' in Roebourne prison. Derik and Nat sing the song, written as part of Big hART's prison music programme (name of song, songwriter?). The ensemble join in the chorus.

Following the song, Mavis Pat, John Pat's mother, is introduced to the audience by Jada, who takes up Mavis' story semi-verbatim: "she has many stories … these are some of her words." After appearing briefly and acknowledging Jada's introduction, Mavis Pat exits offstage. The narration takes us through how she came to live on the Old Reserve, the camp on the other side of the river to Roebourne. Jada relates Mavis' experiences of birthing and raising a child in difficult circumstances as modernity in its most voracious form (large-scale industrial mining) destroys the social fabric of the camp and the town. John grows up on the reserve and is put through law (is initiated) by senior men; "he grew up good way, quiet way." The story turns to how John came to be in the Victoria Hotel that night, and recounts the incident between a group of men, including Pat, and off-duty police officers. Jada states: "if it wasn't John that night it would have been somebody else's kid… that's why John is everybody's now." The commentary on Pat's story foregrounds the central and oppressive place of policing and prison in the lives of the people of Roebourne, inhibiting their capacity to flourish. The telling of Pat's story presents opportunities to openly and collectively grieve inequality and injustice. In this space, the aunties call for commitment to support Roebourne's young people: "they just need support, they just do, every kid, every day."

Finding it difficult to close the play, Trevor/Pat states that "it's not an ending". He notes that each year more men arrive at the ceremonial grounds to be put through law: 30 in the time when Pat went through law has become 1000s today. "The law is not finished, this isn't an ending", he states. The sense of hope in the form of resurgent law/culture rising again in remote ceremonial circles couldn't be any further away from this sorrowful circle (or 'auto-poetic feedback loop' (Fischer-Lichte 2008, pp. 38–39) in a Canberran theatre. Conquergood suggests that cultural performances can register and radiate dynamic "'structures of feeling' and pull us into alternative ways of knowing" (2002, p. 149). Perhaps the knowledge departed so affectively here tonight can catalyse new understandings and initiate alternative ways of doing things. At the same time, *Hipbone* effectively reframes John Pat's story within the context of the near collapse of Indigenous society in the wake of the 1960s mining boom that radically transformed Roebourne; in terms of the longer historical context of Indigenous struggle and survival in the face of colonial-settler provocations; and in terms of the revitalisation of Roebourne and the renewal of a demand for justice centred on dismantling a racialised criminal justice system. That is, *Hipbone* restores Pat's/Roebourne's story to a (long) historical moment that resonates both locally in cultural revitalisation and globally in demanding racial justice: "no more black deaths in custody", "black lives matter". The audience is less witness to testimonies of oppression—the witness role was very much held by community elders mediating the action performed on stage—and more called to take part in the memorialisation of Pat's life in a space established and held open by those same elders (including Pat's mum) in the city at the centre of Australian political life. The performance was ceremonial 'sorry business' and enjoined the non-Indigenous audience to acknowledge—to own—their part in the making of this sorrowful hi/story circle.

'Don't Leave Nothing Behind' (Pauline Peel in Pitts and Watt 2001): Shaping Legacy

Although *Hipbone* was only just moving into a final creative development and rehearsal process, before premiering in July 2013, the YY producers and artists were moving into the legacy phase, which is anticipated from the beginning of projects and can take time and effort to achieve. For instance, the *Northcott Narratives* project turned a high-rise public housing estate regularly represented in mainstream media as 'suicide towers' into a WHO safe community (see Wright and Palmer 2007). The *Namatjira* project produced a feature film documentary of the art and social change project that contributed to the campaign to return the Namatjira copyright to the family, and to establish a trust to fund a remote area arts centre (Iltja Ntjarra) that operates professional art and social support services. Elspeth explained that, Big hART producers and artists were already, before *Hipbone* opened, in the process of "deciding what can be kept going, what can be seeded within other organisations and what we can say goodbye to" (18 May 2013). It was envisaged that *Hipbone* would become "modular" with the ensemble scenes performed by the community cast developed for local/regional performance. This might involve keeping up rehearsals on those pieces so that when the Red Earth Arts Festival comes up we present a 5 minute piece and when there's other festivals or community events happening in the Roebourne amphitheatre we can have people who can sing or have kids who can get up and do the pompom dance so that there is kind of a repertoire still in the community ...what I hope and anticipate is that before each show I'll come up for a month and start that rehearsal process again – with the same kids or with different kids – teaching them up that same material. (21 May 2013)

In addition to a performance repertoire to be performed by local Roebourne people regionally, there were a number of other outcomes primary among which was the completion, in 2017, of the John Pat Peace Place near to the *Ngurin* Cultural Centre.[11] In fact, the *Yijala Yala* project outcomes have been enfolded into a legacy project known as *New Roebourne* (2015–), which includes a performance-making programme; a digital art-making programme (with an additional female inclusive strand); a culture-specific education programme (neo-learning); and Songs for Peace, an ongoing song writing and music producing/performing programme based in Roebourne, with a focus on the Regional Prison, that culminates in an annual high-profile, celebrity-packed celebratory event on the International Day of Peace, adjacent to the John Pat Peace Place in Roebourne. The Songs for Peace programme recommits the people of Roebourne to harmonious communal relations, highlights the community as peaceable and competent creatives (counter to external representations which have tended to focus on dysfunction) and reinstates a broad call for racial justice, particularly in the area of criminal justice (policing/prisons).

Creative Producing Sustainable Cultural Livelihoods

Yijala Yala was a unique project, insofar as an arts organisation came into the complex nexus of relationships between government, a resource-extraction corporation, and traditional custodians of land on a designated national cultural heritage site zoned for industrial development, to promote the cultural heritage values of the site. It is a site with an explicit contradiction enfolding the co-existence of cultural heritage conservation and resource extraction industries.[12] This project was an experiment by a large resource extraction company in managing Indigenous cultural heritage. The corporation turned to a cultural, creative producing organisation to work with traditional landowners and custodians. The *Yijala Yala* project told the story of Roebourne and Murujuga. It drew a line under the past, to distinguish it from the now

---

[11] See https://www.pilbaranews.com.au/news/pilbara-news/roebourne-memorial-unveiled-for-john-pat-ng-b88612886z

[12] In 2020, mining giant Rio Tinto's destruction of Juukan Gorge in the Pilbara made the tensions between industry and Indigenous cultural heritage management highly visible. The corporation was widely criticised and lost its RAP elevate status.

(post-native title era) and to allow the new to emerge. The *Yijala Yala* project took a 'community capacity building' (Myers) approach creating spaces (in addition to and in support of those already existing) for teaching/learning language and cultural knowledge, developing expressive skills and building personal and practical strengths. The outcome was to bring forward a generation of young people as future cultural leaders with capacities to engage in negotiation with government and industry over land use (for economic development) while 'managing' culture. Land and culture are inseparable tangible and intangible assets.

The Australian CCD sector, led by Jon Hawkes (2001), has argued for what it calls "cultural vitality" to be included in the sustainable development framework that informs much of public and private enterprise in neoliberal democracies (after the so-called Brundlandt Report of the World Commission on Environment and Development: *Our Common Future* (United Nations 1987)). This framework sets out a 'triple bottom line' (Elkington 1994) articulating economic development in conjunction with social and environmental sustainability. Hawkes argues that these domains should be increased to four with the inclusion of cultural vitality as the fourth pillar of sustainable development (Hawkes' is also a radical proposal to restructure arts and cultural funding in line with participatory civic planning). Big hART's work in the contested space between industry and cultural heritage management in the Pilbara is attuned to promoting cultural heritage values (the significance of Murujuga) as 'cultural vitality'; it "highlights cultural heritage as something alive and continually evolving in the here and now, rather than only in the past" (Edmunds 2012, p. 58). Future heritage lies with the young people (a major demographic in remote communities)[13] who know land, law, language and culture, and have the capacities to adapt it across myriad cultural forms including comics (see the love punks and satellite sisters), interactive app design, digital storytelling, song writing, music production and performance (both for local/regional cultural festivals and the mainstage). Being strong in culture also enables future leaders to continue the struggle for social justice (not least against racialised policies that disproportionally criminalise and incarcerate Indigenous people—young and adult; against 'black deaths in custody').

At the same time, Big hART's work goes much further than integrating culture into an expanded framework of sustainable development. The work produces 'sustainable cultural livelihoods' (Scambary 2009, 2013; Holcombe 2010), a concept that has been developed after Esteva's new commons critique of the development paradigm (Scambary 2009, p. 183), and draws on post-development discourse such as Gibson-Graham's (2006) community economy which values "non-market economic relations and customary activities as legitimate forms of economically productive action" (Scambary, p. 183). As cultural anthropologists examining the question of "the extent to which mining can contribute to regional development and

---

[13] See Taylor and Scambary (2004).

social sustainability" (Holcombe 2005, p. 107) have problematised land use agreements (negotiated between mining corporations and Indigenous Native Title holders, and meant to materially compensate communities for use of land for mining activities) as "constrained by the very limitations they place on the agency of the Indigenous people they seek to engage" (Scambary 2009, p. 200). That is, agreements negotiated within the dominant paradigm of sustainable development tend to promote Indigenous participation in the mainstream Australian economy (jobs, training, entrepreneurial business/commercial development). This is a significant development especially given the historical exclusion of Indigenous people from the 1960s mining boom (see Holcombe 2005) and deficiencies of the state (welfare) in remote areas. Edmunds has documented this since the 1980s (see 1989) and says, in a study of the 'failed state of remote Australia', that the problem with "governance is government" (2012, pp. 152–180). However, in their focus on mainstream economic participation, these agreements demonstrate poor understanding by the state and mining companies of Indigenous capacity and aspirations (Scambary 2009). It is argued that for the mining industry to have a sustainable impact on regional (remote area) development, it needs to understand the 'deeply acculturated dispositions' of Indigenous people and refocus development on cultural livelihoods (human aspirations and lifestyles) (Scambary 2009, 2013; Holcombe 2010). The livelihoods or community economy approach includes the range of non-economic activity that is nevertheless productive in the sense of reproducing culture through maintaining connections to land and language, for instance.

Big *h*ART's work in the Pilbara has been attuned to the development of cultural livelihoods in place while also forging pathways to mainstream cultural production and distribution—performance, music, digital storytelling (the NEOMAD comics). In addition to producing a national touring piece of theatre, *Hipbone Sticking Out*, the *Yijala Yala* project (and now the *New Roebourne* project) supports the development of performances (theatre, dance and music) for the Roebourne cultural centre and amphitheatre (a venue on the regional festival circuit), and for other times/spaces that have particular, as opposed to mainstream, meaning and significance (such as performances in memorium for John Pat). In other words, Big hART's navigation of Indigenous participation in mainstream culture, whether that's national (Australian) theatre or popular international comics (as hard publications and digital media production), is embedded in the development of specific cultural dispositions, (individual and community) aspirations and livelihoods. Working from a livelihood-based approach, Big hART's work highlights the cultural and creative competence of the people of Roebourne, demonstrating capacities to stage a successful mainstage touring theatre production as well as to sustain vital cultural livelihoods as post-extractive futures.

REFERENCES

900 Neighbours (2006) Directed by B Fletcher for Big hART. Available at: https://vimeo.com/219629661 (Accessed: 12 June 2018).
Commonwealth of Australia. (1997) *Bringing Them Home: Report Of The National Inquiry Into The Separation of Aboriginal and Torres Strait Islander Children From Their Families*. Sydney: Human Rights and Equal Opportunity Commission.
Baker, D. (2001) 'Community Police Peacekeeping Amidst Bitter and Divisive Industrial Confrontation: the 1992 APPM Dispute at Burnie', in Markey, R. (ed.) *Labour and Community: Historical Essays*. Wollongong: University of Wollongong Press, pp. 174–201. Available at: https://ro.uow.edu.au/cgi/viewcontent.cgi?referer=https://www.google.com/&httpsredir=1&article=1008&context=labour1999 (Accessed: 5 June 2016).
Barnes, M., Brannelly, T., Ward, L. and Ward, N. (2015) 'Introduction: The critical significance of care', in Barnes, M., Brannelly, T., Ward, L. and Ward, N. (eds.) *Ethics of care: Critical advances in international perspective*. Bristol: Bristol University Press, pp. 3–20.
Bednarik, R.G. (2002) 'The Killing Fields of Murujuga', http://www.ifrao.com/wp-content/uploads/2014/08/Massacre.pdf (Accessed: 28 May 2014).
Big hART and the Aboriginal Community of Roebourne (2013) *Hipbone Sticking Out*, dir. S. Rankin. Playhouse Theatre, Canberra, ACT. First performance 3. July 2013.
Blunt, E. (2013) Unpublished interview with Kerrie Schaefer, May 18.
Brundlandt, G.H. (1987) *World Commission on Environment and Development: Our Common Future*. Oxford: Oxford University Press. Available at: https://sustainabledevelopment.un.org/content/documents/5987our-common-future.pdf (Accessed: 17 June 2015).
Burvill, T. (1986) 'Sidetrack: Discovering the Theatricality of Community', *New Theatre Quarterly*, 2(5), pp. 80–89. doi: https://doi.org/10.1017/S0266464X00001949
Casey, M. (2009) '*Ngapartji Ngapartji*: Telling Aboriginal Australian Stories', in Forsyth, A. and Megson, C. (eds.) *Get Real. Documentary Theatre Past and Present*. Basingstoke: Palgrave Macmillan, pp. 122–139.
Cohen-Cruz, J. (2005) *Local Acts. Community-based Performance in the United States*. New Brunswick, N.J. and London: Rutgers University Press.
———. (2009) *Engaging Performance. Theatre as Call and Response*. London and New York: Routledge.
Commonwealth of Australia. (1991) *Royal Commission into Aboriginal Deaths in Custody*. Canberra: Australian Government Publishing Service. Available at http://www.austlii.edu.au/au/other/IndigLRes/rciadic/ (Accessed: 7 March 2018).
Commonwealth of Australia (Minster for the Environment and Water Resources) and Woodside Energy Ltd. (2007) *Conservation Agreement*. Available at: https://www.awe.gov.au/sites/default/files/env/pages/4b63db66-1d8e-4427-91d1-951aff442414/files/ca-woodside.pdf (Accessed: 9 May 2019).
Conquergood, D. (2002) 'Performance Studies: Interventions and Radical Research', *TDR*, 46(2), pp. 145–156.
Edmunds, M. (1989) *They Get Heaps: A Study of Attitudes in Roebourne, Western Australia*. Canberra: Aboriginal Studies Press.

—— (2012) 'A New Story – Roebourne: A Case Study' in Walker, B.W. (ed.) *The Challenge, Conversation, Commissioned Papers and Regional Studies of Remote Australia*. Desert Knowledge Australia, Alice Springs, pp. 152–180. Available at: https://eprints.utas.edu.au/15067/3/remoteFOCUS_Compendium_ August_2012%5B1%5D.pdf (Accessed: 24 March 2016).

Exile and The Kingdom, (1993) Directed by F. Rijavec [Film]. Albany, WA: Snakewood Films.

Elkington, J. (1994) 'Towards the Sustainable Corporation: Win-Win-Win Business Strategies for Sustainable Development', *California Management Review*, 36(2), pp. 90–100.

Fischer-Lichte, E (2008) *The Transformative Power of Performance: A New Aesthetics*. Translated by S. I. Jain. London and New York: Routledge.

Gibson-Graham, J.K. (2006) *A Postcapitalist Politics*. Minneapolis: University of Minnesota Press.

Hardt, C. (2013) Unpublished interview with Kerrie Schaefer, January 9.

Hawkes, J. and the Cultural Development Network (Vic). (2001) *The Fourth Pillar of Sustainability: Culture's Essential Role in Public Planning*. Melbourne: Common Ground.

Holcombe, S. (2005) 'Indigenous organisations and mining in the Pilbara, Western Australia: lessons from a historical perspective', *Aboriginal History*, 29, pp. 107–135. Available at: http://press-files.anu.edu.au/downloads/press/p73931/pdf/ ch0650.pdf (Accessed: 14 May 2017).

Holcombe, S. (2010) 'Sustainable Aboriginal Livelihoods and the Pilbara Mining Boom', in Keen, I. [ed.] *Indigenous Participation in Australian Economies: Historical and Anthropological Perspectives*. Canberra: Australian National University E-Press, pp. 141–164. Available at: https://press-files.anu.edu.au/downloads/press/ p122571/pdf/book.pdf (Accessed: 14 May 2017).

James, D. (2015) 'Tjukurpa Time', in McGrath, A. and Jebb, M.A. (eds.) *Long History, Deep Time. Deepening Histories of Place*. Canberra: Australian National University E-Press, pp. 33–45. doi: https://doi.org/10.22459/LHDT.05.2015

Kretzmann, J.P. and McKnight, J. L. (1993) *Building Communities from the Inside Out: A Path Toward Finding And Mobilizing A Community's Assets*. Chicago, IL: ACTA Publications.

Kuftinec, S. (2003) *Staging America. Cornerstone and Community-based Theatre*. Carbondale: Southern Illinois University Press.

Marinos, S. (2013) Unpublished interview with Kerrie Schaefer, January 9.

McConachie, B. (1998) 'Approaching the "Structure of Feeling" in Grassroots Theatre', *Theater Topics*, 8(1), pp. 33–53.

Milne G. (2004) *Theatre Australia (Un)limited Australian Theatre Since the 1950s*. Amsterdam: Rodopi.

Myers, D. (2013) Unpublished interview with Kerrie Schaefer, May 18.

Myers, D. and Palmer, D. (2015) 'What the World Needs Now is Love Sweet Love (Punks)', *Cultural Studies Review*, 21(1), pp. 149–261. doi: https://doi.org/ 10.5130/csr.v21i1.4434

Palmer, D. (2010) *Ngapartji Ngapartji: the Consequences of Kindness*. Perth, WA: Murdoch University. Available at: https://www.bighart.org/wp-content/ uploads/2017/03/BIghART_Evaluation_ConsequencesofKindness.pdf (Accessed: 4 June 2016)

Pitts, G. and Watt, D. (2001) 'The Imaginary Conference', *Artwork Magazine*, 50, pp. 7–14.

Rankin, S. (2018) *Cultural Justice and The Right to Thrive,* Platform Papers 57. Sydney: Currency Press.

———. (2008) Scott Rankin Interviewed by James Waites, September 19 and October 2, in Alice Spring, NT. Transcript. Canberra: National Library of Australia [Oral History Section].

Scambary, B. (2009) 'Mining Agreements, Development, Aspirations, and Livelihoods', in Altman, J. and Martin, D. (eds.) *Power, Culture, Economy. Indigenous Australians and Mining.* Canberra: The Australian National University E-Press, pp. 171–201. Available at: https://press-files.anu.edu.au/downloads/press/p78881/pdf/book.pdf (Accessed: 20 May 2017).

——— (2013) *My Country, Mine Country. Indigenous People, Mining and Development Contestation in Remote Australia.* Canberra: The Australian National University E-Press. doi: https://doi.org/10.22459/CAEPR33.05.2013

Schaefer, K. (2013) 'Something is Happening Here! *Big hART's Ngapartji Ngapartji* at ICAF, Rotterdam', in Van Erven, E.A.P.B. (ed.) *Community Art Power. Essays from ICAF 2011.* Rotterdam: Rotterdams Wijktheater, pp. 198–213.

Smith L. T. (1999) *Decolonizing Methodologies: Research and Indigenous Peoples.* London: Zed Books.

Taylor, J. and Scambary, B. (2004) *Indigenous People and the Pilbara Mining Boom. A Baseline for Regional Participation.* Canberra: Centre for Aboriginal Economic Policy Research (CAEPR), Australian National University. doi: https://doi.org/10.22459/IPPMB.01.2006

Thompson, H. (1992) 'The APPM Dispute: The Dinosaur and Turtles vs the ACTU', *The Economic and Labour Relations Review*, 3(2), pp. 148–164.

Thurow, S. (2019) *Performing Indigenous Identities on the Contemporary Australian Stage: Land, People, Culture.* London and New York: Routledge.

Tronto, J.C. (1993) *Moral boundaries: a Political Argument for an Ethic of Care.* London and New York: Routledge.

Wright, P., Down, B., Rankin, S., Haseman, B., White, M. and Davies, C. (2016) *Big hART: Art, Equity and Community for People, Place and Policy.* Perth, WA: Murdoch University. Available at: https://www.bighart.org/wp-content/uploads/2017/03/BighART_Evaluation_ArtEquityCommunity.pdf (Accessed: 8 July 2018)

Wright, P and D. Palmer. (2007) *People Now Know Me For Something Positive. An Evaluation of Big hART's Work at the John Northcott Estate.* Perth, WA: Murdoch university: Available at: https://researchrepository.murdoch.edu.au/id/eprint/2908/1/People_now_know_me_for.pdf

Van Erven, E.A.P.B. (2013) *Community Art Power. Essays from ICAF 2011.* Rotterdam: Rotterdams Wijktheater. Available at: https://www.icafrotterdam.com/user_files/ICAF_2011/ICAF-community-art-power.pdf (Accessed: 18 May 2017).

CHAPTER 5

The Crossings (Part of the *Islands of Milwaukee*): The Agency of Older Bodies Enacting Pedestrian Crossings

INTRODUCTION

16 June 2016: I'm on East Street, a high street with restricted traffic access, in Bedminster, Bristol, for Entelechy Art's Bed.[1] *It is early afternoon. Haphazardly distributed on the pavements on either side of the street in this busy pedestrian shopping zone are a number of beds (perhaps three, four or five). The beds are gunmetal grey, tubular steel, single beds on wheels. Despite their institutional appearance, each of the beds is brightly decorated presumably in the personal style of the older person contained in repose in them. On each bed is propped a battered brown 1940s/1950s-style rectangular-shaped suitcase. It looks, to all intents and purposes, as if the residents of a nearby hospital, care home or private residence have been removed in their beds and parked (dumped?) in the street.*

This incongruous image of the private and intimate—someone's bed with them in it—placed outdoors in the street is how Entelechy Arts provokes multiple 'conversation pieces' about the invisibility of older people and their lives in public spaces. *Bed* was devised and performed by "older members of Entelechy Arts' Theatre Group who wanted to make a statement about the invisibility they felt when going about their lives in public places".[2] The piece developed over several months and through several iterations as the concept was provisionally enacted and encountered in public spaces. At this particular outing in Bristol, Entelechy practitioners accompanied the performers into the street and stood by to offset any alarm or distress that the image of elderly people abandoned in their beds in the street tended to cause, and to gently coax the public into encounters with the elders.

---

[1] Performed as part of the *Theatre from the Heart* festival, a national festival of community theatre produced by acta Community Theatre.
[2] https://entelechyarts.org/projects/bed/ (Accessed: 7 July 2018).

There were many things that struck me about the performance that day, from the paradoxical image of the private made public, the invisible made visible, to the conversations skillfully enacted by senior performers (in character) with complete strangers of all ages, excavating and negotiating the dynamics of generational relationships in the middle of a busy street. In standing back to watch encounters unfold, knowing *Bed* was a performance rather than following in the wake of an emergency or any other exceptional act, I became aware of a recorded audio track augmenting an act of encounter. Emanating from the area of the bed, a disembodied voice announced that "social isolation was equivalent to smoking fifteen cigarettes a day". The project's direct reference to a body of influential research by American psychologists (Holt-Lunstad et al. 2010) drawing equivalence between the public health risks (50% higher rate of early morbidity) arising from a lack of social relations and the risk to physical health from smoking 15 cigarettes a day, served to link *Bed* to another project, this time in the US. This research 'fact' connecting the physical and social determinants of health had a life, too, in the *Islands of Milwaukee*, a project that aimed to "bring meaningful engagement to older adults living alone or under-connected to community" and to "catalyse a community-wide conversation about the importance of connecting to communities as we age" (IoM Report, p. 1).

Islands of Milwaukee (IoM), coming after The *Penelope Project* (PP), is the second, long-term, cross-sector (arts and non-arts) collaboration undertaken by distinguished artist-scholar Professor Anne Basting, in partnership with Sojourn Theatre (Director Maureen Towey, Designer Shannon Scrofano, Consultant Michael Rohd and devising/performers James Hart, Rebecca Martinez and Edward Massey[3]). The project culminated on the 20 and 21 September 2014 with an interactive installation and performance at Milwaukee City Hall as it played host to 'Doors Open Milwaukee', an event celebrating the city's history and culture as embodied in the built environment. As the public came to register for the Open Doors event in City Hall and to tour the iconic late nineteenth-century (1895) Flemish Renaissance Revival-style building (the Mayor's office on an upper floor was open to the public), they encountered the IoM installation and performance (a ten-minute performance by three to four performers held every hour on the hour).[4]

On the ground floor of city hall, there were three distinct islands carved from the one large polystyrene block on a bright-blue floor canvas. The islands were painted white with the sections where they'd been sliced from the larger

---

[3] Massey was an UWM student who devised and performed in *The Crossings*, and who continued collaborating with Sojourn artists devising the *IoM* performance.

[4] Organized by Historic Milwaukee Inc., the two-day annual event—a weekend in September—offers free behind-the-scene tours of more than 170 buildings throughout Milwaukee's downtown and neighbourhoods. During the 2019 event, more than 29,000 participants visited 170+ sites throughout the city. After the Open Doors weekend, the multimedia *IoM* installation remained in City Hall until 21 October 2014.

block and separated covered in blue-and-white watermark wallpaper. Incorporated into the design (by Scrofano) were ledges or caves where listening devices (headphones) were placed. These listening stations were places where the voices of key participants who had responded (by phone) to the project's primary mode of engagement, 'Questions of the Day', could be heard. Jute cord was stretched from the listening stations on the islands to the upper floors of the building, arranged around a central atrium, encouraging the public to travel up the building by the elevator or the stairs to discover more artefacts made as part of the project. Participants' artistic collaborations (paintings, poems, etc.) created on home visits were turned into feature boards complete with descriptions of the partner organisations they were contacted through and an outline of the subsequent process of artistic engagement and making. The postcard-sized 'Question of the Day' cards, delivered through various contact services such as a meal home delivery service or a community centre providing cooked lunches, were pegged up on multiple lines of twine above the relevant project board. Over the weekend, the boards were attended by representatives of the partner organisations involved, and there were fresh question cards, so the project remained live, interactive and reflective, as well as presentational.[5]

While the *IoM* project comprised question and response, conversations and offerings, radio pieces, intimate (private and domestic) performances and art-making with isolated elders, the live performance attempted to unpack some of that active engagement, introducing some of those whose voices were heard and whose creativity was visible in the installation. As one of the performers said, the performance provides a "sampling of what we heard from forty-five 'Questions of the Day' and two thousand, five hundred responses" (Rebecca Martinez). It was in the middle of the performance as the process was excavated that James Hart asked the question: "Did you know that as a health risk social isolation is equivalent to smoking 15 cigarettes a day?"

In this chapter, I will be examining *IoM* as a project that extended the practical learnings of the *Penelope Project*, set in a long-term care home complex, to a citywide system of senior care. The project was guided by the following questions:

> How do we create a more connected Milwaukee that values and includes older voices in civic life and public decision making? How can we bring meaningful engagement to older adults living alone or under-connected to community? How can we deepen the capacity of existing systems to create a sustainable mechanism to invite and nurture engagement with older adults living alone or under-connected to community? (IoM Report, p. 2)

---

[5] I was stationed at the question about which streets were unsafe to cross maintaining a connection with *The Crossings* project I visited earlier in the year.

Specific focus is given to *The Crossings*, a project within the larger *IoM* project, which staged a series of performances in May 2014 at various street intersections and pedestrian crossings in southern wards of downtown Milwaukee. In *Bed* and *The Crossings*, older people actively collaborated in devising, improvising and performing outdoor performances. Both performances placed older adults in the street to performatively highlight the extent to which social space excludes the participation of older people, and how such exclusion diminishes public health. Streets that are unwalkable or unsafe isolate those who are vulnerable from taking up space. Both performances grappled with the difference between serving as a public-service announcement and enacting provocations to engage the public in elder-led dialogue concerning the place of older people in public space and the public's relationship to them.

The main point of divergence between the two performances is that in *The Crossings* the older adults were not bed-bound or 'playing a character' but pedestrians actively trying—and failing—to do that most mundane, perfunctory act: cross street intersections in the time of the green walk light. This act, performed repeatedly across three crossings, combined community-engaged performance, street or outdoor performance and walking performance with inclusive urban planning. In this chapter I want to explore Basting's sense of community-engaged performance and Rohd's ongoing formulation of civic practice (in its early stages in 2014 when this project took place), that expands public art (here represented by *Bed*)[6] into supporting the creation of vital and sustainable citywide systems of care.

In *Remapping Performance: Common Ground, Uncommon Partners*, Jan Cohen-Cruz examines a shift "from community-based performance to the use of performance in uncommon partnerships" (2015, p. 4). She characterises the move towards "cross sector [arts and social] collaboration" as a natural extension of community-based performance, and as the "integration" of theatre with art as "social practice" (pp. 4–7). Whether this shift is a natural extension of community-based performance or theatre in an 'integrative moment' with social practice, or both, Michael Rohd has placed a wedge in this formulation, meaning integration is not entirely complete or squared. Rohd refers to the *Penelope Project* and *Islands of Milwaukee* as "civic practice", which acknowledges this integrative movement, while at the same time specifying points of difference within the paradigm shift. This chapter is a critical analysis of community-based performance or civic practice, with the awareness that these terms (as is the case with most of the terminologies in this book) are fluid and openly contested, which was evident in the *IoM* process itself.

Before I analyse *The Crossings* as part of the *Islands of Milwaukee*, I am going to turn, briefly, to introduce Basting's work, which has played a major role in defining the field of Creative Care, and the work of US theatre ensemble,

---

[6] Entelechy produces a broad range of participatory arts some of which crosses over with community performance and civic practice. Here, I am using *Bed* as an illustration of a more public art project, albeit devised and performed by an elders, to highlight subtle differences between social and civic practice.

Sojourn Theatre, whose Artistic Director Michael Rohd is simultaneously articulating civic practice alongside social practice. I will touch on their first collaboration, the *Penelope Project*, although my main aim here is to explicate civic practice in greater detail than I have alluded to it above. I will then move on to introduce the *Islands of Milwaukee* project leading into analysis of *The Crossings* as community-engaged performance or civic practice.

The Primary Partnership: Anne Basting and Sojourn Theatre

Anne Basting is an internationally renowned artist, scholar and educator, who is Professor of Theatre in the Peck School of the Arts at the University of Wisconsin-Milwaukee. Her work has long explored the dynamics of older age in theatrical performance, and its performative relationship to the dominant discourse of ageing (as a process of mental and physical deterioration) in US popular culture. Based on practical experiments with seniors living with dementia in care, Basting went on to found *Timeslips* (1998),[7] a creative storytelling methodology that is based on imagination (image association) and improvisation, rather than memory recall. In *Forget Memory: Creating Better Lives for People with Dementia* (2009), Basting identified a broad range of creative approaches, including *TimeSlips*, that utilise the existing capacities of older adults to connect with others, generate meaningful experience and co-produce engaging stories, processes that provide hope and go some way towards replacing fears of memory/identity loss in older age. This led Basting to reformulate memory as a historically contingent form of narrating or storifying experience that is, moreover, an embodied and relational, or social, practice (2009, pp. 13–15).

The *Penelope Project* (*PP*) followed *TimeSlips* (TS) and sought to "expand and disseminate the TS method" (Mello and Voigts 2012, p. 38) so that its impacts went beyond facilitated groups in care and into creative revitalisation of an entire care system. As Basting's colleague at the Peck School of Arts and 'critical friend', Dr Robin Mello states, TPP sought to create a performance that would "illustrate and demonstrate" the capacities of TS participants, many of whom are living with dementia, to create original and meaningful stories and to collaborate in the creative enactment and reinvention of a community of care (Mello and Voigts 2012, pp. 38–39).[8] TPP reaffirmed the partnership between Basting and Beth Arnold Meyer, a specialist in person-centred care

---

[7] In 2013, Basting established, and is president of, the independent non-profit, TimeSlips Creative Storytelling. The organisation is responsible for training and certifying artists/facilitators and caregivers using the approach internationally. See https://www.timeslips.org/

[8] Dr Mello is a Theatre Professor in the Peck School of Arts, UWM. Drawing on her specialism in myth and storytelling performance, she co-wrote and co-taught (with Basting) curriculum for students participating in the PP as part of their degree studies, acted as a critical friend and lead evaluator, and performed the role of 'Nurse' in the piece.

and director of Adult Day Services at Luther Manor (LM), the care facility where Basting developed the TS method with LM residents, many of whom were living with dementia.[9] Unable to locate appropriate local theatre expertise, Basting approached professional friend, Michael Rohd, hoping to partner with him. Sojourn Theatre, became a core project partner:

> [having] a deep understanding, respect for, and commitment to engaging in the community-forming energy that is inherent in theatre work. (Mello and Voigts 2012, p. 40)

This completed the triumvirate of core partners participating in the long-term (Winter 2009–Summer 2012) project.

Sojourn Theatre (Sojourn) is an ensemble theatre company founded in 1999 whose mission is to produce theatre that is 'strikingly physical, politically inquisitive, historically conscious and community engaged' (Sojourn Theatre 2013). The ensemble company is recognised alongside Cornerstone Theatre Company, Liz Lerman Dance Exchange and Urban Bush Women as an exemplary community-based practice (Treuhaft 2008) and as a model of 'best practice' of arts-based civic dialogue (http://www.sojourntheatre.org/company). The PP collaboration came at a time of change for Sojourn and Rohd. While the company had, for a time, a physical base in Portland, Oregon, for several years Sojourn ensemble members (approximately 17 in total) have lived and worked in different cities in the US, coming together for periods of time in intensive residencies to make work all over the country. It is a flexible, mobile and responsive structure—similar to Big hART's —which allows artists to develop skills in aligned and complementary areas of employment, for instance in design (Scofano), live event management (Towey) and counseling (Hart), and then bring competencies back into the company to work on specific projects which rely on these and more traditional theatre skills. In this instance, the partnership with Basting/UWM and Luther Manor was attractive to Rohd because it would be "the first time [Sojourn] had worked in long-term care (where people live while they do a show)" (in Mello and Voigts 2012, p. 40), and, for both Basting and Rohd, it promised to "transform long-term care through creative engagement and extend the tradition of community-based arts into the culture of long-term care, which has traditionally been overlooked by the field [in the US]" (Mello and Voigts 2012, p. 35)

---

[9] LM is a Life Plan community (long-term care facility) just outside of Milwaukee in Wisconsin.

While Sojourn was taking this partnership opportunity to develop practice in new contextual directions, Rohd took the opportunity to remain a collaborating consultant on the project, leaving the project leadership shared between Basting and Towey. Basting's key artistic role alongside the Sojourn artists was as playwright, but she was also creative producer and community organiser, liaising closely with community-based partner organisations in senior community care, in between Sojourn artist intensive residencies. Rohd gained space to reflect on the development of the practice itself, which was, at the same time, moving through yet another evolutionary moment.

Prior to co-founding Sojourn Theatre, Michael Rohd established, in 1991, the not-for-profit theatre organisation, Hope Is Vital, working initially in Washington DC and then in cities across the US, to develop interactive theatre with young people (non-actors) directed towards health (HIV) education. As a form of 'preventative education', Hope Is Vital's interactive theatre programme provided a medium for arts-based dialogue rooted in Freire's notion of popular (peer) pedagogy (see *Community, Conflict and Dialogue: The Hope Is Vital Training Manual* 1998). According to Rohd, the Hope Is Vital project, based on scene-based interactive dialogues, was the first stage of a journey that moved him on from viewing:

> the play as the true meaningful community-building activity at my disposal as a theatre maker. I felt that my role as an artist was to find stories that needed telling, make dynamic context for the telling, and tell them well. (2013a, p. 27)

After almost a decade of work on the *Hope Is Vital* programme, Rohd took forward his investigation of theatre beyond the well-made (political or social issue) play through Sojourn Theatre. Rohd states that he

> became deeply interested in work that builds the possibility of connection through participation. I wanted to further explore moments of deeper and more durational engagement between artists and audiences. The activity of theater, the line that separated my work on Hope Is Vital from production work, at least in my own mind, began to blur. Process and event became linked for me in new ways. Sojourn has been my journey to that discovery and my lab to devise those experiences. (2013a, p. 27)

The exploration undertaken in and through a decade of work by Sojourn Theatre reached a point where, in the 2000s, Rohd was thinking about a move beyond even this summary of the ensemble's experiments. He observes that Sojourn has, since 2001, been moving towards 'civic practice' which he states is,

> a new frame within our field at the intersection of traditional audience engagement activity, current demand-building theory, and community-based art-making methodologies. (2013a, p. 32)

This process crystallised in 2012 with Rohd's co-founding and directing of the Centre for Performance and Civic Practice (https://www.thecpcp.org/).

SOCIAL AND CIVIC PRACTICE

It is late in the evening of the day before Open Doors Milwaukee ushers a public audience into City Hall and into contact with IoM installed on the ground and upper floors of the building. The performance remains to be finalised. Already it is understood that the building is a difficult space for live performance. Sound ricochets off the hard marble surfaces of the walls and floors. The performers' voices disappear into the voluminous seven-story atrium. The rehearsal is pushed back till after 5 pm so that City Hall workers are not disturbed by the cacophony of preparation for simultaneous events. The team have come to understand quickly that any performance taking place in the space simultaneous with a public event will need to be short and direct. Thus they are huddled on the floor by the Islands around Basting's script; Maureen is pacing nearby. The text is being cut, reduced and reformed, edited down to a ten-minute performance to be performed on the hour, every hour. It is a difficult conversation, and it turns to a discussion of how to introduce the participants who engaged with the project and produced art/performance for it and who are, therefore, to be featured in person in particular performances. The question arises of what to call the practice that participants are engaged with. Rohd wants to call it civic practice; Basting argues for community-engaged performance. She says that people won't understand what civic practice means. Rohd gives ground, adding that he's working on making civic practice better known.

Since about 2011, and probably earlier, Rohd has been using the terms 'civic theatre' (2011a, b), 'civic practice' (2012) or 'civic participation' (2013a) to refer to Sojourn's theatre practice. Rohd has found it useful if, as he admitted, somewhat reductive to distinguish between 'two modalities of practice': social practice and civic practice (2013b, 44:20). It is probably worth noting at this point that Rohd is able to identify those of Sojourn's projects which are social practice and, alternatively, civic practice. At the same time, Rohd claims that Sojourn's practice has been moving more towards civic practice since 2001, and the *PP* and *IoM* are leading examples. The term 'civic practice' settled in 2012 with the founding of the Centre for Performance and Civic Practice (CPCP) by Rohd with Sojourn ensemble members, Shannon Scrofano and Soneela Nankini.

Social practice references the already-existing vocabulary that has come to define the broad field of public or social art practice (see, for instance, Kwon 2004, Kester 2004, Jackson 2011, Helguera 2011; also referred to as participatory arts in the UK, see Bishop 2012). While there may be crossovers between social (or participatory arts) and civic practice, Rohd aims to differentiate between practices that are, essentially, artist-led and those that are based on partnership between arts and non-arts (community-based or civic) organisations and whose relationship evolves through engaged dialogue and collaborative creative practice. Social practice, according to Rohd,

> [i]nitiates with an artist's desire to explore or create a conceptual event or moment of their design. The design and/or execution may engage non-artists in any number of ways: it may leverage non-arts partners and community resources; it may intend to specifically impact the social or civic life of the context in which it occurs in measurable ways; it may intend to exist as an aesthetic interruption from which impact is to be derived in an open, interpretive manner. But whatever social or civic needs the project addresses, the leading impulse and guiding origin energy is from the artist. (Rohd 2013b, 45:10)

In contrast, civic practice is a dynamically engaged and dialogic practice in collaborative partnership with a civic (non-arts) organisation, and leads to an exchange of artistic skills (called assets) in relation to the civic partner's needs. Rohd defines civic practice as an

> activity where a theater artist employs the assets of his/her craft in response to the needs of non-arts partners as determined through ongoing, relationship-based dialogue. It's the intersection of two sets of content. Let's call them an x axis and a y axis. The x axis is theater activity that is not limited to the production of plays, but rather is a set of tools, of assets, that theater artists have access to because of our experience in producing plays (and performance). We bring these assets to the table, any table, where we are invited. (2012: https://howlround.com/new-work-building-civic-practice)

It is important to stress that civic practice implies less an application (or even act of applying) of artists' tools to civic needs and more a relational and dialogic partnership established to co-design and creative problem-solve with non-arts partners.

Rohd also uses the term 'civic participation' to distinguish Sojourn's practice given that while 'participation' is not a new concept or practice in the arts, participation is enjoying renewed attention due to "recent awareness of the consumer as a co-creator and to our fascination with audience as self-curator" (2013a, p. 34). Participatory arts practices have come under critique recently. Bishop (2012), in particular, has questioned the politics and ethics of participatory art practices. Drawing on Ranciere's theories of the 'aesthetic regime' (2006) and the 'emancipated spectator' (2010) (see below for further discussion of Ranciere in the context of performance analysis), she asserts that participatory art that seeks to create 'community' as a utopian alternative, in fact, creates 'artificial hells' forcing moral norms of social relation (consensus) on public art audiences. Bishop argues that participatory practices are based on a poor understanding of the critical function of art (in the aesthetic regime) and a naïve notion of community (which is inoperative or defunct she asserts, after Nancy). Kester (2004) is also suspect of participatory art, which he sees as a superficially enjoining the powerless classes to participate in their own socio-economic domination by the powerful. At the same time, for Kester, deep arts and non-arts collaborations can do more than offer aesthetic critique (Bishop after Ranciere), but can actively work towards articulating heterotopian alternatives as a challenge to dominant power modes. While Bishop and Kester may seem to be at loggerheads, they both reject participation, Bishop as pseudo-activism and uncritical art, and Kester as an interpellation of subjects into the dominant mode of power. They both see a powerful, dominant force acting behind that wields cultural participation instrumentally to activate and/or distract.

Rohd's use of the term 'civic' (-theatre, -participation, -practice) points to a longer historiography of participatory theatre and performance practice. The term 'civic theatre' was coined by Percy MacKaye in his book (*The Civic Theatre*) of 1912, on the subject of early twentieth-century pageantry in the US. Civic theatre or pageantry was significantly reinvented in the US in the immediate aftermath of the First World War, as an era of progressive policy took hold and promoted assimilation of culturally and linguistically diverse immigrants as 'American' citizens (see Cohen-Cruz 2005; Kuftinec 2003). Kuftinec notes that an undercurrent of anxiety "about a labour force with increasing leisure time additionally contributed to the development of a pageant and civic theatre movement" (2003, p. 27). In pageantry, the very notion of (class-based) citizenship was enacted, and in the process reformulated.

Scholarship on community-based theatre and performance regards pageantry and civic theatre as an 'emergent mode and method' of community-based theatre (Kuftinec 2003, p. 26), or an 'early antecedent' (Cohen-Cruz 2005, p. 17). According to Cohen-Cruz: "pageants are a source of community performance by being built on a theme, not a plot, necessitating broad-based participation, emphasising place, and engendering civic engagement" (p. 17). According to Kuftinec, civic theatre pageantry placed "formal emphasis on symbolic enactment, community embodiment, and rhetorical emphasis on assimilation and allegiance" (2003, p. 27). Both note that civic theatre pageantry was connected to popular and participatory democratic expression about what it meant to be a US citizen, promoting both active citizenship and participatory democracy. Both also note coercive and controlling elements within the medium itself, enforcing ideal identities and (embodied) behaviours that passed within a top-down definition of national identity. Kuftinec claims that civic theatre's participatory interpellation of 'new' US citizens illuminates processes of community and nation-building in early twentieth-century America and, at the same time, points to the possibilities as well as the limitations of participatory inclusion (p. 30). She asserts that civic theatre pageantry may simultaneously "embody ideological control, participatory diversity, and animating unity—all elements which continue to merit more rigorous assessment in contemporary community-based theatres" (p. 30).

Rohd does not explicitly locate himself in relation to the critique of participation across art theory and performance practice. He does not engage in this debate, nor does he specify the pitfalls of participation highlighted in scholarship on civic theatre, such as the slippage from inclusion to compulsion that

Kuftinec identifies as the other side of participatory art practices (2003, p. 27). But he does discriminate Sojourn's practices as occurring within a field of participation outlined as participation-as-measurement; participation-as-experience, and assets-based participation (2013a, p. 25). Assets-based chimes with a community development approach which I discussed in the previous chapter on Big hART, where those seeking to develop community focus on assets rather than deficits. It has been argued that a deficit focus yields more negativity from within and without the community, and the problem quickly becomes seemingly too big to solve. However, an assets-based approach works with existing strengths (including personal storied experience), and moves forward that way. Rohd uses that concept a little differently: Sojourn's work is not assets-based community development, but Sojourn is using 'assets' in the sense of artists having assets—skills as tools—that can be put to use with civic and community partners in particular social situations. Theatre practitioners and ensembles bring their skills and use theatre-based participatory practice as a way to engage non-arts sectors and settings in meaningful, collaborative work, often aimed at problem-solving or coalition building. Civic participation or practice is

> defined as the process of creating arts activity that originates in partnership between artists and non-arts-centred organisations in service to the needs of the non-arts partner. The activity is not necessarily aimed at an art product (such as a play), but rather uses arts-based process or techniques that engage non-artists in imaginative acts and expressive actions with the intent of leveraging creativity and collaboration to problem-solve in unique, effective ways. (2013a, p. 33)

Asset-based participation, different to measurement of the social outreach of the artwork or the creation of an experience that simultaneously includes the audience/spectator in curated co-production of meaning/signification, places participation at the centre of a relational and dialogic exchange focused on shared values and mutual goals.

THE *ISLANDS OF MILWAUKEE*

The *Islands of Milwaukee* had its beginnings in the *Penelope Project* (PP) project. University of Wisconsin-Milwaukee (UWM) students were an important part of the PP: Basting and Mello had developed a practical curriculum for them and engagement in the creative practice was problem-based learning. During the project, however, students struggled to physically get to Luther Manor due to a lack of reliable public transport. Luther Manor is an approximately ten-mile road journey across the Northern suburbs of the city from east to west. Solutions were explored before Luther Manor solved the transport problem by putting on a free bus service for the student practitioners (Mello and Voigts 2012, p. 69). For Basting, however, it was clear that sections of the community, represented by younger university students and older people in care homes, were cut off from access to each other, in this instance as a result of public transport inadequacies; they were "Shipwrecked" (Basting in Mello and Voigts 2012, p. 70). "Shipwrecked" thus became the working title of the IoM project Shipwrecked: Imagining Ways Off Our Many Islands.

The project idea firmed up in conversation between Basting and Towey in the wake of the PP as they pondered how to extend the kind of meaningful creative engagement they were able to achieve in a long-term care facility, where there is an existing infrastructure, to elders "living alone at home or who were under-connected to their communities" (2020, p. 162). Conversation reaffirmed the core artistic partnership of Basting, with UWM students drawn from the Department of Theatre and graduate programmes, and Sojourn (with Towey as co-project lead and director). The core artistic team then began to build partnerships with organisations responsible for connecting with elders in their homes (outreach) and/or providing services for elders in the community.[10] A team of artists, including Basting and Towey, visited community centres where elders were served a cooked lunch, and they went on 'ride alongs' with Meals on Wheels drivers, delivering meals to people in their homes. They thought about how to introduce imagination and creative play into these service-based relationships to augment the interactions already taking place. The aim was not to invent new connecting systems, to reform interactions or to create relationships where they were lacking; they were not. The aim was, rather, to build on existing networks of connection, to strengthen service provision in partnership with service providers interested in exploring creative methods, and service recipients, and to bring these organisations and the isolated elders they support to the forefront of the awareness of the wider community. My field notes have Anne Basting describing this process as being like "pouring creativity like water into the system that is already there and enhancing its capacity to meaningfully connect" (field notes 26 April 2014).

Basting and Towey hit on the idea of 'Question of the Day' as the "low commitment creative exercise" (IoM report, p. 5) to break the ice and start a feedback loop between the project and lone elders. Scrofano designed the blue-and-white postcards with black-and-gold text that beautifully announced that the 'Question of the Day'. The cards were distributed through service providers (e.g. meal delivery drivers, lunch centres) to service users. They were also disseminated via the project website page and a project social media page. The 'questions of the day' cards posed the question with space for written reply as well as a (free) phone/contact number for verbal response. Apparently the most popular questions were:

> What is something you treasure in your home, and why?
> Is there an intersection you wish you could cross but feel it is too dangerous?

---

[10] Core partners included Milwaukee County Dept on Aging, Interfaith Older Adult Programs, Goodwill Industries of Southeastern WI and Stowell Associates. Funding was provided by MAP Fund, Helen Bader Foundation, NEA Art Works, Greater Milwaukee Foundation, Princess Grace Fellowship and Colectivo Coffee Roasters.

What is the most beautiful sound in your home?
What is the most beautiful sound in the world? (IoM report, p. 7)

Responses were acknowledged at lunch sites (posters collated various responses to questions), online, on social media and in a weekly radio programme produced by Towey on Milwaukee Public Radio. This demonstration of listening and sharing was followed up by the offer, to those who left a name and number, of an 'artistic housecall' (IoM report, p. 4). The 'Question of the Day' format led to responses (written and verbal), conversations, home visits, poetry writing, dance performance, storytelling and other forms of creative expression. This deeper creative expression (painting, dance, poetry making) produced during in-home visits by artists and students, as well as many of the verbal/conversational responses to 'Questions of the Day' were carried through to public exhibition in the installation and performance at Milwaukee City Hall on 20 and 21 September.

My engagement with *Islands of Milwaukee* focuses on a project within the project, *The Crossings* (recalling Peel's "don't do one project when you can do several"), which developed in relation to the popular 'Question of the Day': "Is there an intersection you wish you could cross but feel it is too dangerous?" After attending Sojourn's summer institute in 2013 to learn about the ensemble's mode of theatre-making and civic practice, I arrived in Milwaukee in April 2014 for a two-week intensive as Sojourn artists flew (mostly) into town to work on the *IoM* project and *The Crossings*, joining students devising performances on live street (car/pedestrian) intersections. Sojourn artists offered much-needed support in devising, direction and design. I rode along with Anne Basting as she attended multiple partner meetings maintaining IoM feedback loops and trying to ensure that there would be bodies at *The Crossings*, as well as places to park, unload gear and hold highlight moments in which city officials were offered a public platform to translate experience into action. *The Crossings* culminated in performances at three crossings over two days. This was the most participatory of my series of performance observations. For the short but intensive time I was in Milwaukee in April/May 2014 (I was there again in September 2014), I was part of groups of students, elders and others 'crossing' intersections (on the wrong—or right—side of the road), and I acted as a "docen" at one of six interactive question stands in the exhibition at City Hall, standing near to the Mayor's office with the 'Question of the Day' on dangerous intersections. It's partly due to that experience that I want to focus on *The Crossings*, but also because it was the most public part of the project that was equally performed in (voice over internet) call space and in the private and intimate spaces of people's homes.

The Crossings

In the IoM performance at Milwaukee City Hall, Sojourn performer Rebecca Martinez calls out a question to the crowd: 'Is there an intersection you wish you could cross on foot, but feel it is too dangerous?' *Two performers—James Hart and Edward Massey—respond from the first-floor balcony overlooking the islands and Martinez below. They state: "we got some answers about dangerous intersections", and proceed to unfurl a pack of cards sticky-taped together, concertina-style. The dramatically unfolded cards stretch all the way from the first to ground floor (approximately a 20-foot drop) representing as the performers note, "the 158 dangerous intersections identified by elders of Milwaukee".*

The Crossings are a set of community-engaged performances that took place over two days, 1–2 May 2014, at three specific street intersections with traffic lights and pedestrian walk signs on the south side of Milwaukee. This project within a project came out of awareness generated by project activities and a partner organisation's commitment to address a particular civic issue. While riding along with meal delivery drivers, Basting and artists/students became aware that residences drivers were delivering to were across the road from a restaurant or grocery store but were impossible to access due to the road traffic. This unsafe 'access-to-exchange' (Engwicht 1993, pp. 106–107) situation prompted a question concerning public infrastructure and how it actively inhibits older people, particularly those with disabilities, from maintaining independence and connection to community (walking to local shops and services and in the process meeting other people). This awareness prompted the 'Question of the Day' about dangerous intersections, which proved to be a popular topic.

At the same time, South Shore Connecting Caring Communities (SSCCC), a senior advocacy group led by Debby Pizur and Bob Pietrykowski, had identified pedestrian safety as its organisational initiative of the year (2014). Pedestrian safety is a global issue and subject of intensive research. European and US observatory-style research has found that while all pedestrians are vulnerable road users, age is a critical risk factor in the death or injury of pedestrians involved in motor vehicles accidents. In a critical review of international research into older pedestrians, Dunbar et al. state that "the most inportant finding is that the risk of death from a pedestrian accident is much greater for older people" (2004, p. 25).

The wealth of research evidencing the increased risk of fatality for older pedestrians prompted the EU Parliament to introduce The European Charter of Pedestrians' Rights in 1988. In a list of eight key rights, one states: "Children, the elderly and the disabled have the right to expect towns to be places of easy social contact and not places that aggravate their inherent weakness" (in Engwicht 1993, p. 165).

The partnership between *IoM* and SSCCC was established in October 2013 with the aim to co-produce performances at street crossings to 'make Milwaukee a city that SEES and STOPS for pedestrians" (promotional flyers, 2014).

Basting researched 'pedestrian performances' including the introduction by Antanas Mockus, the iconoclastic former academic turned Mayor of Bogotá, of mime artists onto chaotic and lawless city streets in the Colombian capital, and David Engwicht's work on 'traffic calming' ('Walking School Bus', 'Neighbourhood Pace Car') (1993) and street reclaiming (1999). The traffic mimes were one of several initiatives implemented by the inventive and reformist Mayor, Mockus, as part of a programme of 'civic culture' (*cultura ciudadana*). Doris Sommer (2014), writing on the 'special first case' of the traffic mimes in a study on art and civic agency, explains:

> [t]wenty make-up artists with no authority to detain people or to issue traffic tickets stopped buses, mocked jay walkers, and beguiled a growing pubic. The effective antics encouraged Mockus and his inspired staff to keep playing. Within ten years, traffic deaths decreased from thirteen hundred per year to six hundred. For two weeks each mime would train twenty amateurs – gradually including the homeless and even professional police among the eventual four hundred recruits. Soon the grid of urban space became a massive stage for daily fun poked at offenders of rules about red lights and crosswalks. The spectacle crested a public from discreet and defensive residents [...] In Bogotá, the pantomime performances reconstituted a res publica that appreciates some pedestrian elements of the law. Now people come together in public to abide the law, with pleasure. (pp. 24–25)

In her sophisticated analysis of the traffic mimes as part of a top-down or government-sponsored, citywide creativity programme, Sommer (2014) draws on Schiller's aesthetic philosophy, which stresses play—"creative play and the counterfactual exercise of imagination" (p. 19)—as a third term between reason and the passions, to explain the traffic mimes' aesthetic and pragmatic efficacy. According to Sommer, Mockus's 'civic culture' programme was effective because, as an approach, it effectively "combines the ludic with the legal" (p. 24):

> to "harmonise" the competing norms of moral, legal and cultural practices [...] cajoling citizens to reconcile formal with informal codes of behaviour. [...] The mimes who mocked infringements [...] raised moral support for traffic law and cheapened the cultural cache of ignoring the law, bringing all three codes [moral, legal and cultural] into closer agreement. (p. 19)

While Sommer's focus is on how a government programme adopted creative play as part of a democratic civic and aesthetic process encouraging citizens "to improvise in games of mutual regulation" (2014, p. 31), Engwicht's work offers something of a counterpoint to this top-down or state-led creativity. Engwicht's career began after he, a resident, rather reluctantly joined a neighbourhood group formed in response to the Queensland government's plans to build a highway through his Brisbane suburb to get people into Brisbane city faster. With other residents, he founded the group Citizen's

Against Route Twenty (CART), which called for a social and environmental impact study and then, in a publicity coup, upstaged official publication of a report with prior publication of its own report: 'Traffic Calming – The Solution to Route 20 and a New Vision for Brisbane' (1989 in Engwicht 1993, p. 11). CART's report gained international recognition, and traffic calming was subsequently written into the official report as another option (see Engwicht 1993, pp. 11–12). Elements of what is, according to Engwicht, a rights-based ecological ethos (1993, pp. 87–114) have, not unproblematically, become part of mainstream urban and transportation planning. Engwicht has written books from the report which established him as 'traffic calming guru', and saw some of his innovations such as 'Walking School Bus', taken up officially in Canada, while his own thinking has extended from traffic calming to street reclaiming, and now seems to have settled in the field it also participated in forming, creative place-making.

While there were things to draw on in both research examples, neither focused on the fundamental issue of the safety of (older) pedestrians at street crossings. The Bogotá traffic mimes were focused on the behaviour of all pedestrians, especially those who took pleasure in crossing roads anywhere and anytime, further aggravating the relationship between drivers and pedestrians, and drivers, who refused to stop for pedestrians. The mimes aimed to shame errant pedestrians into crossing roads at designated places, and then to encourage drivers to respect pedestrian crossings, drawing pedestrians and drivers into a relationship of mutual responsibility. Engwicht's initiatives suggested a sea change in approach to the built environment and transportation, which decentred the dominance of the motor car and restored the rights of other road users (cyclists, pedestrians) in the street space. His traffic-calming techniques aimed to reduce the volume and speed of motor vehicle traffic. The 'Walking School Bus' is a good example of encouraging children (and caregivers) to walk together to school safely and healthily while also reducing the number of cars on the road and associated issues of dangerous overparking and pollution. Basting and SSCCC drew on the playful, improvisatory and imaginative mode of creative engagement that these projects employed, and brought these strategies into a performance at street crossings.

The project partners—SSCCC—determined 'intervention sites' (street crossings) through local research, drawing on local knowledge, neighbourhood meeting groups, everyday discussions at service and engagement sites, and the 'question of the day' asking elders to identify dangerous intersections. Towards the end of January 2014, the *Crossings* partnership had determined the three crosswalk intersections for performative intervention, and the dates were set for 1–2 May. Performances at three intersections/crossings was thought to be a manageable number. The three intersections chosen were known to be heavily trafficked, close to residences for older adults and particularly difficult to cross as a pedestrian. The crossings were spread across three municipalities on the south side of Milwaukee, moving increasingly outward from the city centre: Bayview (at the intersection of Kinnickinnic or KK, Logan and Russell Avenues), St Francis (at the intersection of KK and St Francis Avenues) and Cudahy (at the intersection of Packard and Ramsey Avenues). It was not articulated further in the project, but the three intersections exhibit exemplary features that a critical review of research literature (Dunbar et al. 2004) identifies as particularly difficult and dangerous for older pedestrians when crossing street intersections (even at the lights). Bayview (S Kinnickinnic Ave/E Russell Ave/S Logan Ave) has a three-point intersection reflecting older pedestrians' concerns about crossing "where several roads meet"' (Dunbar et al. 2004, p. 13; p. 105). St Francis (S Kinnickinnic Ave/E St Francis Ave) features a junction, peculiar to the US, at which vehicles can turn right against a red light signal. In effect, the red light is treated as a 'give way' for vehicles if the road they are turning into is clear of traffic. A significant percentage of older pedestrians have reported that this was "difficult to cope with" as "this arrangement means that they have to consider an extra source of approaching vehicles" (Dunbar et al. 2004, p. 105). Finally, the intersection of E Ramsey and S Packard Avenues in Cudahy involved crossing a four-lane road. A study of US accident data found that "older pedestrians were particularly at risk crossing wide roads with four or more lanes" (Dunbar et al. 2004, p. 13).

DEVISING *THE CROSSINGS: WE'RE WORTH STOPPING FOR*

The core devising group was made up of ten University of Wisconsin-Milwaukee students, eight from the Peck School of Arts (Jake Colon, Wren DuVernois, Stephanie Kimble, Donald Kozinski, Edward Massey, Catherine Monroe, Megan Scheftner and Kodi Shopper) and two graduate students (Chelsea Wait and Sarah Freimuth). The undergraduate students were chosen via audition, and started in January 2014 with classes and workshops on devising performance, before the group moved into devising in situ throughout the months until the performance in early May (this was a credited module). The group started to explore street crossings themselves (measuring distances from one side of the road to the other, and timing the light changes), as well as the area around the crossings, 'discovering' senior building complexes and mapping other constituencies who might use the crossing based on nearby installations (schools, community centres, business/commercial premises etc.). The project found an additional partner in Wisconsin Bike Fed, a cycling organisation which had nevertheless produced a pamphlet (with Wisconsin Department of Transportation) on 'Pedestrian and Drivers' (2012), which outlined pedestrian rights and explained to pedestrians how to keep safe. The organisation led training workshops for *The Crossings* crew, which led into workshops on 'How to Stop Traffic' offered by the crew to elders living in senior housing close to dangerous crossings. The core partnership of Basting and Sojourn engaged with civil servants drawn from across various City Departments (for instance, Engineering, Transportation, Ageing and Law Enforcement/Police) and elected representatives (including Milwaukee, St. Francis and Cudahy Mayors, and a Wisconsin state senator) gathering necessary information fed into the devising process and also informing them about the project and inviting participation. All the while, Basting had regular meetings with the board of SSCCC at the Kelly Senior Centre; in addition to *The Crossings* events, the group was planning on producing a 'toolkit' to make the project self-sustaining. In mid-March, the project was officially titled *The Crossings: We're Worth Stopping For*, with the new subtitle coming after input from a senior during a workshop: when asked what would you say to drivers to get them to stop, the senior replied, "I'm worth stopping for". April was an intensive month of devising and rehearsing, with Sojourn (Towey, Hart, Scofano, Rohd and performer Malkia Stampley) arriving towards the end of this time to prepare for the public performances. I arrived shortly before Sojourn, and will discuss the final few weeks of the devising process as it moved between intersections, classrooms at UWM and community spaces, before introducing and analysing the performances.

Site-Specific Devising at the Corner of Packard and Ramsey, Cudahy, 22 April 2014

My first time out on a crossing with the student group and elders (three ladies, one with a walker, and two men) from nearby housing is at the Packard and Ramsey intersection in Cudahy, the municipality furthest from downtown Milwaukee. Packard is a straight, wide (four-lane) road, while Ramsey is less of a thoroughfare. The intersection is beside a strip mall which sprawls across the intersection, with a grocery store and post office on one side of Packard and a pharmacy on the other side of road; a restaurant is across Ramsey. The walk sign to cross Ramsey is out of action. The group assemble on the pavement readying to cross Packard. Someone presses the 'Walk' signal.

It's my first experience crossing. I'm wondering how hard it can be to cross the street. I'm standing with an older lady who has walked up with students from the village. She has a walking frame. I stand by her. The light changes to green. The students dart out onto the crossing to do their routine—two students performing the bridges run to either side of the crossing followed by the two students holding the bars. The bridges mime being raised while the bars come down. Students standing in the middle of the road face the traffic clanging triangles. Beside them are students with small hand-made signs. Most of the group set off as soon as the light turned. I walk beside the lady with the walker, and as we are not even half of the way across the crossing, the walk light changes to red leaving us stranded in the middle of a very wide intersection. There aren't many cars stopped as there isn't a lot of traffic, and they manoeuvre around us from a standing start as we pass by, but I'm worried about the cars travelling back from the traffic and whether they'll see us and stop in time! I feel like a pin in a Bowling alley waiting to be struck. I wonder whether to go back to where I came from or forge on. The lady with the walker is quite sanguine and suggests that we 'keep going'. She says it is always like this. I think about running but I can't because it would leave her there and I'd look like a real coward abandoning an older lady in the middle of the street. The students are sort of holding their ground too, guardians of the crossing, but it's a large crossing, and they can't cover it all. I remain by the lady's side and put my head down so as not to lock eyes with any driver angered by the impediment we are putting in their place. We make it across and the group regathers. The elders have the floor and explain how this is a standard occurrence. I listen to stories of navigating crossings, near misses and altercations with drivers. In the discussion that follows, Anne remarks that a site-specific workshop at a crossing had to be abandoned because it was just too dangerous. I wonder how much worse it can be.

Taking It Back to the Classroom (22 April 2014)

Anne followed up the site-specific devising session with an email to students and the project team. She pointed out, firstly, the issue of the "size of the crossing" and that it was "in danger of overwhelming the performance" (Basting 2014). In the same point, she asked the questions: "How do we create a performance that will make people in their cars see things differently or make them think differently? What story or narrative or performative image will capture the attention and transform the perspective of drivers" (Basting 2014). The second point touched on "conversations on the walk" and how important to the project "dialogue with elderly residents/pedestrians" was (Basting 2014). Finally, Basting indicated that the crux of the project depended on getting powerful people—mayors, district and departmental elected representatives, city engineers—to the event to experience a crossing: "so that they get a sense of what it feels like to step out on a crossing only to have the light turn to red, [so that they have the opportunity] to listen to the elderly people talk about what it is like for them, what [are] their difficulties and challenges" (Basting 2014).

Back in the classroom at UWM in the afternoon, Basting explored with the students the possibilities of 'walking and talking'. She asked the students to recall what they heard the elders saying on the crossing, how they tended to speak about the dangers of crossing. She wanted the students to prompt these sorts of statements in the act of crossing. She also acknowledged that it was 'difficult to focus on conversation when you might be run over' (field notes 22 April 2014). The devising group created lists of statements, things they'd heard the elders saying on the crossing, and played around with these. They created actions to go with statements, they sang the words and they put that altogether into a collage. Embodying the statements in this manner encouraged students to remember the difficulties the elders faced and to raise questions that would enable the elders to expound on the dangers of pedestrian crossings with civil servants and elected representatives present. From this devising work, a list of ten conversation starters was composed. This 'walking and talking' was something that was worked on right up until the final public performances, and was a challenging aspect of the process. For the students used to more traditional acting studies, it was difficult to envisage conversational performance pieces with an as-yet-unknown group of different participants. It was also an incredibly demanding task to create a performance for a crossing, to keep pedestrians and themselves safe on the crossing and then to facilitate conversations while in an insecure situation.

Community Engagement

In community meetings that Anne attended as part of the *IoM* project, *The Crossings* often came up and offered an opportunity for Anne to disseminate learning. On 23 April, Anne collected me to go with her to Nutrition Council Meeting at Hart Park Senior Centre. She was mainly talking about *IoM* and 'Questions of the Day' cards sent out to meal centers. She mentioned *The Crossings* also, and got into a conversation with a woman there who wanted to get the police involved in looking into pedestrian crossings. Anne urged her to do a community assessment of the crossing by timing the length of the green light and assessing its timing against the measure of two seconds per step. The woman surmised that the timing of the walk light was shortened because motorists get angry having to stop too long, and returned to the issue of the police somehow enforcing the crossing. Anne reiterated that the police are only interested in 'infractions', and encouraged the woman to contact the council as it was not a police matter. She encouraged the woman to do her own assessment, and mentioned that the SSCCC and the *IoM* project were working to develop a DIY Crossings kit so that people could test their own crossings, and raise awareness of rights of pedestrian safety (field notes 23 April 2014).

My field notes from the process reveal some of the challenges of 'civic practice' in sustaining a relational dialogue with community partners and local residents. On 24 April, I accompanied Anne to an SSCCC meeting in the Kelly Senior Centre. Anne voiced concerns about having a hard time getting certain organisations involved. She felt she was close to 'harassing' people to engage. Anne named a long list of people she'd contacted to ensure participation in the crossings performances, many of whom she hadn't heard back from. She was at the point of running out of time to do any further relationship building: her philosophy at this stage was whoever will be there will be there. There was no time for making new contacts. At the same time, the SSCCC group realised that they needed to get the word out through their networks and ensure that their contacts would be at the performances. In the afternoon, after the meeting, we (Anne and I) dropped by a school on the KK/St Francis crossing. Anne hadn't had a response to her invitation. She did not get past reception, who were rather short, and left a final message; she let me know the following day that the school had got in touch and were 'on board'. That afternoon we also visited the church on the KK/Logan and Russell crossing. There were two ladies there, and they responded to the project immediately. One expressed that she was so fearful of crossing the road that she would not put post in the mailbox across the street, but gave it to the postman when he delivered mail to the church. They showed us around and Anne cleared with them using the car park, to park and unload props, and the chapel, to temporarily store materials and to change and prepare for the performance. She also gained permission to use the front steps to the church (on KK) for a short press stop that she had planned into each Crossings performance. This highlighted to me some of the behind-the-scenes work that Anne undertook in inviting participation and clearing permission to utilise spaces connected to each intersection to support the performances and the planned post-performance doorstep presentation to publicly (with media present) address the issue of pedestrian safety on crossings.

On Sunday 27 April, the Sojourn-intensive residency began. Company members began arriving on Sunday, and flew in throughout the day. They were there for the week until Friday, with performances on Thursday and Friday. The *Crossings* was the main focus, but they also worked on the *IoM* project.

Sojourn Residency

On Sunday afternoon, we meet at UWM, and go over the routine the students have devised. James Hart asks about the devising process. The students explain that they began without props, just using their bodies on crossings, and then because of the rude gestures and abuse the students were getting from drivers, they introduced props to mimic the vernacular design of downtown Milwaukee (built on three rivers) where drivers have to stop at bridges to let ships pass: the bells ring, bars come down to block traffic and bridges raise up to let water traffic pass. The students take the performance out onto a crossing near the University to demonstrate what they have come up with in the context of an intersection. James offers positive feedback on aspects of the performance, and pinpoints where he feels the piece needs more entertaining elements to it. Most importantly, James says that the student performers need to make a contract that served drivers and pedestrians. James suggested losing the bridges stationed at either end of the crossing. He wanted more bodies more dynamically involved in the performance, and the performance throwing the focus onto pedestrians communicating with each other and the pedestrian collective communicating with drivers.

On Monday evening (28 April, 6 pm), Maureen Towey, the director, begins working with the student performers in the PSoA, UWM. She has planned a strenuous but fun physical warm-up with stretches, body popping and popular dance. After the warm up, Maureen delivers the news that the bridges have gone, and the idea has morphed into sails instead. Shannon has taken over design of the sails of a boat, and they are in the workshop. Meanwhile, the students, picking up the high energy of the earlier warm-up, work repeatedly on running out into the crossing and bringing down the safety bars that stop traffic.

Tuesday (29 April 2014) is first day Maureen gets out on a crossing. James is now the captain of a boat, and three students become pole bearers (while the sails are still in the workshop). In an afternoon rehearsal back at UWM, Maureen and Anne introduce a sea shanty, which the group learn and rehearse. Anne introduces the routes she has planned for each of the performances. They are circuitous taking in not only the crossings but the surrounding area as well. She imagines the boat touring a larger area than the crossings and stopping to pick up and let off passengers. Anne has also written a loose script for the highlight moment with press and media. The group discuss the sites for the highlight and block the positioning of the student performers flanking 'the specials' and try speaking the text.

Before the end of the day (Tuesday), the group perform crossing another intersection close to campus. The student performers are seriously cut off on the crossing by two cars (one driven by an elderly driver with a disability badge) and a yellow school bus. On the way back from rehearsal, James, at the head of the group, is stopped by UWM police, who think the performance is a demonstration (a problem that will reoccur unexpectedly in the actual performances). Anne provides the name and details of the project, and the conversation turns to the legality of cars turning on red lights with pedestrians on the crossing. The officers seem resigned to the rule of cars; the position seems to be that it is ok for cars to turn right on a red light with pedestrians on the crossing as long as they don't force a pedestrian to literally jump out of the way. This is difficult because *The Crossings* doesn't want to break the law or stop cars from doing what they are legally able to do, but the ship formation crossing the street may mean drivers won't be able to turn right because it will probably take all the time, if not more, to get the group of people across with the green light, which is shared with drivers turning right. The discussion moves to what to do if not everyone gets across with the light—do some go back to the crossing? What about the slow walkers/wheelchair bound? Do they do multiple crossings?

The difficulties of the crossing lead Sojourn performers to query Anne's route maps. There is a shared sense that the routes are too complicated. Anne has good reasons for wanting to go here and there, but Sojourn are thinking things through pragmatically, without connection to the communities that utilise the crossings and who Anne, mainly, has painstakingly engaged with on the project. Sojourn performers push to simplify, to focus the performance on the crossing. Discussion narrows to consideration of the practical and logistical complications of multiple boat crossings of the intersection. Maureen wants the boat to be a tighter formation, and she'd prefer each performer had a clear sense of responsibilities: Who is going where? Up front, in the middle, holding up the end? James considers there might be 10 to 12 people who can cross on 'the boat' at a time with others needing to stay behind at the church or on the crossing, watching and waiting for a turn.

On Wednesday 30 April, the entire crew get out to the KK/Logan/Russell crossing with the completed props. The sails are large, and the inclement weather makes them hard to manage. It is decided that harnesses are to be secured to enable student performers to better manage the sails and, by implication, the boat in the case of wind. The long safety barriers have bright red-and-white stripes. There are large—poster-sized—signs with key information in striking black-and-gold capitals lettering. Each person in the performance now has a designated role to play, so each is looking after a specific part of the performance: Chelsea is in charge of the volunteers (as one I am to carry flag or seagull stick and to ask elders questions about their experiences of crossing), Anne marshals the special visitors and press, Maureen guides the audience, while James, is to master sea shanties, and captain the boat. Malkia is to strike up strategic conversations. This leaves the students free to face drivers—pre-warned by signage—offering an energetic and entertaining framework around the boat crossing. In the follow-up to the final dress rehearsal, Michael Rohd, who joined for the crossing, reminds the group: "make certain you prioritize making an encounter between a politician and a senior happen, a small conversation and documenting that within the structure of the eventover a perfect boat ride" (Rohd 2014).

Pedestrian Performance: Navigating Safe Passage

1 May 1 2014. A crowd is gathering on the pavement outside the Immaculate Conception Church on the corner of the intersection of S. Kinnickinnic, S. Logan and E. Russell Avenues, a three-way intersection in Bayview, a residential neighbourhood a few miles south of downtown Milwaukee. A ship's captain (in fluorescent yellow rain jacket and sea captain's hat) breaks from leading a sea shanty chorus with the growing crowd and calls over a megaphone for passengers to board the ship for the first crossing. The 'ship' he's calling for passengers to board is constructed from three variously sized sails (small, medium and large) comprised of tall metal poles, each with two to three cross bars draped with sail material, now billowing in the breeze. Each pole is held aloft by a student-performer in harness. On the pavement, they form the outline of a tall ship. Boarding commences as pedestrian passengers move into the space between the forward and rear sails. Passengers with spare hands are given long sticks topped with brightly coloured triangular flags or cut outs of seagulls to wave as they cross. When the captain feels the ship is full and ready to sail, he gives a signal. A student-performer presses the Walk light.

At the moment, the Walk light changes from red to green, student-performers spring into action. Two barrier holders run into the middle of the crossing like they're running onto a football/athletics field with legs pumping and a high energy chant 'hup! hup! hup!'. They are accompanied by student-performers carrying large signs and others with triangles (percussive instruments). The effect is somewhat comical, and the student-performers play it up. The barrier-holders dramatically lower their red-and-white-striped safety bars in front of the cars to create safe passage for the pedestrian boat. The sign carriers plant themselves firmly in the middle of the crossing and wave large white signs with oversized black-and-gold text in the direction of motorists. The signs thank drivers for stopping, let them know that the performance will last for 20 seconds (roughly the time of the green Walk light), and that the purpose of the performance is to create a city that "sees and stops for pedestrians". The triangle players laughingly attempt to conjure a cacophony from their tiny instruments.

The pedestrian-filled ship follows straight on the heels of the student-performers. As they buoyantly engage motorists, the vessel navigates a slow passage across the street, the walking collective accommodating the speed of (some) seniors walking with aids (sticks, frames) or pushed in wheelchairs. The Captain, aware of the slow pace of the group and the timing of the green Walk light, maintains a constant dialogue with the pedestrian-passengers and the student-performers holding the crossing. The mood of passengers is jaunty, with pedestrians freely engaging in animated conversations. Some of these conversations touch on how it feels to cross the road in the moment, moving as part of a celebratory collective body. Pedestrians remark that crossing the road is something they haven't been able to do or have felt uncomfortable doing. Today, a frightening experience has been made pleasurable. The Walk light turns red while part of the ship remains in the crossing. The captain calls for the students to hold their ground while he brings up the rear of the ship until it is moored on the opposite side of the road. Today, the mood is good; the motorists are, mostly, engaged and patient. The students stay in the crossing until the ship's passage is complete and, once all passengers/pedestrians are safely on the pavement, they exit the crossing. Traffic resumes flowing along the street.

The *Crossings* event is approximately a couple of hours long in total. The walk—the ship's passage—goes with the green walk light each time until a round is complete. The passengers disembark at the end of their journey, and a new set of passengers is invited on board for another round of crossing. Every time they go round, this ship of happy (sea shanty singing, chatting) pedestrians performs the impossibility of crossing: a celebratory passage performs the impossibility of a safe and comfortable crossing. Performing what elders and others already know provides the opportunity for visitors and 'specials' to know via active, embodied experience. The 'specials' have a 20-minute segment which enables a crossing or two, and then a 'highlight' moment at a nearby site (a church in this instance). Students flank the invited special guests in V-shaped line of honour on each side, up a row of steps, with signs announcing "make Milwaukee a city that sees and stops for pedestrians". The speakers include the mayor, a senator and a UWM Professor of Public Health. It is a way to capture media attention and to bear witness to a response to the issue raised.

Performing a pedestrian crossing takes in several types of performance: site-specific (the site is the pedestrian crossing, rigorously observed), walking (the mode of crossing) and outdoor or street performance (a creative intervention happening outdoors in the street). These modes overlap with community-engaged performance: the performance has been made and is performed specifically with and for vulnerable—age, ability—pedestrians; the performance is staged as a dialogue between pedestrians and drivers, and between experts in precarious crossings and 'specials', as people who have power to effect changes in urban design and planning. In other words, there are several ways to read *The Crossings* as performance, and I'm going to work through three modes (street, walking and site at which mobilities meet), highlighting along the way what each one tells us about this complex form of civic practice.

Susan Haedicke's discussion of street performance (including an example of a community performance), which draws on Ranciere's figuration of the relationship between aesthetics and politics, sheds some light on the effectiveness of *The Crossings* performance. Ranciere defines the current (modern) period of aesthetic production, in which art ceased being merely representational of life and the boundaries between art and everyday life began to dissolve, as the 'aesthetic regime' (2006; see also Tanke 2011, pp. 73–109). He asserts that in such a system, the everyday material realm is a collection, or collage, of aesthetic and ordinary artefacts. Art-making has inherent political purchase because it produces a material rearrangement of that of which it is part, or as Ranciere terms, effects a "re-distribution of the sensible" (2006). Haedicke explains and uses Ranciere to explore "a politicised dramaturgy of contemporary street arts interventions" that is less about the political content of art and more about practices that intervene in the visible, sayable and thinkable through "material rearrangements of signs and images" in public spaces so that spectators must reassess what they see and understand (2013, pp. 6–7). For Haedicke, two points emerge from this. Firstly, street art collages of fictional and everyday worlds produce an enhanced understanding of the sociopolitical world as the experiential shock of this disorienting contradiction is processed: "[An] experiential shock of disorienting contradiction elicits an initial somatic response that then stimulates a desire to critically understand what seemed natural moments before and is now unfamiliar" (2013, p. 7). Central to this, and this is Haedicke's second related point, is that these kinds of street arts are non-representational events. Street artists go beyond the telling of a story (or reject storytelling altogether) and try to make something happen, to produce an experience that is embodied and affective insofar as it initiates a visceral reaction in audiences (2013, p. 8). According to Haedicke, this is a necessarily political (or *democratic*) process because it doesn't force a message—a meaning (content) contained in the event—onto the spectator, who, Ranciere is clear, is always already 'emancipated', but produces a discombobulating sensation, he calls this 'dissensus' (2010), in their being that they process, physically and mentally (2013, pp. 13–14).

The Crossings re-enacts the ordinary, everyday act of crossing the street at a signaled pedestrian/traffic intersection. As well as performing the event of pedestrian crossing, the ship and safe passage directly references the vernacular architecture of other crossings in the urban landscape: the many road/river crossings in downtown Milwaukee where there is a system of loud signals and barriers on bridges that stop traffic for the bridges to open or rise allowing ships to pass. This overlay or 'experiential palimsest' (Haedicke 2013, p. 6), along with the participative and performative action of journeying on an imaginary boat across the crossing, makes sensible the *impossibility* of safe passage: it is impossible to cross the street in the time of the green walk light (especially while walking *with* seniors). This shock realisation, an enhanced understanding of the sociopolitical world produced through the experience of walking with elders across a pedestrian crossing, an experience that the elders know all too well, is given public witness.

The *Crossings* would seem to have much in common with walking performance since it turns the everyday act of pedestrian crossing into performance, walking as an aesthetic act. The field of walking performance, however, tends to avoid analysis of the 'instrumental A to B walk' (see Morris and Rose 2019, p. 3; pp. 13–14) as in the pedestrian commute (to the shops, to the bank, to the hairdresser, to the doctor) or rule following behaviour as in pedestrians following road traffic rules (crossing at traffic intersections, waiting for the green walk light to cross). Walking art/performance specifically seeks to overcome everyday rhythms of the functional or purposeful walk from A to B, since that is to obey capitalism and its construction of daily rhythms and its infrastructure. As Deirdre Heddon observes, there is a pervasive critical tendency to characterise walking as a form of resistance "to habit, to capitalism, to rules, to expectations" (2008, p. 104). However, in this under-exploration of the A to B commute is the failure to register, as Edensor (2011) states, "the enforced rhythms and repetitive hazards that typify particular forms of commuting":

> For while spaces, timings, materialities and mobilities are orchestrated to provide 'relatively smooth "corridors"' for some (Sheller and Urry 2006: 213), for others, travelling rhythms are far from smooth. (p. 201)

Research into older pedestrians demonstrates that the mundane commute is worthy of consideration because it is when accidents are most likely to occur, that is, "in urban areas, especially at junctions (crossing the road) ... in good weather ... in daylight, on weekdays and near to home ... despite [older pedestrians] exhibiting 'best crossing behaviour'" (Dunbar et al. 2004, p. 28; p. 77; p. 120).

The celebration of walking as an aesthetic act of singular (individual), heroic, resistance to social norms has tended to overlook subaltern embodiments until recently. Along with Heddon and Turner's (2012) work which initiated the turn to consider women walking artists, and Murali's (2016) exploration of Algerian Abdelhafid Khatib's and her own difficult derives as racialised body-subjects in European capital cities, Rose (in Morris and Rose 2019) gives consideration to disability and disabled drifters (see also Heddon and Porter 2017; Kuppers 2015). Rose states that "a key tension in my walking art is reconciling intangible potentials with actual material conditions" (p. 14). These developing critiques of walking art/performance are instructive, and I draw on them in this analysis in order to avoid celebrating *The Crossings* as inherently resistant; in fact, the performance rigorously obeys traffic/road rules. Nor do I want to deploy metaphors of pedestrianism in relation to community performance that romanticise both the pedestrian (as the everyday, ordinary) and community performance as re-marking place as stasis and a return to human values counter to the alienation and the anomie of the urban autopia (Hopkins 2003). This is the nostalgia thesis of community performance that Hawkins critiques (see Chap. 1). According to the dynamic of call and response that underpins much of community-engaged performance (see Cohen-Cruz 2009), *The Crossings* publicly calls out "thoughtless [street] design" (Rose in Morris and Rose 2019) and invites the city's response.

Fiona Wilke's work, which has moved from analysis of site-based performance towards a 'mobilities paradigm' (Wilke 2015, pp. 3–8), offers an optimal critical frame for analysis of *The Crossings*. The 'mobilities paradigm' is based, at least partly, on cultural geographer, Cresswell's, identification of two dominant and all-encompassing ways of conceptualising place and mobility: one is 'sedentarist' and the other is 'nomadic' (see Wilke 2015, p. 5). In the 'sedentarist' framework, place is a fixed property and "mobility is perceived as a threat to fundamental human values" (Wilke 2015, p. 5). In the 'nomadic' framework, "mobility is coded as freedom, figuring centrally in post-modern culture and positively linked to subaltern power (as, for example, in the work of Michel de Certeau)" (Wilke 2015, p. 5). Cresswell is critical of both approaches to place and mobility; that is, he criticises both "'fixity as an ideal' (2006, p. 28) [...] [and] a romanticization of flux and movement" (Wilke 2015, p. 5). In terms of the latter, an equivalence could be drawn between the tactical walker or flaneur and the postmodern figure of the rhizomatic nomad whom Cresswell notes to be "a remarkably unsocial being [. . .] – abstract, dehistoricized, and undifferentiated" (in Wilke 2015, p. 5). In the final analysis, Wilke argues that "mobility needs to be understood as socially produced" (2015, p. 5) after Cresswell's sophisticated account of mobility: 'any politics of mobility and any account of mobilities in general has to recognise the diversity of mobilities and the material conditions that produce and are produced by them'" (in Wilke 2015, p. 5).

Employing the lens of the mobilities paradigm, the pedestrian crossing can be read as a material site, part of a public infrastructure, at which different types of mobility—pedestrian and automobile/driving—intersect. *The Crossings* enacts this intersection of two different modes of mobility—pedestrian and automobile—at the live sites of pedestrian crossings where pedestrians meet cars with the ever-present threat of literal collision, violence and, sometimes, tragically, death. Devising crossings of intersections, the UWM crew noted frictions between drivers and pedestrians, and that "the dialogue that exits between pedestrians and drivers tends to revolve around the horn, revved engines and the middle finger" (Basting in field notes 25 April 2014). *The Crossings* attempted to engage with drivers and to establish an alternative dialogue between them and pedestrians.

In the event of performance, the drivers are engaged by students standing on the sidewalk several meters out from the crossing bearing large signs with black-and-gold text. The signs state that there is a performance ahead at the next pedestrian crossing and that it will last for 20 seconds only. The signs thank the drivers for seeing and stopping for pedestrians:

> AHOY! PERFORMANCE AHEAD!
> THIS PERFORMNCE WILL END IN 20 SECONDS1
> THANK YOU FOR SEEING AND STOPPING FOR PEDESTRIANS!

The performance registers the stopped drivers with the student-performers playing up to them while the boat passengers wave appreciation. Stopped vehicles are approached, and information leaflets are shared. It is important that the performance does not occupy the crossing for any longer than it needs to. The aim is not to delay or impede the driver's commute. The regard shown to the driver is tested when the boat, geared to the pace of senior pedestrians, some with walking aids, remains in the road for a few seconds after the signal change. The drivers who remain stopped, waiting for the boat to fully dock on the other side of the crossing, display the mutual regard, or mutual responsibility, that points to the possibility of a new kind of relationship between drivers and pedestrians. In this way, pedestrians "remind drivers of their status as drivers, thus inviting them to examine this condition rather than experiencing it as the natural state of the space" (Wilke 2015, p. 97). *The Crossings* makes clear that "older pedestrians depend on drivers accommodating their crossing" (Dunbar et al. 2004, p. 120). In addition to registering passage, Wilkie suggests that these encounters between mobilities also make passage "invit[ing] alternative ways of moving in those spaces" (2015, p. 33). *The Crossings* invites drivers to be more accommodating of older pedestrians, a change that may improve the walking environment, making it safe for all pedestrians.

Not every *Crossings* performance is the same and, as the project moves further into the suburbs of Milwaukee, unexpected events occur. At the intersection of St Francis and KK, which is flanked by a school and a senior housing complex, a police car parks up staking a claim to the crossing. A traffic officer stands in the middle of the intersection and directs traffic, managing the right turn against the red light from St Francis onto the main thoroughfare (KK). *The Crossings* performance threatens to cut off this right turn on the red light because it takes all the time of the green walk light to get people across the road. The performance highlights how the right turn on the red light is not safe given that people need the maximum time to navigate the crossing. In the event, there is no communication between the traffic officer and *The Crossings* performance (the presence of law enforcement wasn't invited and was not factored into devising or rehearsal processes). While the police officer's actions ensure the safety of those participating in the performance, the official and orderly management of traffic flow somewhat nullifies the problem the performance poses which, after Freire's theory of pedagogy (education/learning), is meant to lead to the emergence of (embodied) consciousness and reflexive action.

The Packard and Ramsey crossing, as in the devising process, presented more complex issues. The four-lane crossing swallowed up the performance despite the honed routine that Sojourn developed with the student-performers, and an excellent turn out from nearby residents. The attempt to make a safe passage at Packard and Ramsey is wholly impossible. The hierarchical power and dominance of the car reasserts itself, and any pedestrian's claim to the road—at a crossing—is countered. The Mayor of Cudahy, walking with the group, is visibly unnerved, as I was (again), at being unable to cross the road in the time of the green walk light. Car horns beep, and at one stage the mayor lunges to safety on the sidewalk as drivers insist on their right of way. A police car appears, again, at the side of the road. Apparently, this time, the police are responding to reports of a political demonstration. The act of crossing a pedestrian intersection is viewed as contesting the rights of drivers to unimpeded movement; the road is their thoroughfare. This intervention reveals that the relationship between car drivers and pedestrians is grossly unequal. The performance is abandoned early, and while it didn't instigate a relationship or dialogue between pedestrians and drivers, it did affectively and effectively highlight the precarity of pedestrians at the crossing due to the timings of the green walk light (poor city design). The performance was followed by a short highlight on the sidewalk, where the 'specials' confirm they will have the timing of the walk light extended by several seconds. And while apparently not appreciated locally, the group is buoyed by a message (sent to Anne) from the EU commission parliament for pedestrians which sends its support to the project for acting in the interests of and raising awareness of pedestrian safety.

Conclusion

Entelechy's *Bed*, made by a senior theatre group, startles passersby through the incongruity of an older person in repose in their bed appearing in the middle of a public street. The institutional (grey, metal) bed registers another context: the care home. It re-marks a spacing between the care home and public space. *Bed* prompts members of the public to respond, to care: How did the senior end up in their bed in the street? Has there been an emergency? Do they require assistance? In this way, the artwork leads members of the public into an encounter with the senior performer (in role, playing a character). The theatrical frame offers a construct in which to process the initial shock, to converse and to reflect, maybe even critically, on the exclusion of older bodies from public space and the public health costs of social isolation.

The ultimate outcome aimed for in *The Crossings* was, according to Basting, to create "a space where Angie and Nancy could perform their inability to cross in time with the policy makers" and to have the policy makers thus realise that "THEY can't cross in time" (2014; original emphasis). Writing about cross-sector (art and non-arts) collaborations, which also go under the name of civic practice, Cohen-Cruz asserts that concrete, long-term social change is achieved by professionals augmenting art's efficacy in their social sector (2015, p. 4; pp. 15–17). *The Crossings* placed older adults at the heart of the performance making process and event. It established a problem common to many seniors—the *im*possibility of crossing pedestrian intersections in the time of the green walk light—as something to be co-performed, widely experienced and felt, and publicly witnessed. It brought seniors into dialogue with drivers and 'specials' (civil servants and elected political representatives). Posing the problem as it did, in an active and embodied manner, cross-referencing pedestrians and drivers and pedestrians and city planners, and enacting dialogue between them, *The Crossings* surfaced (embodied) consciousness of a problem that had hitherto been ignored, so as not to trouble hierarchical power relations confirming the dominance of cars on our roads. *The Crossings* engaged the dynamic of mutual responsibility to address highlighted inequalities in mobilities. In the event, the professionals were held to account for poor street/road design by elder experts and activists who were nevertheless extremely obedient and rule abiding citizens in asserting their rights. This instance of civic practice—publicly performing the impossibility of the 'everyday' cross-walk—effectively focused attention on public infrastructure as a bridge to "creating more connected communities as we age" (Islands of Milwaukee flyer 2014). Most importantly, it centred the delightful agency and creativity of older bodies in achieving immediate and long-term infrastructural improvements.

REFERENCES

Basting, A. (2009). *Forget Memory. Creating Better Lives for People with Dementia*. Baltimore: The John Hopkins University Press.
———. (2014) Email to Kerrie Schaefer, 29 August.
Basting, A., Towey, M. and Rose, E. (eds.) (2016) *The Penelope Project: An Arts-Based Odyssey to Change Elder Care*. Iowa City: University of Iowa Press.
Basting, A. (2020) *Creative Care: A Revolutionary Approach to Dementia and Elder Care*. New York; San Francisco: HarperOne.
Bishop, C. (2012) *Artificial Hells: Participatory Art and the Politics of Spectatorship*. London: Verso.
Cohen-Cruz, J. (2005) *Local Acts. Community-based Performance in the United States*. New Brunswick, N.J.; London: Rutgers University Press.
———. (2009) *Engaging Performance. Theatre as Call and Response*. London; New York: Routledge.
———. (2015) *Remapping Performance. Common Ground, Uncommon Partners*. Basingstoke: Palgrave Macmillan.
Dunbar, G., Holland, C.A. and Maylor, E.A. (2004) *Road Safety Research Report No. 37 Older Pedestrians: A Critical Review of the Literature*. London: Department for Transport. Available at: http://publications.aston.ac.uk/id/eprint/24396/1/Older_pedestrians.pdf (Accessed: May 19 2018).

Edensor, T. (2011) 'Commuter: Mobility, Rhythm and Commuting', in Cresswell, T. and Merriman, P. (eds.) *Geographies of Mobilities: Practices, Spaces, Subjects*. London: Routledge, pp. 189–203.
Engwicht, D. (1993) *Reclaiming Our Cities and Towns: Better Living with Less Traffic*. Gabriola Island, BC: New Society Publishers.
———. (1999) *Street Reclaiming: Creating Liveable Streets and Vibrant Communities*. Gabriola Island, BC: New Society Publishers.
Entelechy Arts Elders' Theatre Group (2016) *Bed*. Devised street performance. First performance East St, Brighton, 5. May 2016 [East St, Bedminster, Bristol, 15. June 2016]
European Charter of Pedestrian Rights EU 1988
Haedicke, S. (2013) *Contemporary Street Arts in Europe: Aesthetics and Politics*. Basingstoke: Palgrave Macmillan.
Heddon, D. (2008) *Autobiography and Performance*. Basingstoke: Palgrave Macmillan.
Heddon, D. and Turner, C. (2012) 'Walking Women: Shifting the Tales and Scales of Mobility', *Contemporary Theatre Review*, 22(2), pp. 224–236.
Heddon, D. and Porter, S. (2017) 'Walking Interconnections', *CSPA Quarterly*, 18, (dis/sustain/ability), pp. 18–21.
Helguera, P. (2011) *Education for Socially Engaged Art: A Materials and Techniques Handbook*. New York: Jorge Pinto Books.
Holt-Lunstad, J., Smith, T.B. and Layton, J.B. (2010) 'Social relationships and mortality risk: a meta-analytic review'. *PLoS Medicine*, 7(7). doi: https://doi.org/10.1371/journal.pmed.1000316
Hopkins, D.J. (2003) 'Mapping the Placeless Place: Pedestrian Performance in the Urban Spaces of Los Angeles, *Modern Drama*, 46(2), pp. 261–284.
Islands of Milwaukee, Using the Arts to Build Relationships and Create More Connected Communities As We Age. (2014) Unpublished report. Available at: https://islandsofmilwaukee.org/assets/IoM%20report%2012.4.14.pdf (Accessed: 16 June 2018).
Jackson, S. (2011) *Social Works: Performing Art, Supporting Publics*. London and New York: Routledge.
Kester, G. (2004) *Conversation Pieces: Community and Communication in Modern Art*. Berkeley: University of California Press.
Kwon, M. (2004) *One Place After Another: Site Specific Art and Locational Identity*. Massachusetts: MIT Press.
Kuftinec, S. (2003) *Staging America. Cornerstone and Community-based Theatre*. Carbondale: Southern Illinois University Press.
Kuppers, P. (2015) 'Disability Performance in the Streets: Art Actions in Post-Quake Christchurch'. *The Drama Review (TDR)*, 59(1), pp. 166–174. Available at: http://www.jstor.org/stable/24585062 (Accessed: May 26, 2018).
Mello, R. and Voigts, J. (2012) *The Penelope Project: Using the Power of Myth to Transform Long Term Care*. Unpublished Program Evaluation Report, pp. 1–98.
Morris, B. and Rose, M. (2019) 'Pedestrian Provocations: Manifesting an Accessible Future', *Global Performance Studies*, 2(2). doi: https://doi.org/10.33303/gpsv2n2a3
Murali, S. (2016) 'Walking the Walled City. Gender and the Dérive as Urban Ethnography', *Etnološka tribina*, 46(39), pp. 189–212.
Ranciere, J. (2006) *The Politics of Aesthetics: The Distribution of the Sensible*. Translated by Rockhill, G. London; New York: Continuum.
———. (2009) *The Emancipated Spectator*, translated by Elliott, G. London: Verso.

———. (2010) *Dissensus: On Politics and Aesthetics*. Edited and translated by Corcoran, S. London; New York: Continuum.
Rohd, M. (1998) *Community, Conflict and Dialogue: the Hope Is Vital Training Manual*. Portsmouth, NH: Heinemann.
———. (2011a) 'Civic Theater.' Available at: https://howlround.com/civic-theater (Accessed: 13 March 2015).
———. (2011b) 'Civic Theater Part 2.' Available at: https://howlround.com/civic-theater-0 (Accessed: 14 March 2015).
———. (2012) 'The New Work of Building Civic Practice.' Available at: https://howlround.com/new-work-building-civic-practice (Accessed: 23 May 2015).
———. (2013a) 'Artist's Notebook: Civic Participation', *Theater*. Available at: http://search.ebscohost.com.uoelibrary.idm.oclc.org/login.aspx?direct=true&db=edsbl&AN=RN345574509&site=eds-live&scope=site (Accessed: 25 May 2016).
———. (2013b) 'Civic Practice Workshop.' Symposium on Entrepreneurship, the Arts, and Creative Placemaking at the Pave Program in Arts Entrepreneurship, Arizona State University Friday 12–13 April 2013. Available at: https://howlround.com/happenings/symposium-entrepreneurship-arts-and-creative-placemaking-pave-program-arts (Accessed: 5 August 2015).
———. (2014) Email to Kerrie Schaefer, 1. May.
Sojourn Theatre Summer Institute Papers (2013) Unpublished.
Sommer, D. (2014) *The Work of Art in the World: Civic Agency and the Public Humanities*. Durham, NC: Duke University Press.
Tanke, J.J. (2011) *Jacques Ranciere: An Introduction*. London: Continuum.
Treuhaft, H. (2008) *Community-based Artistic Practice: Perspectives From A Gathering of Eexmplar Artist Companies*. Available at: https://www.animatingdemocracy.org/sites/default/files/documents/reading_room/CommunityBased_ArtisticPractice_Evanston_Report.pdf (Accessed: July 8 2016).
Wilke F. (2015) *Performance, Transport and Mobility: Making Passage*. London: Palgrave Macmillan.

CHAPTER 6

Community Performance in Singapore: Drama Box's *IgnorLAND of Its Time* Performing the 'HDB Nation' at Bukit Ho Swee

PROLOGUE

Between 29 March and 2 April 2017, Drama Box performed The Lesson (2015) at the International Community Arts Festival in Rotterdam. The company erected GoLi, their crowd-funded inflatable pop-up performance shell, in a city square and invited an 'audience' into a very Singaporean dilemma. Billed as Forum Theatre and facilitated by several Drama Box practitioners, the audience was informed that they were citizens of a town targeted for redevelopment and invited to participate in a public consultation to determine the site of construction of a new MRT station by identifying one of seven landmark sites for removal. Through contact with symbolic representations of the sites installed in the space [e.g. a cinema for foreign workers, a columbarian, marshlands, a wet market and hawker centre and so on], the mobile audience gleaned information about the sites, the (more-than-human) communities they served and their social, cultural, ecological and heritage value/s. Choosing a site to defend, audience members engaged in dialogue between different interest groups before a vote was called. The audience had to come to a consensus on the site for removal to make way for the MRT, or the decision would be passed on to the relevant government authority. On the evening I attended, one group rejected what they viewed as the limited 'democratic' process and staged a walk out. They moved outside the performance shell to write their own manifesto, which the group returned to deliver with the audience verdict.

The performance did its job beautifully insofar as the 'planning problem' posed to the group became a "lesson on democracy" (Nanda 2017) in

Rotterdam as it had been in Singapore.[1] At the same time, I did wonder about the extent to which we can take practices out of context and the limits of intercultural exchange: in this instance, was there space to explore differences between sociopolitical frames such as Singapore's 'anti-liberal or communitarian state capitalism' (Chua 2017) and residual forms of social or participatory democracy in a (neo-)liberal state in Europe? Writing on the long period of one-party rule in Singapore, sociologist Chua Beng-Huat, states:

> the long duration of PAP [People's Action Party] leadership … has changed the public sphere to one that is largely in need of administration rather than one fraught with political contestations. The everyday life of the people becomes conducive to rational planning and administration by large public service agencies and statutory boards. These agencies are operationally relatively unrestrained in the absence of strong opposition parties. The only check on them is one of instrumental effectiveness in achieving the targets of their respective plans. (1997, p. 950)

Twenty years after this initial analysis, Chua asserts that the political system of government, which "features a decidedly anti-liberal social management system that places social interests above individual rights and freedoms and an economy that is a mix of state-owned and private capital" (2017, p. 193) is a stable and enduring one. He notes that "Singapore's cultural sphere has been expanded and liberalized, but the political sphere has not made any concession to ideological pluralism" and that things will probably remain that way for as long as political leaders maintain the "efficacy and efficiency" of the system and as long as the system remains "responsive to [citizens'] largely material demands, which the PAP government is" (Chua 2017, p. 194). With this chapter, I offer an account of how a community performance-making process intervenes in the production of a social space managed according to what another sociologist, Terence Chong, terms an "interventionist corporate government" that is in the process of transforming from an 'exclusive' to 'inclusive' mode of governance (2005, p. 554).

Introduction

This chapter investigates a community-engaged performance project by Singaporean theatre company, Drama Box. *IgnorLAND of Its Time* (2014) was the third of four instalments in the *IgnorLAND* series, initiated by Drama Box Artistic Director Kok Heng Luen in 2007 to excavate hidden histories of spaces within the fast-changing Singaporean landscape, effectively recirculating forgotten cultural narratives contesting a hegemonic narrative national identity. After the first two productions, Kok handed over artistic leadership of the

---

[1] See https://artsequator.com/dramabox-the-lesson-2017/#:~:text=The%20Lesson%20was%20first%20staged,theatre%3A%20audience%20empowerment%20and%20intervention.&text=The%20public%20%E2%80%93%20we%20the%20audience,their%20choice%20through%20a%20vote [Accessed 21 May 2019].

IgnorLAND series to Koh Hui Ling (associate artistic director) and Han Xuemei (resident artist) for *IgnorLAND of Its Time* (IOIT) and *IgnorLAND of its Loss* (2016). IOIT was a year-long project that culminated in a promenade performance, a walking tour, of Bukit Ho Swee, the housing estate famously erected in record time to re-house the victims of a large fire on 25 May 1961. The fire destroyed the existing *kampong*, an urban village of closely built timber and attap (palm frond thatch) dwellings, leaving thousands of survivors (approx. 16,000) homeless and destitute overnight. IOIT excavates the historical significance of the Bukit Ho Swee estate as one of the first housing estates constructed by the new government statutory authority, the Housing Development Board (HDB). As one of the first HDB estates, Bukit Ho Swee, comprised of 'relatively modest, early generation flats' (Jacobs et al. 2012, p. 137), holds a mythical place in the creation story of the HDB nation. IOIT was, itself, a significant moment in Drama Box's performance history as it was the company's first experiment with community engagement methodology in a geographic location: "the creation process, instead of being led by the artists, now invites various community stakeholders to become collaborators and co-creators" (Drama Box 2014).

Modern Singapore is a city renowned for its 'rags to riches' (Chua 1995, p. 87) transformation. Once a colonial entrepôt and military base for the extension of British imperial power in Southeast Asia, present-day Singapore is an independent nation state[2] whose flourishing is due, in large part, to a comprehensive (island-wide), government-initiated and government-led programme of urban development according to "high-modernist philosophical principles" (Loh 2008, p. 1). The Singaporean government, essentially led by one political party, has taken a fundamental role in the material production of social space through the creation of a mass public housing system which has, in turn, delivered a solid and enduring base of popular support for the government (Chua 1995, 1997).

---

[2] Since the fourteenth century, *Singapura*, the small island at the end of the Malay Peninsula, has been a 'settled' site as one in a chain of seaports whose complex network formed the 'Silk Road of the Sea', as Miksic (2013) terms the long and significant history of maritime trade in Southeast Asia. The founding of modern Singapore was a colonial enterprise which began with the establishment of a British trading post on the island in 1819. Incorporated into a network of strategic Malay settlements, the Straits Settlements, administered by the British East India Company from Calcutta, India, and then by the British Colonial Office in London from the 1860s, Singapore was an important base for the extension of the Empire's economic and military power in Southeast Asia. In 1942, invading Japanese forces swept down the Malay Peninsula and captured Singapore. After the Japanese Occupation (1942–1945), Singapore was returned to British military administration (1945) and established as a separate Crown colony after the dissolution of the Straits Settlements (1946). In the post-war period, Singapore slowly began to move towards (internal) self-government (1955–1963). In 1963, alongside the Crown colonies of Sarawak and North Borneo, Singapore gained independence in union with the already-independent Federation of Malaya, creating the larger federation of Malaysia. The union was, however, difficult and short-lived. Malaysia moved to expel Singapore from the federation and, in 1965, Singapore, on separation, became an independent, sovereign nation.

The Peoples' Action Party (PAP) has driven the process of nation-building and modernisation in Singapore since it became an internally self-governing state in 1958, and elected its first government in 1959. One of the premier acts of the PAP government, in 1960, was the creation of the key statutory authority, the Housing Development Board, to oversee the building of quintessentially modern high-rise, high-density housing estates to re-house the majority of the population relocated from inner city 'slum' housing. Legitimacy for government intervention was grounded in the discourse of 'spatial emergency' (Loh 2008, p. 10). In part this was a pragmatic response to the 1960s 'housing crisis'[3]; acknowledgement of the abject conditions in which most Singaporeans were living as a result of colonial neglect and the Japanese Occupation during the Second World War. At the same time, Loh (2008) problematises labelling of 'squatter' settlements or *kampongs*—semi-autonomous urban village communities—as dangerous (the timber and *attap* dwellings were particularly prone to fire), unhygienic and unruly or ungovernable (crime-filled) spaces. This aspect of the discourse justified the interventionist programme of mass clearance of urban villages and relocation of inhabitants into government housing.

According to sociologist, Chua (1997), the relocation of the majory of the urban population into newly constructed HDB flats has had the effect of incorporating semi-autonomous inhabitants of informal settlements into the formal structures of the new nation state. Former 'slum' dwellers, living on the margins of society, became citizen and HDB flat owners.[4] Ultimately, the transformation of the population into a capitalist labour force, a process Chua (1997) describes as "active proletarianisation" (p. 135) has benefited the PAP government. He notes that the material benefits that have accrued from the near universal public housing programme have conferred political legitimacy on the long-serving PAP government and established a "hegemonic consensus" on its capacity to govern effectively (Chua 1997, pp. 127–132). In order to maintain this hegemonic consensus, the government ensures ever increasing material improvements in living standards: HDB estates are "maintained and upgraded by the government to considerably high standards" (Tan 2007, p. 21).

In the mid-1990s, the phenomenon of en bloc—wholesale or in total— redevelopment of HDB estates appeared, under the administrative title of Selective En-Bloc-Redevelopment Scheme (SERS), and the physical and built environment underwent an ongoing phase of redevelopment.[5] The constant ungrounding of the ground in the city state exemplifies the condition of "liquid

---

[3] See https://www.hdb.gov.sg/cs/infoweb/about-us/history

[4] Approximately 80% of Singaporeans are enrolled in the national system of public housing through subsidised ownership, typically via a long-term (99-year) lease, of an HDB apartment.

[5] In Singapore, all aspects of land use, planning and redevelopment are managed by the government through the Urban Redevelopment Authority (URA), a statutory board under the Ministry of National Development. The URA has established the Singapore City Gallery over several floors of its administrative building in downtown Singapore to communicate the challenges it faces in maintaining the high quality of life of a growing population on a small island. It does this through a collection of historical images, interactive exhibits and models including a scaled, architectural

modernity" described by Bauman (2000). Yet, despite constant change in the physical and built environment, the HDB authority remains a mainstay of redevelopment.[6] The Bukit Ho Swee estate has undergone some modest redevelopment. However, it has been noted that, while "still vibrant and viable homes", the newly built, 40-storey tower blocks built nearby signal "that this older style high-rise [is] becoming increasingly anachronistic in local housing visions" (Jacobs et al. 2012, pp. 137–138).

In response to ongoing redevelopment of the built landscape and the rapid rate of change, a resistant phenomenon has emerged: '*kampong* nostalgia' (see Chua 1995; Loh 2008). Chua (1995) asserts that this nostalgia presents a persausive affective critique of the high-modernist, hyper-technical rationality of PAP governance through the not unproblematic desire for urban village life in the past. It points to the fact that what has been most lost in the modernisation process is a sense community as neighbourly social relations and mutual interdependence. Chua also notes that this mode of critique is ineffective as it overlooks the material deprivation, chronic un(der)-employment, lack of educational provision and general (colonial) government neglect that produced the conditions for the emergence of apparently more organic forms community in the space of the urban village. It is, he asserts, 'rooted in a past that no one would seriously want to return to, as is evident in the electoral popularity of the PAP government' (1995, p. 95).

As a modern housing estate famously built on the fire remains of a *kampong* and now shaded by later, more modern redevelopments, Bukit Ho Swee is a rich site at which to explore the materialities and meanings of built space. The HDB estate that emerged like a 'phoenix from the ashes' of conflagration (Loh 2008) holds the 'imagined' communities (Anderson 1983) of the HDB nation and *kampong* nostalgia in critical tension. By entering into this space, Drama Box (re)animates these and other enactments of community, which is the subject of this chapter. According to Drama Box, IOIT took as its focus:

> the theme of "displacement", starting from the Bukit Ho Swee fire in 1961 when people were forced to move out of their homes into one of the very first HDB flats in the aftermath of the fire. The situation back then serves as a parallel to the present-day situation in which estates are constantly *enbloc-ed* and its residents relocated. We hope to explore the effects of this continuous cycle of tearing and re-building of places/homes as well as work with the residents to discover and record what is it that they want to remember about this place they call Home. (Dramabox 2014)

---

model of the Central Area of Singapore (see https://www.ura.gov.sg/Corporate/Singapore-City-Gallery/Key-Highlights-details/CentralArea-model-details).

[6] In relation to the built environment, this shift is becoming visible in the increasingly innovative and diverse design architecture of public housing. This has followed from public criticism of redevelopment which targets both the homogeneity of public design and the loss of history of vernacular architecture. The situation is beginning to change with the inclusion of citizen/owners' concerns in redevelopment plans.

Koh Hui Ling and Han Xuemei led a year-long engagement process which included company research, cultural mapping, photography and reminiscence workshops, oral history interviews, and scripting community participant scenes. These participatory elements were woven into a performance tour of the Bukit Ho Swee estate. The performance script was written by professional playwright Jean Tay. Tay also edited the community participants' scripts developed from transcribed interviews. Over ten nights (24 July–2 August 2014), a cast of two professional performers led an audience on a tour of the Bukit Ho Swee estate which included memories and stories of the estate performed by former or current residents (storytellers, dancers, a singer). In addition to the community performance, there were daytime 'heritage tours' of the estate led by fire victim and former resident-turned 'nostalgic blogger',[7] James Seah, and two open 'town meeting' events, one oriented to young people and the other to adults.[8] My focus is on the engagement process and the performance event.

This chapter is broken down into several sections. First, "Singapore's Cultural Policy: The Politics of Nation-Building and Global Positioning" examines the development of cultural policy in Singapore and suggests that a corporate mode of governance remains firmly in place managing parallel processes of globalisation, underpinned by neoliberal capitalist economic goals, and national augmentation, in line with communitarian regional or 'Asian' values. Second "Drama Box and the Arrested Development of Community Performance in Singapore" investigates the development of community theatre practice in Singapore. While it is possible to align Drama Box's practice with international definitions of community theatre, local practices have been shaped over time by government intervention into the field of theatre. At the same time, community theatre practitioners operate in a field where, since the 1960s, 'grassroots' community organisations are in effect managed by central government. There is, in other words, not a purported lack of community but an excess of it. The issue for a community-engaged theatre is co-optoin as just another government agency producing, through disciplinary technologies of culture, politically docile and economically active subjects. Finally, "*IgnoreLAND of Its Time*: The Performance-Making Process" explores the process of making a piece of community-engaged theatre *in* Bukit Ho Swee, the mythic 'birthplace' of modern Singapore, and a government managed HDB space, *with* residents of the estate.

---

[7] See http://blogtoexpress.blogspot.co.uk/2012/02/nostalgic-blogger.html
[8] See http://www.dramabox.org/eng/productions-ignorland-2014.html

Singapore's Cultural Policy: The Politics of Nation-Building and Global Positioning

In July 2014, during my observation of the making of IOIT,[9] the National Library Board (NLB), a statutory body under the Ministry of Communications and Information, took a decision to withdraw three children's book titles from circulation in all public libraries: *And Tango Makes Three*, *Who's in My Family?* and *The White Swan Express*. These books, exploring diverse family types in the animal and human world, were "deemed to contravene pro-family values" (Chua 2014). In response to various forms of protest by writers (resignations from the NLB, threats to boycott literary events, donations to LGBTQ charities), the minister for communications and information, Dr Yaacob Ibrahim, stated his support for the NLB decision as "guided by community norms, which public libraries ought to consider since they serve the community" (in Chua 2014). This act brought into sharp focus the coexistence of official practices of censorship, based on normative community values, and government policy pronouncements promoting Singapore as a 'Renaissance City' (see 2000) and 'Global City of the Arts' (1995).

Cultural policy researcher, Lily Kong, identifies censorship as an impediment to the realisation of the sort of vibrant cultural scene one might connect to a city-state undergoing a culture-led renaissance or one staking a claim as a global hub (a keeper and attractor of global economic talent). She asserts that the Singapore arts sector exists in a state of "bounded creativity" (Ooi in Kong 2012, p. 290) due to the existing "paternalistic and authoritarian" (Leo and Lee in Kong, p. 290) mode of governance evident in practices of censorship. Cultural management researcher, Ruth Bereson (2003), has traced the development of arts policy in Singapore from 1957 onwards, noting that the discourse of renaissance is historical and pervasive across government sectors serving to connect patronage of arts to key political goals: social cohesion (this acknowledges the racialised/ethnic tensions in the founding era and applies to the construction of a new national identity in the wake of independence) and economic development. She asserts that neither the development of an arts and cultural bureaucracy in the 1990s—the establishment of the Ministry of Information and the Arts (1990) and the National Arts Council (1991)—nor the shift to a global knowledge economy has had an impact on the 'political agendas' that govern arts and cultural policy development (Bereson 2003, p. 13). Political scientist Kenneth Paul Tan similarly questions 'Renaissance' discourse, perceiving instead 'old politics' in new policy (2007, pp. 3–5). He explains that, within this old/new system, acts of censorship are critical to cohering the population around normative (communitarian, Asian) values, which the globally oriented economy threatens to destabilise:

---

[9] I was in Singapore for an intensive three-week period in July 2014 to observe and document the final weeks of the performance-making process.

> Community has been situated firmly within romanticised notions of the 'ethnicized' or 'Asianized' national heartlands, where Singaporeans are flatteringly defined as patriotic keepers of core values that have helped Singapore to survive and become prosperous in a dangerous world full of negative, destabilising, and disintegrating influences that come with modernisation and globalisation. (Tan 2007, p. 86)

Terence Chong has focused on the way in which the PAP government has managed nation-building and economic development in alignment with processes of globalisation which otherwise threaten to decrease the power of nation states (and governments). He characterises PAP governance as transitioning from exclusive to inclusive corporatism: Exclusive corporatism

> signifies a greater degree of authoritarianism …the state is dominated by technocrats-bureaucrats… institutionalised cooperation is restricted to a small elite…the interventions of experts are necessary and fruitful …the non-expert masses are not to be trusted with autonomous political participation,

whereas inclusive corporatism "is built on a more genuinely consensual partnership between state and society" (2005, p. 554). In line with this transition, he sees the state taking an increasingly dual approach to policymaking, on the one hand, positioning the city state as a global cultural hub and, on the other, reinforcing an ongoing process of nation-building according to PAP ideology (2005, p. 556). In the field of cultural policy, this is evident, according to Chong, in the "increasingly sophisticated Janus-faced state strategies that regulate the production of art while purporting to encourage arts liberalisation and deregulation in the journey towards Global City for the Arts" (2011, p. 33).

Shortly before Drama Box started on IOIT, *The Arts and Culture Strategic Review* (2012) was published setting out key strategic directions in cultural policy to 2025. Listed as a key aim is to 'Bring Arts and Culture to Everyone Everywhere Everyday' (2012, p. 19). Officially, this shift towards 'everyday participation' in arts and culture is couched in terms of reward for economic achievement. Having raised living standards well beyond the point of meeting basic needs, arts and cultural pursuits may now be universally enjoyed. It has also been mooted as an attempt to produce more 'cultured and gracious' (or less individualistic, materialistic and demanding) citizens. Alternative readings, however, suggest that cultural participation remains linked to economic goals. With corporate governance having excluded the majority of the population, as non-experts, from the political decision-making process there is now a need to instil capabilities in the labour force essential for success in a global economy subject to unpredictable peaks and troughs. According to Varney et al. (2013), this economically driven policy is unlikely to result in the production of critical (aesthetic-political) art. It is more geared to the creation of economically active, creative and flexible subjects rather than culturally active, critical ones:

The [Arts and Culture Strategic] review promotes a wholesale expansion and concentration of Singapore's cultural policy into a 24-hour, seven day a week modality designed specifically to merge cultural industries and the everyday into a new economic paradigm... It has a likely intended result of discouraging arts with more critical aesthetic-political orientations. (Varney et al. 2013, p. 210)

Within the cultural participation agenda is a strengthening of grassroots community organisations in the promotion of a national programme of amateur arts: PassionArts (the PA stands for People's Association, which leads up grassroots organisations). In Singapore, 'grassroots' refers to a broad network of neighbourhood community centres located in public housing estates, and associated community-based and voluntary organisations that come under the umbrella of the People's Association (PA), a statutory body established in 1960 and headed by the office of the prime minister. According to Tan:

> Today, the grassroots sector, a wide range of overlapping organisations all linked in some way to the PAP government, has co-opted traditional community leaders and is dominated by leaders and members who are also affiliated in some way or other to the PAP government. This creates an informal but reliable system of patronage. The grassroots sector serves as a feedback mechanism and a mouthpiece for the government... The grassroots sector is also tasked with monitoring social and political trends at the constituency level, including the behaviour of individuals and groups of residents suspected of anti-social, subversive, or politically oppositional activities. The grassroots sector helps not only to maintain internal security, but also to sustain a climate of surveillance and fear that can be harnessed both for nation building as well as political gain. (2007, pp. 20–21)

This is the evolving context Drama Box found itself working in, which raises a question: When culture becomes a tool of government via centrally aligned grassroots organisations which seed arts/cultural participation via community centres in public housing estates, how do you practice community theatre, and what is its value?

DRAMA BOX AND THE ARRESTED DEVELOPMENT OF COMMUNITY PERFORMANCE IN SINGAPORE

The Necessary Stage (est. 1987) and Drama Box (est. 1990s) have driven the development of political and community theatre in Singapore. Chong, who recognises community theatre as a form "integral to [the] theatre-making process in Singapore" (Chong 2011, p. 243), defines community theatre after van Erven's definition deriving from an international collection of (post-political and post-pedagogical) theatre practices that share values, methods and processes. According to van Erven, community theatre:

> Privileges the artistic pleasure and sociocultural empowerment of its community participants. Its material and aesthetic forms always emerge directly (if not exclu-

sively) from "the" community, whose interests it tries to express. Community theatre thus is a potent art form that allows once largely silent (or silenced) groups of people to add their voices to increasingly diverse and intricately interrelated local, regional, national and international cultures. (Van Erven 2001: 3)

Jo Ronan, a pioneer of political and community theatre in Singapore as one of the co-founding members of The Necessary Stage (TNS) (along with Artistic Director Alvin Tan), applies the term 'progressive' to qualify

> theatre making activity which attempts to engage with the concerns of marginalised communities and awaken critical thinking by countering the relentlessly monologic narratives and ideology broadcast by the PAP state's official media. (2018, p. 75)[10]

In this section, I want to note that it is difficult to locate a continuous history of community theatre in Singapore. 'Progressive' practices have been shaped by PAP government intervention to curtail 'Marxist' opposition to its ruling ideology and practitioner responses to the exercise of state control. Peterson notes that the epithet of political Marxism contains "dark and sinister tones in Singapore", and is rooted in the struggles of the 1950s when the state and economy were fragile and threatened by ideological contestation (2001, p. 50). Peterson also notes that the PAP frequently recalls this 'crisis' period to legitimate intervention into and regulation of the cultural sphere. Thus, while it may be possible to locate the work of Drama Box in relation to international community theatre practice, broadly defined, the practice has an interrupted rather than continuous history in Singapore. I'm going to briefly outline this history as arrested development.

Drama Box was started by Artistic Director Kok Heng Luen in 1990 shortly after he graduated from the National University of Singapore (NUS). As a student, Kok was a member of the NUS Chinese society and was involved in society productions of Mandarin-language plays. Drama Box evolved out of this extracurricular activity but the company fell dormant as co-founding members left for work and life-related reasons. Kok, himself, went to work at The Necessary Stage (TNS) as the company's business manager from 1993 to 1999. This was a formative period for Kok as he went through the 'crisis' that curtailed TNS's experimentation with Forum Theatre practice.

Under the artistic direction of Alvin Tan and with Haresh Sharma as resident playwrights, TNS developed a reputation for producing Brechtian-style theatre of social critique (see Chong 2005, p. 563). In 1992, TNS established a Youth Theatre, renamed the Theatre for Youth and Community (TFYC) in 2002, "to reflect the wide-ranging work of this aspect of TNS, including work

---

[10] Ronan has drawn on her experience with TNS (and other theatre practices she has worked with, especially 7:84 Scotland) to articulate political theatre as a process of making theatre, rather than the content of play text, and to develop a political theatre-making methodology which she calls "dialectical collaborative theatre" (2018).

with community groups, and our community festivals and plays" (The Necessary Stage 2014, p. 5). In 1993, TNS introduced Forum Theatre techniques into their work after Tan and Sharma attended Theatre of the Oppressed workshops conducted by Boal at the Brecht Forum in New York.[11] Kok was involved both administratively and creatively in TNS's youth and community theatre and in Forum Theatre in theatres, schools and community centres. As Tan notes (2013), as a form of "unscripted performance that encouraged spontaneous audience participation", Forum Theatre posed difficulties for the licensing (censorship) authority. For this reason, the National Arts Council ceased funding Forum Theatre to discourage the practice (in Tan 2013, p. 201). Shortly after this decision, a sensational editorial piece appeared in the state-directed newspaper, *The Straits Times* (5 February 1994), accusing Tan and Sharma of attending Marxist workshops and alleging use of the "provocative and agitational" form of Forum Theatre for political purposes (Tan 2013, p. 200). Tan and Sharma were forced to deny the political intent of their work in a "soft dose of public humiliation" for a pair of socially committed theatre practitioners (Lagenbach in Tan 2013, p. 207). The matter was resolved when the National Arts Council (NAC) stepped in to publicly reiterate support for the company. NAC support did not extend to resumption of funding for Forum Theatre which effectively banned the practice in Singapore. At the same time, NAC 'rehabilitation' of TNS raised questions about state "recuperation and co-optation" of the theatre company (see Rae in Tan 2013, p. 208).

This episode is significant as the third in a series of 'crises' in which theatre practitioners/ensembles were charged with the promotion of Marxist ideology necessitating PAP government intervention into the field of progressive (counter-hegemonic) theatre practice in Singapore (Peterson 2001, p. 50). The TNS Forum Theatre 'crisis' of 1994 echoes two previous instances of 'crisis': namely, the arrest and detention of Kuo Pao Kun, 1976–1980, and the 1987 'Marxist Conspiracy' in which members of the independent theatre company, the Third Stage, were arrested and detained. Unlike the previous two episodes, the TNS incident was resolved without recourse to practitioner arrests and detention.

Chinese-born, Australian-trained, Singaporean-based theatre practitioner, Kuo Pao Kun, was arrested along with other socially committed artists as part of a wholesale purge of the opposition movement emerging in Singapore in the 1970s. According to Kuo, Singapore at that time was volatile: "it was a time of strife … there was the pressure to succeed, particularly economically, on the part of the government, which was expressed in radical economic and social changes like the evacuation of people, of farmers, from their land for new development" (in Lo 1993, p. 139). The PAP's nation-building programme produced popular opposition, "a radical alignment among mainly

---

[11] Tan and Sharma were each at the end of separate, sponsored working tours and took an opportunity to attend the workshops.

Chinese-language theatre practitioners, artists, intellectuals, organised workers and student movements" (Tan 2013, p. 201). Kuo's part in all this was to initiate the 'Go Into Life' programme within the Practice Performing Art School. The programme involved artists living amongst the labouring masses for any amount of time—days, months, years—and using that experiential understanding of the working-class condition as a basis from which to create theatre. Kun was arrested in 1976 and detained under the Internal Security Act[12] until 1980. Tan states that "the government, aware of how 'theatre had become a handmaiden to communist ideology in mainland China', regarded Singapore theatre that featured working class concerns as 'having the potential to undermine the security of the state'" (p. 201). On his release, Kuo re-established his theatre career (and was eventually awarded the prestigious Cultural Medallion for his services to theatre), but he noted that modern Chinese-language drama had ceased in the years he was detained and on its revival in the 1980s shifted away from political, working-class, collective concerns to reflect on "the individualisation of the person, in a modern political economy that produced the individual" (Lo 1993, p. 142).

In 1987, members of independent theatre company, the Third Stage, were arrested and detained among a group of 22 young people including lawyers, members of the opposition Workers' Party, Catholic social workers and members of a women's research organisation. The detainees were accused of plotting a "Marxist conspiracy to overthrow the government" (Tan 2013, p. 201) led, allegedly, by a former student leader self-exiled since the 1970s in London. In fact, the Third Stage was in the process of developing a musical comedy that was also consciousness-raising. It had applied its popular and political theatre to critique aspects of government policy and the PAP's style of governance, as well as to raise broad awareness of the conditions of migrant workers in Singapore. Members had recently participated in summer courses with Philippines Educational Theatre Association (PETA) with a view to implement their newly acquired skills, on return to Singapore, in workshops in some Catholic parishes and labour organisations (Van Erven 1992, pp. 233–234). The arrest and detention of Third Stage members, for over a year in some cases, led to an abrupt end to the development of theatre of liberation, as Van Erven notes, "government repression virtually destroyed the small, peaceful theatre of liberation movement of Singapore" (1992, p. 233).

In 1999, Kok left TNS to re-establish Drama Box as a full-time, not-for-profit organisation. Tan notes that while TNS moved their work inside a dedicated theatre space, stopped using the terminology or nomenclature of Forum Theatre and began to adopt official cultural policy discourse, Drama Box openly practised what they have continued to call Forum Theatre in public, outdoors spaces (foregoing public funding and testing regulatory authority to

---

[12] The ISA is a colonial inheritance that allows government to detain without trial for public security/order offenses. The initial two-year detention period can be renewed indefinitely, and the detainee has no recourse to judicial review (Tan 2013, p. 202).

grant a performance license). In its insertion of Chinese-language Forum Theatre into the everyday spaces of working-class communities, Drama Box, according to Tan, "embrace[d] an aesthetic and site specificity [...] closer to the form's popular roots" (2013, p. 214). Tan maintains that Drama Box is part of "a more radical Chinese theatre tradition, which ... articulates well with the more 'revolutionary' origins of forum theater" (p. 217), although as Peterson notes, the "history [of Chinese language workers theatre] is virtually unknown" and "because of its perceived oppositional stance in relation to government policy, no one in Singapore has attempted to document this phenomenon" (Peterson 2001, p. 35).

Kok explains his decision to establish the Mandarin-language company, Drama Box, not in political or class-based, but in personal and familial terms. Drama Box's decision to take Forum Theatre to the Chinese (Mandarin and other dialects)-speaking community was motivated by the example of his father who while speaking Mandarin at home was confined to expressing himself in terms of the dominant language (English) of economic, educated elites in the workplace. As Kok notes, like many others of his generation, his father was effectively silenced in the workplace and in political decision-making (Kok 2014). Meanwhile, in the suburbs, "cultural shows are organised by grassroots organisations like the PA (People's Association), your RCs (Residents Committees), CCCs (Citizens' Consultative Committees) and CDCs (Community Development Councils)" (Kok in Chong 2011, p. 244). This fare serves to interpellate the majority of citizen-subjects who live in HDB estates to the ideology of the dominant ruling party. Thus, the insertion of Chinese-language Forum Theatre into the everyday spaces of working-class communities can be seen to challenge marginalisation by a professional elite and to unsettle control via reproduction of traditional cultural values and norms in the heartlands sphere.

IgnoreLAND of Its Time:
The Performance-Making Process

Now that I've related context on histories of cultural policy and theatre practice in Singapore, I want to move into exploration of the process of making *IgnorLAND of Its TIME* (*IOIT*) in Bukit Ho Swee. I'll discuss how Drama Box engaged with relevant research on the 1961 fire (Loh 2008) and then examine the 'grassroots' (the pseudo-state organisational network embedded across all aspects of everyday life) and 'community' engagement process. I will examine how the company utilised mixed creative methods to engage stakeholders and invite participation in the creative process including cultural mapping, creative workshops and performance-making with individual community participants via (oral history) interview, transcription, dialogue, re-scripting, rehearsal and performance. I will argue that Drama Box's performance-making process in the Bukit Ho Swee estate space with former and current residents, pseudo-state ('grassroots') and statutory authorities responsible for oversight of use of multiple spaces within the estate space itself, powerfully illuminates dynamic processes of community enactment in a public housing estate in Singapore. While Drama Box's work was compromised by being set within the estate space, subject to the regulatory (pseudo-)state mechanisms that operate in that space, that setting also supported Drama Box's generative practice in ways that cannot be simply concluded as uncritical (Varney et al. 2013).

Influential in the making of IOIT was research into BHS, and a critical source was Loh's research (2008) on the place of fires in the social history of cities, with a focus on the symbolic significance of the *kampong* Bukit Ho Swee fire in the history of Singapore. Prior to the 1961 fire, Bukit Ho Swee *kampong* was constructed in official discourse as 'the quintessential urban slum' (Loh 2008, p. 10). The destructive fire spoke to the official discourse of 'spatial emergency' applied to urban village housing and the associated way of life. In the aftermath of the event, the *kampong* was erased and replaced, with extraordinary efficiency, by modernist high-rise housing blocks, the foundation stones of the modern city state of Singapore. Loh (2008) interrogates the fire event and aftermath as part of a powerful myth in the making of the modern Singaporean nation: a meta-social narrative accepted by fire victims and the public at large. Through extensive oral history capture, Loh reconstructs a social history of *kampong* Bukit Ho Swee drawing on the memory of former residents, some of whom continue to live in the Bukit Ho Swee estate. This leads him to trouble both the official narrative of the urban village ('slum') and associated ('degenerate') way of life and the transformational myth of nation forming. Loh contends that Singapore was not created "like the proverbial phoenix rising from the ashes" (2008, p. 458) and that

> to understand the true extent of the BHS fire's impact requires us to examine how far the life of a formerly semi-autonomous community, and its social and economic relations with the state, were transformed in the wake of the catastrophe. The full story may not be one of the complete destruction of community but a more complex reconstitution on which both modern and customary ways of life co-exist in a state of tension. (2008, p. 9)

Drama Box's entry into the estate space examines, after Loh, the dominant myth of nation founding through excavation of popular memories touching on (semi-)autonomous, interdependent livelihoods and social agencies, past and present. The company aims, in this manner, to participate in the generation of narratives—a process of (mytho)poesis—opening onto a dynamic social history of the city.

After analysing research sources, Drama Box moved into the engagement part of the process. The first step in this process involved engagement with the 'entire government system' (Koh 2016) embedded at grassroots level, after recommendations put forward in the Arts and Culture Strategic Review (2012). This engagement was essential to gaining the necessary permissions and support to access and operate in the estate space. Associate Artistic Director Koh Hui Ling created a 'huge map of complication' to outline complex engagement with the broad grassroots sector indicating the increased layer of bureaucracy added to the creative process by the Arts and Culture Strategic Review (ASCR) recommendations:

> So because of the ACSR proposal in 2012, suddenly we have to check with PA [People's Association] [which equals the relevant] Advisor, CCC [Citizens' Consultative Committee] and RC [Residents Committee] and get their support before we could get any approval [on the use of space] from the respective authority; usually the HDB, LTA (land Transit Authority), SLA (Singapore Land Authority) or Town Council. In the past, we just [went] directly to HDB, LTA, SLA or Town Council and got the land [use permission] [...] The network web just got more complex. (Koh 2016)

Cultural Mapping: 'A Day in the Life of Bukit Ho Swee'—Spaces and Times for Being Together

In the first instance of engagement with estate stakeholders, Drama Box planned to employ the method of 'cultural mapping'. An emerging interdisciplinary field of enquiry employed since the 1990s in public planning practices, cultural mapping is

> a systematic tool to involve communities in the identification and recording of local cultural assets with the implication that this knowledge will then be used to inform collective strategies, planning processes or other initiatives. These assets are both tangible, or quantitative and intangible or qualitative. Together these assets help define communities (and help communities define themselves) in terms of cultural identity, vitality, sense of place, and quality of life. (Duxbury et al. 2015, p. 2)

Initially, Koh had planned to use cultural mapping techniques to "get the community to plan their town together, so we could see and understand what people want and what best suits their needs" (in Koh and Han 2016). However, concerns were raised about these ideas by the Residents Committee (RC) and the Citizens' Consultative Committee (CCC) team. There were "fears that the residents might pressure the grassroots organisations to deliver what they were consulted on. For instance, if people on the estate decided that they wanted an ice-skating rink on the estate, the RC/CCC was concerned that they would need to provide it" (Koh in Koh and Han 2016). This indicates the tendency of grassroots organisations to follow the 'ideology of pragmatism' (Chua 1995, p. 5) central to PAP governance. In Singapore, community development is carefully managed, with expectations of what can be delivered kept in check, so that government appears to be responsive, effective and efficient within set limits, thus reinforcing its legitimacy to govern. The RC/CCC's qualms led Drama Box to reconsider their aims including what promises they might make to people and whether these could be supported in the time of the project. Therefore, "after much negotiation and deliberation", the creative team decided to base the cultural mapping exercise on the theme: 'A Day in the Life of BHS'. The main objective was "to get a picture of what people did and where on the estate over course of a day" (Koh in Koh and Han 2016). To this end Drama Box produced a large plastic canvas with an asymmetrical red, blue and green colour block design. Buildings (apartment blocks, community centre, shophouses, market, Tiong Bahru plaza with MRT station etc.) were marked on the map in black outline and grey colour block. DB took the map with them on site visits, and to workshops and events they were invited to. They hung it in or placed it across tables in public spaces. The team travelled with a set of coloured round stickers, the size of a thumbprint. The pink, yellow and silver stickers represented different times of the day: morning, afternoon and evening, respectively. Participants took three stickers and placed them on the map according to where they spent most of their time for that part of a normal day on the estate. Koh elaborates: "Their responses were just stickers with no writing. We don't have a written documentation of the stories, it was more in our heads, but certainly gave us a clearer idea of what life is like for the people there, what they usually do, because people of different ages participated in the activity" (in Koh and Han 2016).

The map/s proved to be extremely useful in the initial engagement process. The large, colourful canvases sparked curiosity and interest, and all ages participated in the simple task of placing stickers on the map. As there was no formal written information capture, participants could remain anonymous. The maps provided an informal, low-risk, open and primarily visual point of contact with a broad segment of the estate population. In the course of explaining the task to people, the Drama Box team used the opportunity to also talk about the project, explaining what it was about, what activities would be taking place on the estate and how people could participate. Over time, as Koh noted, the maps provided a basis for continued contact extending, in some cases, into deeper conversational relationships: "when we brought it around to different community events, some of the residents became more familiar with us … allow[ing] us to form better conversations with people" (in Koh and Han 2016). Through those conversations, the team was able to better understand the interest in the project and to express the project aims and objectives in terms of "what we wanted to say, stories we want to find" (Han in Koh and Han 2016).

While enabling initial conversational relationships to form, the maps produced useful visual information. The patterns produced by the coloured stickers visualised collections of people in space and time, and also highlighted underused or less-frequented spaces. Koh noted that as the map built, residents began to discuss with the Drama Box team their own experiences of estate space/time, to share interpretations of why certain spaces were more or less frequented, and to offer insight into the temporal rhythms of use (or not) of spaces (2016). Seeking to address the rise of '*kampong* nostalgia', and to address the notion that what has been lost to the past in Singapore's modernity is precisely a sense of belonging and community, Chua undertook a longitudinal study of resettlement of a Chinese village to HDB estate in the 1980s (1997, pp. 81–85). The study found that a different "sense of community has emerged in the new environment for the resettled residents" (p. 69):

> the ubiquity of incidental social activities in all the informal social spaces in a village … gave villagers a sense of belonging and of security, as expressed in their generalized sense of 'knowing everyone' in the village, an organic sense of community. …In contrast to this the residents of high-rise estates form limited restricted communities – 'small collectives of residents in selective void decks or along selective 'corridors of activities' …a generalized sense of community feeling in the village is …replaced by much more personalised sentiments localised at a particular void deck or in one's routine routes in the high-rise housing estate. (1997, pp. 85–86)

What was communicated strikingly—visually—in the mapping project, along with the potential for community in spaces marked for social congregation (void decks) and in the pathways along which residents' routines are carried out ('corridors of activities'), was the centrality of the Beo Cresent Market in the life of the estate. In discussing the significance of economic factors in the transformation of residential basis of community life, Chua notes that, while

> middle income professionals may now belong concurrently to several trans-spatial social collectives that are based on interests and class homogeneity rather than residential proximity … financial constraints tend to confine working-class individuals to their residential areas for their simple recreational needs. For example, they are inclined to patronize the neighbourhood hawker centre nightly, and a sense of community is likely to exist among them, which is localized at the hawker centre itself. (1997, p. 87)

As an older housing estate, with a greater proportion of lower-income groups and a higher proportion of senior residents, Bukit Ho Swee conformed to type. The cultural mapping process confirmed the centrality of the hawker market in communal life, and Drama Box drew on this awareness in sourcing community participants/performers and in situating the performance. Koh noted that from the stories shared "we gained insight into the usage (or not) of some of the spaces within the estate […] and also how residents saw different spaces and the spatial characteristics that attracted or repelled them" (2016). Drama Box used this developing sense of space/time as community process and potential in creating the performance tour.

Photography Workshops: Prefiguring a Visual Archive

The engagement of a broad range of estate residents in cultural mapping went on while Drama Box sought to establish group workshops—a staple of community theatre/arts practice—with social service organisations on the estate in order to generate ideas, material and participation in the performance. One organisation approached by Drama Box and invited to participate ultimately declined the offer of workshops, while another accepted. I didn't speak to anyone from the former (family support based) organisation, but the feeling in the team was that an arts workshop over eight weeks was seen to be drawing human resources away from the core programme of service delivery and that any reduction in service could threaten the organisation's finanical support. The lack of buy-in from this group had an impact on the project. It meant that whereas "there would have been several layers of information coming into the project from both the seniors and younger people", that "complexity was lost" (Koh in Koh and Han 2016). In the end, Drama Box conducted four three-hour workshops sessions with a senior citizens group from the Salvation Army—Family Services. Drama Box held two photography workshops, one workshop on cultural mapping 'A Day In The Life of BHS', and concluded with a reminiscence-based workshop drawing on the residents' own photographic self-portraits and objects of affection, that the senior citizens themselves brought from their own homes.

Drama Box hired professional photographer Zinky Aw to deliver workshops to the senior citizens. As well as work shooting corporate events, Aw also mentors young people in the art of street photography for Photovoice.sg. For this project, Aw tutored a group of senior citizens on basic aspects of film photography with disposable film cameras brought by Drama Box. Drama Box gave the group a task which was to photograph anywhere or anything on the estate that they felt it was important to preserve, something they would still like to see around in five years' time. Aw tutored the senior citizens in the basics of photography from loading the film in the camera to image framing and the art of image composition (scene, subsets, colour, shapes etc.). After the tutorial participants had one hour to take their images. They went out into the estate in pairs accompanied by a social worker and/or member of the Dramabox team to support their photography. In the follow-up session the following week, Aw, who had developed the images, led a process of analysis and reflection. In small groups, participants reflected on the subject and composition of the image with Aw encouraging a "more specialized way of seeing" (2014). In their groups the senior citizens chose their three favourite images and then chose their group favourite, which they presented back to the group for discussion.

Aw hadn't worked with older adults before; for this exercise she'd had to transcribe her teaching notes into Mandarin, and was limited in her interactions with the group by an inability to engage in complex conversation in dialect. Nevertheless, she felt, for the first time, through the process of working with the senior citizens, that "photography could be used as a tool" and that "a way of seeing could resonate with a community":

> The format of this workshop is quite new in that the photography component is an excuse or a tool, yes, but more an excuse for the [participants] to uncover new areas within the neighbourhood and, subsequently, by asking them questions about what they have captured, the images, it unlocks certain memories or allows them to share what matters to them or not …[it can be] mundane things … mundane concerns … through what they have shared you get a sense of what matters to them – whether its social interaction, the greenery aspect, a clean environment, the market, kids/playgrounds or animals. (2014)

Drama Box incorporated a final selection of images in the performance. They were installed at the Kim Seng Community Centre, where the audience gathered at the beginning of the performance tour of the BHS estate. The images were also included as a pull-out within the performance programme. As a collection of unofficial yet professionally tutored and artfully composed scenes, the images stand as a striking expression of affective attachment to place. Loh notes that the Bukit Ho Swee estate was a popular early target of official photographers. Photographic images tended to juxtapose images of the new buildings against the fire ground or the former 'slum' (Loh 2008, p. 461). In other words, images of slum squalor or the conflagration against images of modern, newly built high-rise apartment blocks served to legitimate "a politically powerful vocabulary and discursive language of societal transformation in post war Singapore" giving "moral and social authority to terms like 'clearance' and 'relocation', which in practice frequently meant the destruction of not only houses but of established social and economic ways of life centring around the residences" (Loh 2008, p. 7). The collection of images produced by the senior citizens speaks to the past in some respects and also prefigures future loss. As an early generation estate, Bukit Ho Swee has now become older and, even, anachronistic in the high modernist landscape of twenty-first-century Singapore. It is increasingly subject to the discourse of degeneration and disrepair applied to the *kampong* in the 1950s. This collection of images expressing attachment to place in terms of colour, line, pattern, light and shade and so on, therefore, forms a rich archive that remains as a visual counter-narrative to the dominant discourse of renovation through redevelopment.

Playwriting and Performance-Making

Drama Box engaged professional playwright Jean Tay to create a play about Bukit Ho Swee based on this community engagement process and with community participants/performers. Tay is an established, prize-winning author, who has written several plays, including *Plunge* (2000), which explored the impact of the 1997 Asian Economic Crisis on the lives of ordinary people, and *Boom* (2008), which investigates economic recovery, the ongoing modernising process and the attendant pressures on land and housing. In *Boom*, the dramatic narrative encompasses the en bloc sale of an older HDB estate and the exhumation of graves in a cemetery to release land for housing. The play examines how these phenomena affect the lives of one family, one of whom is a rotting corpse evicted from his eternal resting place. In these plays, Tay, who has a double degree in economics and creative writing from Brown University, USA, questions the model of progress underpinning the modern Singaporean state and how the constant redevelopment process impacts ordinary citizens, living and dead. The IOIT project involves Tay for the first time in crafting a play written with community participants. The play is probably best described as a docudrama as it combines a dramatic narrative with the real stories of present and former estate residents.

The community performers were engaged over the course of a year. The Drama Box team with Tay worked closely with past and present Bukit Ho Swee residents to gather, shape and perform their stories of everyday life on the estate as part of a larger site-specific performance tour. A couple of well-known local figures (Mr Seah and Mr Tay) were directly invited to participate by Drama Box, while others (Ms Alison Koh, the cobbler, Yap Ah Leck, his wife and their dance group and the 'Chess King') accepted invitations to participate in the performance issued through the process of site visits. Mr Tay, Ms Koh and the cobbler (Mr Leck) had scripted speaking parts. The community performers scripts were gathered (through oral history interview), transcribed, edited, scripted, performed and rescripted—in a feedback loop between the community performers and Drama Box with Tay—and then set within a dramatic narrative created by Tay. The cobbler (Mr Leck), his wife and dance troupe performed a dance piece in a nature strip between two rows of coconut palms, and the 'Chess King' sang in accompaniment of the final scene performed from the roof of a parking garage with a vantage point over the estate. The play was performed by two professional performers and the community performers. One performer plays a teenage girl, Tan Kim Choo, speaking a mix of Hokkien and Mandarin. The other plays a man in his 1960s, Samuel Tan Kim Huat, speaking in English and Mandarin. Samuel is the tour guide.

The character of Samuel was loosely based on Mr James Seah, who was invited to perform in the role but couldn't commit to a full run of evening performance dates. Hence, the role was given to a professional performer. Seah grew up in the *kampong*, and was a victim of the fire. With his family, Seah was rehoused in emergency flats built on the fire site. He participated in oral history collection by Loh and went on to establish his own social media (Facebook) page called 'I grew up in Bukit Ho Swee' (est. 2008), which invited others who grew up in the *kampong* to share memories and attempt to collectively remember and reconstruct the *kampong*, the fire event and relocation to new HDB estates. His inspiration, as he explained it to me, was partly to correct the notion that the *kampong* was a "black zone" and that those living in the slum were "criminal gang members" rather than "working families living in affordable housing located conveniently close to places of work (city factories)"

(2014). James subsequently developed his blog, 'Blog to Express', and has become quite a famous figure for his erudite blogging. His blog was mentioned in Prime Minister Lee Hsien Loong's 2011 National Day Rally speech.[13] Although he couldn't perform in the play, Mr Seah led daytime heritage tours of the estate during the performance run, supported by the DB team who provided programmes and carried his photographs (sourced from national archives) to reconstruct the *kampong*, the fire event and the early rebuilding process. The tours were based on Seah's own documented revisit to the estate with friends after he first started to recall his early life at Bukit Ho Swee.[14] Seah's Facebook page and blog were key sources for researching the performance.

Bukit Ho Swee: A Tour of Invisible Things

The play weaves a dramatic narrative involving 'tour guide', Samuel (played by Fanny Kee), and a younger girl/ghost (played by Tan Wan Sze), around the 'real' stories of community participant-performers drawn from the estate. The play moves through 15 scenes each of which corresponds to a specific site, or station, and story episode. The performance tour takes two hours, and there are stops/stations at which the audience may sit and take in refreshments as the evenings are still warm and humid. I am going to deal with the dramatic narrative and community performances separately and in turn, as they are somewhat distinct, and examine why this might be. The gathering point for the performance is the Kim Seng Community Centre (KSCC) on Havelock Road, on the perimeter of the main Bukit Ho Swee estate. There the audience assembles, collecting free tickets and taking in the photography exhibition of the Bukit Ho Swee estate by senior residents. The beginning of the performance is marked by Samuel, our guide, introducing himself and leading us onto the footpath outside the KSCC. Pointing to patch of grass on other side of the road, our guide asks:

> You see anything? Nothing, right? Just empty space? A peaceful patch of green? For me, it's the opposite. I lived here for over forty years ... my block of flats, 16 stories high. Block 29. This big solid block made of concrete and corridors ...and life. And now to see just air here. It's a very funny feeling ... For such a big building, to suddenly disappear like that. (Tay 2014)

Thus, we are introduced to Sam's 'tour of invisible things'. The empty space where a building used to be is symbolic of the absence that Sam's memory must represent for us. Lacking memory, we are asked to imagine the past that Sam recalls on this tour: "full of things you can only see with your imagination, that I can only see with my memory" (Tay 2014).

---

[13] See http://www.pmo.gov.sg/mediacentre/prime-minister-lee-hsien-loongs-national-day-rally-2011-speech-english-sunday-14-august

[14] See http://blogtoexpress.blogspot.co.uk/2010/09/tttt.html

The group crosses the road and walks along the pavement beside the nature strip heading towards busy nightlife around the shophouses (cafes, restaurants, medicine shops) further down on Havelock rd. In the distance, a small figure holding a lantern appears in the far corner of the nature strip and comes towards the audience, skipping down a grassy slope. A girl in a blue dress emerges out of the darkness and converges with the audience before the entrance to the Bukit Ho Swee estate. Sam mentions that we are standing at the site of a former Cantonese cemetery, Mah Kau Tiong. At this point, our guide goes to leave off and the girl speaks to chastise Sam, reminding him that the cemetery is also a playground and that, here, children play with abandon free of the oversight of those who "have one foot in their coffin already" (Tay 2014). She tells the story of a woman who married a dead man, buried in the cemetery. He was a gangster who died through misadventure. The woman was so in love with him that she insisted they be united in marriage. In order for the marriage rites to be performed, someone/thing had to stand in for the dead man. In the end, the rites were performed with a rooster in his place. For the girl, the story is a fabulous example of the stupidity of adults. Sam doesn't seem to see or hear the girl, even though she seems to be talking directly to him. He moves us on into the space of the Bukit Ho Swee estate.

A moment later, we are inside the estate oriented to the outline of the former *kampong* which existed between the boundaries of Havelock Road, to the west, and Tiong Bahru Road, to the east. Sam tells us that all that remains of the former *kampong* is a couple of roads: Beo Cresent Lane and Bukit Ho Swee Road. As we ascend some stairs leading to a raised walkway passing between apartment blocks, Sam remarks on how clean, quiet and orderly the HDB estate is compared to the noisy, crowded and smelly *kampong*. His comments prompt a rebuke from the girl who has followed the group. She is in the playground below the raised walkway we have climbed to. Playing on the equipment, the girl interjects to tell Sam to stop pretending to be dignified and noble. She then proceeds to tell the story of his birth as she—then seven years old—helped their mum deliver him, "you were covered in blood, wet, sticky, so disgusting I could die" (Tay 2014). With this interruption, we learn she's our guide's older sister. But while Sam has grown into an older man recalling his past from present-day Singapore, the girl remains in the past of her childhood in the *kampong*. Her interruptions represent a vibrant past that is less faded by remembering through a long life that has experienced significant change. The girl questions Sam's memories. She points out that he has forgotten the *kampong*, of which few physical or material traces remain, although he claims to remember it. Sam and the girl do not communicate—there is no dialogue between them. The girl is invisible to him. She represents his blind spots. She sees Sam but doesn't acknowledge his adult self. She sees and speaks to her younger brother. They are both connected yet discontinuous in time and space. In these early episodes of performance, the dramatic narrative serves to call (Sam's) memory into question as something not definitive or solid, but partial. The performance cautions us not to rely on memory (as it is forgetting), nor should we rely on the girl's limited purview of the all-but-erased *kampong*. There is, in other words, not one authoritative perspective here. The estate is a puzzle that the audience is invited to reimagine through recharged powers of critical perception as they move deeper into the estate space.

It is at this point that the first community performer is introduced to the audience. Mr Tay Ah Chuan warmly greets the group on a walkway by a parking garage built over where his family home used to be. He welcomes us and talks a little about growing up in the *kampong*, although he notes that he was, for a period of time, sent away to live with family elsewhere for his own safety because he got into trouble at school with *pai kia* (gangsters). After introductions, Mr Tay walks us to the Beo Crescent Market and explains how hawking (the low-income, subsistence lifestyle that nevertheless sustained many *kampong* dwellers) moved from a large sprawling street market made up of indoor/outdoor stalls to an indoor centre of small stalls as this critical mode of self-employment came increasingly under government regulation and control. Central to Mr Tay's story of the stalls is his role in establishing a Hawkers' Association. From outside his former office, Mr Tay talks about how as chairperson of the Hawkers Association he both managed relationships between hawkers themselves and acted as their advocate in negotiation with government bureaucracy. Mr Tay then hands over to the current chairperson, Alison Koh, who works at a soybean drink (*Tau Huay*) stall on the other side of the market. Alison invites the audience to sit down at the tables outside her soybean drink stall. She has prepared drinks and serves the audience much-appreciated refreshments. The tables have a collage of images on them of the estate, and Alison talks about how she collected the images with people from the estate to show how the place has changed over time from *kampong* and through processes of redevelopment to what it is today. Alison parallels the changes in the development of the estate to those involved in making Tau Huay in the 1960s to now and the processes of modernisation that have affected her work as hawker of soybean drink.

From the Beo Crescent Market centre, Sam, retaking the tour, guides us to the site of the old wet market (an outdoor market selling meat, fish and vegetables) at the back of the Malaysian and Chinese Association shop houses that front Havelock Road. These buildings have, he tells us, survived both the fire *and* redevelopment, providing a rare link with the past. The site, between the Beo Cresent Market and Havelock Road shop houses, is now a space dedicated to songbirds. There is a metal frame-like cage set up in 'song bird corner' that the older men (uncles) who participate in this hobby hang their intricately hand-made wooden birdcages from. As well as hosting gatherings of songbirds, the space also hosts competitions to find the bird with the best singing voice. Sam tells us that this group of songbird enthusiasts is famous and used to be based at Tiong Bahru. When their estate was sold en bloc and redeveloped the group relocated to Bukit Ho Swee where they managed to reinstate a space for their competitive hobby. While telling the story of the relocation of the songbirds, Sam's memory goes back to the day of the fire. He had plans to meet his big sister at the wet market. But when the fire started, Sam made his way to safety. His sister, on the other hand, went to look for her little brother in the wet market where they were due to meet. The scene of the girl searching for the boy in the midst of the conflagration is enacted within the metal frame-like cage in the space. Light flickers on metal as thick grey smoke (from a smoke machine) billows into the space overwhelming the girl's frantic search efforts. Sam's memories are overtaken by this painful event from his past, the loss of his sister's life in the fire. He moves into a more reflective state commenting on the human toll from the fire. The death toll was officially given as four people. Sam seems to question how definitive this number is. More than numbers of fire dead, however, Sam reflects on how the fire marked the loss of an entire way of life. Nevertheless, in the space where songbird traditions were relocated and adapted, Sam's critical reflections on the past are interrupted by the present.

The audieece is moved on to the next performance stop and introduced to the cobbler, Mr Yap Ah Leck, at his stall in the void deck a short walk from songbird corner and the Beo Cresent Market. The cobbler is not from Bukit Ho Swee but he has managed to secure a space from which to work on the estate. The cobbler explains to the audience how he carved out this semi-officially sanctioned work area for himself, despite regulations against setting up shop in the void deck, and how a friendly 'parliament' of different characters—customers and passersby—forms around his stall for a chat during the working day. While outlining the unusual friendships formed, the cobbler also outlines threats to his rather unorthodox business, such as the man who set up and operated in his space while he was on holiday. The cobbler's scene ends with him joining his wife, and their local dance troupe for a spin in an outdoor avenue between two rows of palm trees. The scene indicates how (non-)residents make use of the HDB estate space for work and how the space—its open areas and wide, tree-lined avenues—lends itself to pleasurable work conditions and leisure pursuits (group dancing).

After the cobbler's scene and group dance, Sam guides the audience to the roof of a mutlistorey car park. The view from the top of this block provides a vantage point overlooking Bukit Ho Swee and "all these beautiful shining blocks of flats' risen like a phoenix from the ashes" (Tay 2014), as Sam says citing official literature refering to the modern buildings built on the Bukit Ho Swee fire site (see Loh 2008, p. 462). As the dusk sky darkens, a man begins to sing. The song by 'the chess king', a community participant drawn from a collection of men who regularly gather together to play chess at the outdoor tables, transports Samuel back to the *kampong*, which he also sees laid out below. As Sam describes aspects of the old village, our eyes are drawn to an adjacent block of flats by the movements of a small figure in blue. The girl/sister can be seen walking up and down the long white corridors of the block of flats, searching for something. As she makes her way up each level, her seeking becomes an increasingly frantic dance. Sam, who sees her now, observes her useless activity noting that she, "this girl, who can find her way from one end of the *kampong* to the other, running through its zigzag alleyways, into people's doors and out their side entrances" (Tay 2014), is unable to find her way in the regular, ordered, monotonous space of the HDB block. "She is no phoenix", he says. And so the girl in the blue dress, trapped in the past of the *kampong* like a bird in a cage, becomes a symbol of the human costs of the transformation of one way of life for another. This is when Sam suggests that the fire, a 'blessing in disguise' according to the discourse of social reform uttered by a powerful elite leading a modern reconstruction process, caused pain and unrecoverable/irreplaceable loss for others:

> So, she's not one of the four people who were officially lost, on paper.
> On paper is one story.
> Off the paper, is another story.
> Off the paper, who knows what happened?
> Who knows how many people were actually lost?
> Do you count all those people who *tiao lau* [Hokkien for 'jumping off a building'] after they moved to their new flats in the sky? Do you count all those families, friendships broken up by the fire? (Tay 2014)

Through the course of the tour, Samuel moves from remembering (and forgetting) the past in the present and into a more reflective and questioning space. The character's shift is partly prompted by the girl/ghost who corrects aspects of Samuel's memory that have faded or taken on, over times of great change, a consensus view of the transformation of the *kampong* into a modern high rise housing estate. As Sam moves deeper into the estate space and confronts the fire event, his sense of detachment wavers, and he begins to reflect on the death of his sister as symbolic of the end of an entire way of life and his own personal transformation. In his reflective state, Samuel begins to question unofficial narratives of the fire event through rumours he has heard spoken, for instance, that official agencies started the fire to carry forward their planned programme of transformation, that the unofficial death toll was much higher than official sources, and stories of suicides from the new apartment blocks as people failed to adapt to a radically new way of life. These oft-spoken, if whispered, narrative fragments (many of which are documented in Loh (2008, pp. 485–490)), begin to trouble the myth that modern Singapore emerged like a phoenix from the ashes of the fire. The question is how does this dramatic part of the performance tour of the Bukit Ho Swee estate that attempts to unravel, or at least complicate, the myth of nation formation gel with the performances of the community cast? How does the company's interrogation of the dominant narrative of nation founding sit with the motivations and viewpoints of the project participants?

Community Performers

A main aim of the project was to have residents of Bukit Ho Swee perform their stories of the estate themselves in the places where their experiences and memories inhere. While the dramatic narrative dealt with the fire as a central symbolic event, the interruptions from the residents shed light on actual experiences of living and working in Bukit Ho Swee, past and present. Writing on oral history, Della Pollock suggests that it may open:

> a great vista of postmodern agency, embracing the lives of those whose accomplishments might not be the stuff of conventional history, but whose agency thrives in the tactical politics of everyday living. The achievements of oral history suggest a postmodern history made up of small stories or what Lytoard calls "petit récits": history relieved of pretensions to a "master narrative", history as a somewhat humbler quilt of many voices and local hopes". (Pollock 1998, p. 18)

The discussion here centres on the participants, their voices and their stories, themselves, and in relation to the dramatic narrative which attempted to open questions in relation to the Bukit Ho Swee conflagration as the 'ground zero' of the HDB nation. There were three interviewees: Mr Tay (Tay 2014a, b), the cobbler and Alison (Koh 2014; in the text, I'm using the terms of reference the participants preferred, also used by the Drama Box team). Mr Tay and Alison could be classed as grassroots leaders, and were drawn from the milieu of the market centre. As 'community leaders', they arguably have a stake in presenting a certain view of the market at the centre of the estate, or in promoting it, and are more confident in coming forward. Drama Box worked with participants separately. In the case of Mr Tay and the cobbler, the feedback loop remained between the participant and the company. Alison's process sought to include residents in remembering the Bukit Ho Swee *kampong*, perhaps because she hadn't grown up there. Alison gathered groups of older residents together and collated their stories and images of the *kampong* (the images—old photographs—were displayed on the tables outside Alison's soy bean drink stall), as well as narrating her own experiences on the estate. This process reveals interesting contrasts between individual and collective remembering, and hints at the gendered differences in practices of oral history-based community theatre. The Drama Box process revealed that oral history is not immune to capture by official narrative uses of history. Mr Tay's oral history deploys narrative in a way that reinforces a powerful consensus and aims to discipline younger Singaporeans. At the same time, Alison catalysed a process of collective reminiscence to socially and economically revitalise the market place in the present.

Mr Tay is a well-known source of oral history on the Bukit Ho Swee *kampong* fire (see Loh 2008), keenly sought after for media interviews on the topic, adding to his prominent public profile. He is the former chairman of the Hawker Association at Beo Crescent Market, and a grassroots volunteer leader. Although retired, and attempting to wind down from public life, Mr Tay agreed to take part in the performance because "if nobody tells the story of Bukit Ho Swee or preserves memories then people will forget" (Tay 2014a). The project offered Mr Tay the opportunity to tell stories other than those he'd previously been invited to share. He said that the "stories of life around the market here were new" and that he was "sharing them for the first time" (2014a).

Mr Tay stressed that there are "many many many stories in Bukit" and that it was "an exciting place to be". While acknowledging the sheer volume of stories that could be told about Bukit Ho Swee, Mr Tay said he was very careful to "share those stories that he felt comfortable telling in public" (Tay 2014a). These stories tended to revolve around his own childhood in the *kampong* and his involvement in the development of the hawker centre and association at Beo Crescent. He indicated that the stories he didn't personally feel comfortable in telling were political in nature (2014). Mr Tay's discomfort in entering into political discourse may be linked to a sense of fear that, according to Varney et al. (2013), is "a feature of the social landscape in Singapore [...] The use of extreme pragmatism and instrumental bureaucratic reason has meant government intervention in almost every aspect of social life has created what some observers have dubbed a 'Republic of Fear'" (p. 134). While this anxiety may explain a reticence to publicly engage in political discourse, it appeared that Mr Tay had clear intentions in telling the stories he did, and that his storytelling aligned with official discourse disciplining younger Singaporeans through stories of an older generation's struggle and sacrifice in the early period of nation-building. He states, "coming from the pioneer generation, I hope to share our struggle, so that they [younger Singpaoreans] can cherish our stability and not be easily swayed. Our pioneer generation sacrificed much to build Singapore's peace now. I hope the younger generation can recognise and understand this" (Tay 2014a).

According to My Tay, his aim was for his storytelling to have an effect on younger people coming from outside the estate to watch the performance. It was very important to him that a younger generation learnt about Bukit Ho Swee's place in the national story, "how she's overcome and progressed" (Tay 2014a), particularly as Singapore was moving towards celebrating its 50th anniversary (in 2015). He stated, "Bukit stories are very crucial to Singapore nation building" and "it's very important to record memories otherwise the younger generation will be a blank page" (2014a). In a post-performance interview, Mr Tay expressed a sense of having achieved his aims and intentions for the performance:

> I was so proud that my stories of the market were well received by the younger people. According to my observation, the audience were engaged... I feel rewarded that people came up to talk to me. How attentive they were, really moved me. Some audience even asked me questions during the show, so heartening, because it means they were really paying attention. (2014b)

Reflecting on the oral histories of the victims of the 1961 Bukit Ho Swee fire, Loh notes that many "have generally assimilated at least part of the official discourse in their memories of the fire" (2008, p. 474), leading him to wonder the extent to which "independent personal memory is simply a filtered form of official myth" (p. 15). In the Bukit Ho Swee performance there is an element of memory as 'filtered official discourse' in Mr Tay's case. He falls back on the PAP government discourse invented in the early 1980s after its electoral dominance was slightly dented by an opposition party by-election win. Quick to respond, the PAP reversed its "pragmatic dismissal" of the place of history in society on the basis that it would impede the ideology of progress, and staged a return to history in order to frame 'lessons' to discipline young Singaporeans' individualistic tendencies (Loh 2008, p. 465). A key lesson was framed around the generation of former *kampong* now HDB dwellers, who had endured the brunt of the nation-building process. Venerated as having steadfast and socially-oriented values this group was elevated to the status of model citizens and younger Singaporean's were warned not to upset the "nation state's hard-won stability and prosperity" (Loh 2008, p. 465).

Loh notes that this generational difference has become an ongoing point of antagonism in Singaporean society. While the older generation narrates life as a hard-won struggle full of personal sacrifice in the achievement of social goals, the younger ones are depicted as self-centred and somewhat complacent. What this serves to do is construct social struggle as firmly in the past. The only threat from the present derives from the demeanour of young Singaporeans who are willing to risk the national prosperity for self-serving ends. Against increasing claims for increased civil liberties and personal freedoms, this discourse stresses social responsibility. It has again been reinforced recently by the government's recognition and reward of the 'pioneer generation', something Mr Tay said he felt gratified by. This new terminology was introduced into official government discourse in 2013–2014, and backed up by material welfare support to Singaporeans over the age of 65 years. In passing on the story of Bukit Ho Swee and how it had 'overcome and progressed', Mr Tay was aligning his identity unambiguously within the so-called pioneer generation and official PAP government discourse. Mr Tay and James Seah's participation in the project does seem to mobilise personal narrative as a disciplinary mechanism. Seah's participation, like Mr Tay's, was predicated on making the younger generation aware of what had changed over the last 40-odd years, that the older generation had lived through an amazing experiment and that the luckier youngsters should 'make the most of opportunities, such as education, not available to their seniors when they were young' (2014). Nevertheless, within Mr Tay's personal narrative is also a will to autonomy that contradicts the dominant narrative: "I've been on the hawker committee for so long, and we were self-created, self-motivated and independent, not linked to RC and CCC" (2014a), somewhat blunting the disciplinary power of the narrative.

Alison was approached by Drama Box practitioners at the market where she works out of the soybean drink stall and invited to participate in the project.

She admits that "when she first heard about the project she was a little 'blurgh' but then thought it would be interesting to challenge herself about what these bukit stories are. She felt she had a lot to contribute since she married into BHS and had a lot to do in her working life with the market" (Koh 2014). As well as working the stall—for which she was up at 2.30 am everyday, closing the store at 3.30 pm—Alison had family responsibilities and was the first female chair of the Hawkers Association.

Alison's stories told of her own experience of hawking. She talked about how her work producing and selling the soybean drink had changed since the 1960s. At the same time, Alison used her position as a community participant/performer to gather residents together to produce a photo montage/collage of the Bukit Ho Swee *kampong*. She passed on some of these stories of everyday life on the point of transition while detailing her experience of the changing landscape of the estate space, and the market within it. While Mr Tay aimed to communicate BHS's central place in the national story to the younger generation, what was critical for Alison was restoring the place of the market itself at the centre of community life in the neighbourhood. She explained that "this market used to be famous". It was the "site of huge, bustling market that extended from indoors to outside" (Koh 2014). Once it moved indoors and under cover, it has become smaller: "people started not to come here anymore" (Koh 2014). She notes that while "a lot of old market blocks have been torn down", the Beo Crescent Market was, to the contrary, "undergoing an economic renaissance" (Koh 2014), and Alison wanted to support that process of revitalisation by drawing people to the market (via the performance) and telling them about its past and present significance within the Bukit Ho Swee neighbourhood. In addition to drawing new people into the neighbourhood and, hopefully, converting them into customers of the market centre, Alison found that the performance drew together people on the estate as well. In particular, the performance provided an opportunity for older people to reminisce: "the old photos of the *kampong* that DB curated with us, and displayed brought a lot of joy. It got the uncles and aunties back out to chat in community again, like the old days in the *kampong*" (Koh 2014). According to Alison, there was an influx of new people to see the performance, and the performance activities taking place on the estate 'made the area lively'. She, personally, "really enjoyed all the people coming here" and "was grateful because it felt like the old days" (Koh 2014).

The Cobbler fixes shoes from a self-made stall in the void deck, a short walk from the market centre. Unlike the other community participants the cobbler moved to Bukit Ho Swee in 2010 after a physical injury led to the loss of his job. He was 64 and unsure of what work to do. He learnt cobbling from an uncle and attempted to set up his business in the market where his wife had a stall selling clothing. But the stall was too small for two, and, according to the cobbler, business wasn't good. He walked around and decided to set up in the void deck, close to the market where his wife's stall was, to catch the passing trade. He made himself a work space that he could assemble/disassemble and wheel to his wife's stall at the end of the day. On the day I met the cobbler, I observed his rehearsal; he told the Drama Box crew that he'd rewritten his script so the rehearsal became a reading of the new and better script. He performed in the style of a stand-up comedian and presented a long list of the people/personality types that pass by and stop to chat. It was a roll call of the good, the bad and the ugly. He had the team laughing. At the end of his reading, the director, Hui Ling, remarked that the rewritten script wasn't so different that it needed to go to the certification body (censor), but that it was worth getting it back to Tay for editing as it was a bit long and, while engaging and funny at the start, it might get a bit tiring for audience.

The crux of the cobbler's story is about being new to the estate, carving out a work place in the void deck space (in the process getting around strict rules about the use of these types of spaces), and making friendships from the 'small parliament' of people who congregate around his stall for a chat. Although the cobbler seemed to enjoy writing and performing, his main aim in participating in the performance was to increase his business. To that end, he had prepared a $1 off voucher to give to 40 people over ten performances. It was written into his script. Based on a post-performance interview, it was clear that the cobbler was most interested in increasing his business via performance. He also seemed to enjoy performing and, if anything, expressed that he wanted a greater stake in the performance but didn't articulate why or what it meant to him.

Reflections on Community Performance in the HDB Nation

IOIT performed a site loaded with (official) symbolism and rich with un/official (counter-)narratives. The process of making a performance in a housing estate in collaboration with a variety of in-dwellers in the midst of people's homes, places of work and leisure, routine activities and ritual practices (religious festival, marriages, funerals) is difficult enough. At the same time, the company was involved in complex negotiations with the wide-ranging network of pseudo-state and statutory organisations that constitutes the government-owned and regulated infrastructure of the HDB estate. The performance process provided Drama Box with real insight into the experiences of residents as they sought, as Mr Tay so succinctly put it (speaking about the Hawker market), to "claim a space from government for people" (2014a).

In order to undertake a NAC-funded performance project in an HDB estate, and after having gained support of the local MP and relevant grassroots (PA/RC/CCC) organisations, Drama Box had to still apply to government departments for licences to perform in particular spaces: namely, the market/hawker centre, controlled by the National Environment Agency (NEA), and the roof top of the multistorey car park, which came under HDB control. Drama Box had trouble securing licenses for both spaces. In regard to use of the multi-story car park, Drama Box had approached HDB for a license early in the project planning process. The HDB gave permission for the company to use block 44a, an older block with fewer cars, and less traffic. At the beginning of the rehearsal process, Drama Box returned to the HDB, who withdrew permission to use the car park citing safety concerns. Drama Box reasoned that the site was important and that they couldn't replace the vantage point it provided over the estate. They raised the issue with various estate stakeholders—the Residents Committee and Town Council—and came to a collective consensus to use the car park without a license.

The NEA had also been positively consulted in the planning stages of the performance project. Then, in the midst of rehearsal Drama Box received communication from the NEA withdrawing permission to use the hawker centre for performance. A substantial section of the performance is located—physically and thematically/conceptually—in the marketplace due to the participation of Mr Tay (former chair of the Hawker Association) and Alison (current chair). Koh explains that the problem stemmed from a change in NEA personnel. Mr Tay and Alison knew the former NEA officer and assured Koh that they needn't keep checking in with the officer. However, this meant that they hadn't realised there had been a change in personnel. The new NEA officer, the RC chairman surmised, was perhaps playing around and making things difficult for the company because he hadn't been approached in a timely manner and shown appropriate respect (or "face"). Again, Drama Box drew on support from community stakeholders from within the RC and CCC. A grassroots volunteer organised a letter of support from the area MP to appeal the decision. The NEA officer refused use of the office, the site of a key scene in Mr Tay's narrative, citing the reason that it contained confidential information. The NEA also required Drama Box to rent an empty stall inside the market. There was a lot of conjecture, and some anxiety, about this move by the NEA officer particularly as there had recently been a change of Chairperson of the Hawker's Association from Mr Tay to Alison. It was wondered whether the NEA officer was reinstating a more authoritative relationship between the NEA and the Hawker Association. The team adjusted the scene so that Mr Tay performed his scene as it was outside the office stating that permission was not granted to perform inside the office as planned. In addition to the community stakeholders who intervened to assist Drama Box in their negotiation with the NEA officer—Mr Tay, Alison, RC chairman, PA volunteer, MP—there was a response from within the hawker centre as well in the form of offers of help and support. DB's rented stall didn't have access to electricity, which they needed to run lights, sound and smoke machine. Other stall owners offered for Drama Box to use their electricity. The cleaners assured Drama Box that the NEA didn't come in at night and offered to open the office for them (the offer was graciously declined). The songbird uncles also gave Drama Box permission to use their space, secured after petitioning Town Council, even though they were initially concerned that a performance within the birdcage structure might damage it. As well as positive support offered the project, there was an unknown attempt to curtail it too.

One evening, after a performance preview, the storeroom containing the company's gear was left unlocked. A person/people broke in and cut the electricity cables on the generator.

However, on the whole, the environmental and social challenges that confronted Drama Box as a result of performing in/with Bukit Ho Swee were resolved in a productive manner. Koh and Han noted that towards the end of the rehearsal process tents were set up next to the songbird station for the Hungry Ghost Festival. The '7th month ritual' involves singing and chanting of prayers usually through a PA system all day through till 10 pm. Koh and Han approached the neighbourhood committee members and spoke with them in order to ask about and understand their schedule. They politely informed them of the performance schedule. According to Koh and Han:

> we didn't ask them to change their schedule but they did of their own goodwill. They planned their schedule such that they stopped during the time of our show we were in and around the bird care – about 30mins. They also came to watch the show. We didn't know they were going to do this beforehand. We went to thank them thereafter. Similarly, there was a funeral planned during the performance run. Funerals usually last from Sunday to Friday and on the last night there is a lot of chanting and noise. Coincidentally, perhaps, when we were performing it was very quiet then right after we ended the music came on. We didn't ask them to stop so we're not sure if it was coincident or planned. (2016)

While admitting that community in the high-rise environment is "more restrictive in the sense in which it operates"—and we can see this in the hierarchical order and control of estate spaces and the regulation and surveillance of human activity in these spaces—Chua notes that the 'void deck' as a large open space made to host simultaneous communal gatherings and activities might be where a more open sense of community is forged. He asserts that "in their simultaneous presence, these activities and the participants constitute an 'open' community characterised by multiple uses of the same space" (1995, p. 121). For Chua, a sense of community is established and reinforced "by the informal processes of negotiation between different groups in taking turns to use the same spaces. Such is the spontaneous and organic community which develops out of the necessary reproduction of everyday life of and by the residents themselves" (1995, p. 121). Drama Box's intervention into the estate space to engage in a process of performance-making activated both quasi-state (grassroots) and state systems geared to an communitarian or corporatist mode of government. At the same time, the company's presence in the estate space created possibilities for enacting open community as collective practices of simultaneously sharing social space. The process of performance-making enacted both dominant and emergent modes of community in the estate space.

IOIT explored the site where, as myth would have it, modern Singapore, the HDB nation, rose from the ashes of a fire that erased a past way of life. The PAP government played no small part in leading this remarkable 'rags to riches' transformation, and much of Singapore's success as an independent nation in a global world stems from the decisive actions taken by government then, as now. In a time of continual redevelopment, critical resistance to this myth of nation-building has taken the form of *kampong* nostalgia. Through processes of making and performing IOIT, Drama Box exposes the poetics of myth making, opening a space to explore the HDB estate space that replaced the *kampong* as interconnected and interdependent spaces. Residues of the *kampong* (of a semi-autonomous way of life) remain in the present, not least in the memory and narrative practices of former and current residents of Bukit Ho Swee. At the same time, Drama Box explored the present estate space with residents uncovering its affective characteristics and experiencing (through participation in and sharing of social space) ways in which community is enacted in the HDB estate space. In this way, IOIT moved away from the idea that community resides only in recovery of the lost *kampong* space and that the act of recovery of community is resistant critique. IOIT posed a different category of problem. It explicitly invites spectators on their physical tours of the estate space to question constructions of the *kampong* as a space of exception or as repository of lost community and to question the dominant myth of the nation state that has completely transformed itself from its (difficult) past. By revealing that the past is active in the present, DB opens up the idea that the making of the future remains possible, and it lays out practical possibilities by performing being together in a shared space.

Drama Box applied learnings from the experimental community-engaged methodology tested in IOIT in the final performance in the IgnorLAND series, and beyond (see Schaefer 2022). Situated in an older estate scheduled for en-bloc redevelopment, *IgnorLAND of Its Loss* (2016) opened space in which to explore the embodied, affective experiences of residents forced to leave their homes in the Dakota estate, amidst heightened tensions between preservation and progress. This project coincided with the unveiling of GoLi, the crowd-funded, pop-up performance shell specifically commissioned by Drama Box to work around some of the difficulties of securing permissions to use public space for performance. Recently, Drama Box has started moving beyond activation of heartlands HDB spaces into cross-sector partnerships (see previous chapter). In 2018, the company created a performance tour of its own 'home' space, Chinatown: the company's physical base is in a converted shophouse in the tourism zone. Working with heritage and tourism agencies, the common concern for the company and state agencies was to mitigate the effects of policies that had produced a one-dimensional space that was fast losing its cultural vitality and commercial draw. In between the *IgnorLAND* series and *Chinatown Crossings*, Drama Box brought Goli and its community engagement methodology to Rotterdam in 2017. The company demonstrated an approach to performance making that strives to navigate complex webs of government organisation also embedded at the grassroots level. Within constraints, Drama Box negotiates space for meaningful (even if disagreeable) cultural participation, places the past and present in dialogue to open possible futures and seeks to extend the bounds of inclusive corporate governance underpinned by communitarian ideology. These practical skills, or 'assets', are increasingly necessary in our world and an important addition to the field of community performance.

REFERENCES

Anderson, B. (1983) *Imagined Communities. Reflections on the Origin and Spread of Nationalism*. London: Verso.

Arts and Culture Strategic Review (2012) National Arts Council, Singapore. Available at: https://www.nac.gov.sg/dam/jcr:1b1765f3-ff95-48f0-bbf9-f98288eb7082 [Accessed: 15 June 2015]

Aw. Z. (2014) Unpublished interview conducted by Kerrie Schaefer, July 15.

Bauman, Z. (2000) *Liquid Modernity* Cambridge: Polity Press.

Bereson, R. (2003) 'Renaissance or Regurgitation? Arts Policy in Singapore 1957–2003', *Asia Pacific Journal of Arts and Cultural Management*, 1:1, pp. 1–14.

Chong, T. (2005) 'From Global to Local. Singapore's Cultural Policy and Its Consequences', *Critical Asian Studies*, 37(4), pp. 553–568.

Chong, T. (2011) *Theatre and the State in Singapore. Orthodoxy and Resistance*. London and New York: Routledge.

Chua, A. (2014) 'NLB's decision 'guided by community norms'', *Today*, July 11. Available at: https://www.todayonline.com/singapore/nlbs-decision-guided-community-norms [Accessed: December 5, 2014].

Chua, B-H. (1995) *Communitarian Ideology and Democracy in Singapore*. London and New York: Routledge.

Chua, B-H. (1997) *Political Legitimacy and Housing: Stakeholding in Singapore*. London and New York: Routledge.

Chua, Beng-Huat. (2017). *Liberalism Disavowed: Communitarianism and State Capitalism in Singapore*. Ithaca: Cornell University Press.

Drama Box (2014) *IgnorLAND Of Its Time*, dir. Koh, H.L. A performance tour of the Bukit Ho Swee estate, Singapore. First performance: 24. July 2014.

Duxbury, N. Garrett-Petts, W.F. and MacLennan, D. (2015) *Cultural Mapping as Cultural Inquiry*. London and New York: Routledge.

Jacobs, M. Cairns, S. and Strebel, I. (2012) 'Doing Building Work: Methods at the Interface of Geography and Architecture', *Geographical Research*, 50(2), pp. 126–140.

Koh, H. L. and Han, X.M. (2016) Unpublished interview (skype) with Kerrie Schaefer, June 18.

Kok, H.L. (2014) Unpublished interview with Kerrie Schaefer, July 7.

Koh, A. (2014) Unpublished interview with Kerrie Schaefer, July 15.

Kong, L. (2012) 'Ambitions of a Global City: Arts, Culture and Creative Economy in "Post-Crisis" Singapore', *International Journal of Cultural Policy*, 18(3), pp. 279–294.

Lo, J. (2004) *Staging Nation: English Language Theatre in Malaysia and Singapore*. Hong Kong: Hong Kong University Press.

Lo, J. (1993) 'Theatre in Singapore: an Interview with Kuo Pao Kun', *Australasian Drama Studies*, 23, pp. 135–146.

Loh, Kah Seng. (2008) *The 1961 Bukit Ho Swee Fire and the Making of Modern Singapore*. PhD thesis. Murdoch University.

Miksic, J.N. (2013) *Singapore and the Silk Road of the Sea, 1300-1800*. Singapore: NUS Press, National University of Singapore: National Museum of Singapore.

Nanda, A. (2017) 'Lesson on democracy in an inflatable theatre'. *The Straits Times* [review], July 15. Available at:https://www.straitstimes.com/lifestyle/arts/lesson-on-democracy-in-an-inflatable-theatre (Accessed: 14 November 2018).

The Necessary Stage. (2014) *Theatre for Youth and Community* [magazine]. Singapore: The Necessary Stage.
Peterson, W. (2001) *Theatre and the Politics of Culture in Contemporary Singapore.* Middletown, CT: Wesleyan University Press.
Pollock, D. (1998) 'Making History Go', in Pollock, D. (ed.) *Exceptional Spaces. Essays in Performance and History.* Chapel Hill and London: University of North Carolina Press, pp. 1-45.
Renaissance City Report: culture and the arts in renaissance Singapore. (2000) Ministry of Arts and Information, Singapore.
Ronan, J. J. (2018) *Capital, Cooperation and Creating Performance: Blood Water Theatre Develops Ownership in Collaborative Theatre Practice.* PhD thesis, The Royal Central School of Speech and Drama. Available at: http://crco.cssd.ac.uk/id/eprint/1423/1/Ronan_Capital_Cooperation_and_Creating_Performance_BloodWater_Theatre_Develops_Ownership_in_Collaborative_Theatre_Practice.pdf [Accessed: 5 December 2020].
Singapore, Global City for the Arts. (1995) MITA and STPB, Singapore.
Seah, J. (2014) Unpublished interview with Kerrie Schaefer, July 10.
Schaefer, K. (2022) 'Drama Box and the Place of Community-Engaged Performance in the Production of the Singaporean Space Scape', in Rajendran, C. and Gough, R. (eds.) *Drama Box and Spaces Of Performance: Experience, Encounter, Engagement.* Aberystwyth: Performance Research Books (Inside Performance Practice).
Tan, K. P. (ed.) (2007) *Renaissance Singapore? Economy, Culture and Politics.* Singapore: NUS Press.
Tan, K.P. (2013) 'Forum Theater in Singapore: Resistance, Containment, and Commodification in an Advanced Industrial Society', *positions: asia critique*, 21(1), pp. 189–221.
Tay, A. C. (2014a). Unpublished Interview with Kerrie Schaefer, trans. Khee, S. July 11.
Tay, A. C. (2014b) Unpublished Interview with Kerrie Schaefer, trans Khee, S. July 31.
Tay, J. (2014) *Bukit Ho Swee: A Tour of Invisible Things* [unpublished playscript].
Van Erven, E. (1992) *The Playful Revolution: Theatre and Liberation in Asia.* Bloomington: Indiana University Press.
Van Erven, E. (2001) *Community Theatre. Global Perspectives.* London and New York: Routledge.
Varney, D. Eckersall, P. Hudson, C. and Hatley, B. (2013) *Theatre and Performance in the Asia-Pacific. Regional Modernities in the Global Era.* London: Palgrave Macmillan.

CHAPTER 7

Conclusion: An Invitation

In this book, I've explored the re-signification of community (Chap. 1) from common being to being-in-common articulated by Gibson-Graham (2006), after Nancy (1991, 2000). Gibson Graham and Rose (1997) emphasise a notion of community as navigating interdependent social relations, generating new productive possibilities in and through that process. I have introduced this re-signification of community in the context of the crisis of community in postmodernism and post-structuralism, whose commodification of culture and celebration of difference, respectively, is seen to invalidate the concept of community.

In Chap. 2, I examined historical and theoretical perspectives on community-based cultural practices. I argued that a dynamic notion of community is central to community-based performance practice. Community, in other words, is not a pre-existing entity waiting somewhere out there to be found but is (per)formed. The act of creating community as a social and cultural formation is an interactive, relational and embodied process that may draw on the past (historical narratives) but is firmly focused on dynamic becoming. For me, the issue has been to explore connections between a dynamic notion of cultural community and to take that forward into analysis with the re-signification of community as the enactment of being-in-common.

Despite, or perhaps because of, social and economic changes over the past decades, community remains a vital concept that is, as sociologist Martin Mulligan states, "better understood as an unquenchable aspiration or desire rather than a social structure" (2013, p. 107). Mulligan asserts that community, even as "grounded" or "way of life", is "imagined" and must be 'wilfully constructed", or "projected" (p. 107). This process is going on all around us, and Mulligan argues that the arts should have a stake in the process of reimagining community not least because leaving the construction of community to others risks the dangers of common-being community—nationalisms, sectarianisms, authoritarianisms—coming home to roost. I've argued that community performance has been engaged in performing community since at least the 1960s. In the broader participatory arts/social practice field, Nancy's (1991) notion of community as 'inoperative' has been used to support the idea that community is a tantalising, yet naive social ideal, or is impossible to define, and therefore dangerous in the sense of open to appropriation and misdirection. Kwon (2002) recommends that artists not work under sign of community but, rather, work to unwork community. Mulligan himself is only a little more positive insofar as he suggests that Nancy offers the key insight that community is not simply a cruel mirage—beyond experience—but neither can it ever be completed (2013, p. 110). The incompleteness of inoperative community does not take away from the fact that, as being-in-common, community is always already given to us. It is something we can't choose to ignore since it is given to us with our being insofar as Being is being-with. Being singular plural is the relational dynamic that animates our coexistence. I want to suggest that community performance, as 'improvising being together' (Kuppers 2007), is at the forefront of processes of actively reimagining community. For Rose, community artists create spaces not necessarily directed towards articulating an oppositional or resistant world view (community against society), but in which to explore being-in-common (interdependence) and the possibilities of (per)forming community differently.

The case studies in the book offer a deep dive into complex processes of enacting community in community-based performance practice. I hope the re-signification of community as being-in-common and the resurfacing of a dynamic notion of cultural community central to theories of community-based performance practice inspire further analysis of community performance and enacting community as being-in-common. Below, I summarise the case study findings and indicate areas for further research into community dramaturgies.

BEING-IN-COMMON CASE STUDIES

There is a logic of practice, in community performance practices that wilfully and artfully re-construct community. This is evident in the methodologies and principles, the ways of operating, adopted by practitioners whose work I have unpacked in case studies. In this book, I have extended the notion of being-with to the practices of these community performance groups, as well as to the engagement process that is essential to their practices. I've examined how the practices themselves have been shaped by the contexts in which they operate and develop and how they adapt methodologies in/for broad communities they reimagine. In each case, the case studies offer themes for future research in community (studies and) performance studies.

acta's work has always been based on a regional cultural ecology set within radical welfare structures redirecting mixed (local government and charity/third sector) support to develop community theatre-makers and audiences. Their work is devised and performed by company members who are developed first as audiences (often people who don't normally go to the theatre) or participants, and then as participants in varying stages of engagement, from a basis that is 'fun, free and local', to experienced producers making engaging, relevant performance and touring it to new audiences throughout the region. The 'cycle of engagement' ensures a dynamism to acta's community theatre work. Members cycle or flow through modes of engagement or 'participation pathways' such that audiences become participants who become experienced theatre-makers and, recently (through funded Foundation Worker and Cornerstone programmes), facilitators and cultural producers (see Schaefer et al. 2020).

I've applied the concept of 'community of practice' to conceptualise acta's practice now that the company operates from a centre (a building) in an inner-city neighbourhood in Bristol. This base tends to restrict the concept of community to specific groups (of location or identity)—young carers, young people, adults, older people, ethnic communities (Somalian, African Caribbean), refugees and people who are free on a Thursday morning (the Thursdays). At the same time, such containment enables groups to learn theatre (aesthetic) skills, recover cultural practices and excavate social (local history/memory) meaning which is ploughed straight back into embodied practice, and the next project. The acta centre acts as a hub for the activities of many 'communities of practice'. As a social and aesthetic space, it manages the inclusion of diverse groups where what they share is theatre practice. That practice affirms group identity and foments appreciation of each other as each group has been through the process of making theatre. The way that acta bridges difference exemplifies the way that neighbourhood community theatres (see also Rotterdams Wijktheater) operate. Social differences are recognised and acknowledged—they are not denied or erased—and social connection is forged through processes of theatre-making and audiencing. This dynamic and growing (expanding) model of community theatre avoids entrenching division by appealing to a base and, instead, constantly navigates group differences through common practice: a community of practice. As a company, acta plays a vital role in establishing national networks (through seminar series and festivals) and is part of international networks, such as ICAF, which share practical learning on community theatre methodologies. The challenge remains to maintain dynamic growth and extended networks in times of funding scarcity.

Big Hart's methodologies are grounded in community cultural development practice and have also uniquely managed to bridge the local and the national, taking the margins to the mainstage. With *Yijala Yala*, John Pat's death-in-custody became national 'sorry business' in the capital city of Canberra, an indictment of colonisation and a call for justice and peace. Big hART's tenure in Roebourne—ongoing at the invitation of the community—locates the Roebourne community, so often depicted as dysfunctional by outsiders, as competent creative producers: a resilient creative community with cultural resource (country, language, story) to sustain livelihoods well beyond the limited futures of extractive industries. What is distinct about Big hART's work is the company's multilayered methodology which incorporates debates about community and art as tensions that animate complex community dramaturgies. Big hART's innovative methodology allows the company to operate at a scale rarely seen in community performance while achieving combined objectives, namely to "make art, build community and drive change" (https://www.bighart.org/).

The Anne Basting/Sojourn collaboration focused on the different mobilities that meet at street crossings, and the public infrastructure that makes this meeting so difficult, and the crossing impossible. It can seem that 'community' recedes in this civic practice, but engagement is there in Anne's dogged persistence behind the scenes on and across so many levels—researching traffic codes and pedestrian performances, bringing together students and seniors at crossings to devise performances, and liaising with key social partners, schools, care homes, 'specials' (government officials) and so on—to ensure that the bodies on the crossings are the bodies that matter in order that Sojourn's focused performances promote the dialogue that will lead to change. All this was in the context of making a larger project that aimed to inject creativity into a city-wide system of elder care to break down isolation between seniors and the broader community not least by ensuring that streets are safe for all pedestrians. *The Islands of Milwaukee* tackled social inclusion from the dual and interconnected perspective of forced and voluntary social exclusion (Mulligan et al. 2006). If forced exclusion refers to "ways in which people are systematically cut off from the resources – economic, social and political – that are necessary to fully participate in society" (p. 26), voluntary exclusion "refers to situations where people can afford to effectively secede from the rest of society, and their obligations to it, exemplified in such practices as tax evasion or choosing to live in a gated community" (p. 27). Mulligan et al. (2006) state that "in theory, voluntary and forced exclusion are … causally connected – that is, opting out of social and financial obligation by those at the top has the effect of further excluding those at the bottom, such that reducing voluntary exclusion is seen as key to solving forced exclusion" (p. 28). However, Mulligan et al. (2006) also note that in practical policy contexts both the fuller notion of inclusion and finer point of difference in definition have been lost: "the focus of much recent policy around social inclusion and exclusion has almost exclusively been on the forced exclusion of those at the bottom, with little attention paid or actions taken to re-connect those at the top into the social bonds of community" (p. 27). *Islands of Milwaukee* practically insists on the fuller sense of inclusive community. The project places emphasis on a fully inclusive notion of social inclusion drawing together vulnerable pedestrians, overconfident drivers and powerful political/civic agents responsible for planning public space. Performances of street crossings share experience of failure or inability and build empathy with vulnerable users of street crossings. How can community-based performance as a practice that is variously embodied and affective, build social inclusion while re-engaging political/policy agents to reconnect forced and voluntary social exclusion?

Drama Box embarked on an experiment in using community engagement methodology in theatre/performance making in Singapore with its complex layers of grassroots pseudo-state organisations feeding into national governance in a corporate mode. At Bukit Ho Swee, Drama Box nevertheless worried the foundational myth of nation formation: that Singapore arose like a phoenix from the ashes of a *kampong* fire and that it was the modern and efficient management of PAP government that achieved this outcome. At Bukit Ho Swee, the company dug up residues and remains of the past (in living memory)—former 'slum dwellers'—in the modern Housing Development Board space and recirculated these stories/narratives enabling them to interact with the dominant one. There was no need to fall back on unproductive, uncritical nostalgia since traces of community remained and the performance created forms of community through sharing space—all this was revealed by the act of making theatre/performance in the Bukit Ho Swee HDB estate space. There may be limits to community engagement methodology in Singapore where active censorship is in operation and where to openly counter government consensus, or to dissent, runs a risk of arrest and detainment. As systems of democratic government are placed under strain by increasingly authoritarian and corrupt tendencies (not necessarily in Singapore), Drama Box's skills in navigating restricted citizen agency (remembering forgotten agencies of a generation subsumed into a single governmental narrative) and corporate or communitarian forms of governance may prove instructive. Drama Box continued to develop the company's community engagement methodology through several other projects in the city state (see Schaefer 2022). In 2021, Drama Box co-hosted, with Rotterdams Wijktheater, a virtual ICAF from its base in Singapore illuminating for international audiences practices of cultural democracy in the Southeast Asian region.

References

Gibson-Graham, J.K. (2006) *A Postcapitalist Politics.* Minneapolis: University of Minnesota Press.
Kuppers, P. (2007) 'Community Arts Practices: Improvising Being Together', in Kuppers, P and Robertson, G. *Community Performance Reader.* London and New York: Routledge, pp. 34–47.
Kwon, M. (2002) *One Place After Another: Site Specific Art and Locational Identity* Massachussetts: MIT Press.
Mulligan, M. (2013) 'Thinking of community as an aspirational and contestable idea: A Role for the Arts in Creating Community', *Journal of Arts & Communities*, 5(2/3), pp. 105–118.
Mulligan, M., Humphery, K., James, P., Scanlon, C., Smith P. and Welch, N. (2006) *Creating Community: Celebrations, Arts and Wellbeing Within and Across Local Communities.* Melbourne: VicHealth and Globalism Research Centre.
Nancy, J-L. (1991) *The Inoperative Community.* Minneapolis: University of Minnesota Press

Nancy, J-L. (2000) *Being Singular Plural*. Redwood City, California: Stanford University Press.
Rose, G. (1997) 'Performing Inoperative Community. The space and resistance of some community arts projects' in Pile, S. and Keith, M. (eds.) *Geographies of Resistance*. London and New York: Routledge, pp. 184–202.
Schaefer, K., Abdulla, A., Beddow, N., Cook, J., Elhindi, H., Jones, I., Harvey, T., Hopkins, K., Pordes, R., Snook, S. and Tomlin, H. (2020) 'Acta community theatre's 'cycle of engagement' and foundation worker programme: creating pathways into cultural participation and work', *Studies in Theatre and Performance*, 40(3), pp. 334–345. doi: https://doi.org/10.1080/14682761.2020.1807214
Schaefer, K. (2022) 'Drama Box and the Place of Community-Engaged Performance in the Production of the Singaporean Space Scape', in Rajendran, C. and Gough, R. (eds.) *Drama Box and Spaces of Performance: Experience, Encounter, Engagement*. Aberystwyth: Performance Research Books (Inside Performance Practice).

Index[1]

A
acta Community Theatre, 47–78, 125n1
Activism, 26–29, 32, 33, 41, 95, 104n9
Aesthetic regime, 133, 149
Aesthetics, 10n6, 29, 33, 37, 42, 57, 63, 69, 77, 85, 86, 103, 133, 134, 139, 149, 150, 165, 169, 195
Affirmative aesthetic, 57
Anti-liberal, 158
Applied theatre, 9, 16, 22, 38, 42–43
Arrested development, 165–169
Asset-based community development (ABCD), 2, 5, 81, 86–88, 135
Authenticity, 62, 63
Authoritarian, 163, 164, 197

B
Basting, Anne, 40, 126, 128–132, 129n8, 135–143, 153, 196
Beddow, Neil, 48, 50–56, 58, 59, 61, 67, 68, 71
Being-in-common, 3, 6–8, 43, 193–197
Being singular plural, 8, 194
Being-together-with-others, 109, 193
Big hART, 4, 5, 38, 39, 44, 81–120, 130, 135, 195, 196
Bukit Ho Swee, 157–189, 197

C
Censorship, 163, 167, 197
Cheeseman, Peter, 50, 66, 69, 71, 73
Civic culture, 139
Civic practice, 38, 40, 44, 128, 128n6, 129, 131–135, 137, 144, 149, 154, 196
Class, 2, 7, 17–24, 26, 28, 31, 32, 35–37, 66, 70, 72, 133, 141, 168, 173
Cohen-Cruz, Jan, 6, 16, 18n2, 33, 34, 37–42, 50, 66, 87, 128, 134, 151, 154
Common being, 3, 6–8, 193
Communitarian, 157–189, 197
Community, 1–11, 15–44, 47–78, 81–93, 89n3, 96–109, 111, 112, 117–120, 125n1, 126, 127, 128n6, 129–131, 130n9, 133–136, 138, 141, 142, 144–146, 149, 151, 154, 157–177, 179–189, 193–197

---

[1] Note: Page numbers followed by 'n' refer to notes.

INDEX

Community arts, 3, 16, 17, 18n2, 19, 21, 22, 26–33, 36–38, 43, 44, 54, 62, 82, 83
Community cultural development (CCD), 1, 3–5, 10, 17, 19, 23, 29n7, 30, 37–40, 40n10, 44, 83, 85, 106, 119, 195
Community dramaturgies, 86, 194, 196
Community-engaged methodology, 189
Community of practice, 48, 57, 75–78, 195
Community theatre, 5, 6, 10, 11, 15–19, 18n2, 23–26, 30, 36–38, 41, 42, 44, 47–57, 63, 66–69, 75–78, 125n1, 162, 165–167, 174, 182, 195
Counter-hegemony, 8, 21, 33, 167
Creative Care, 128
Creative place-making, 140
Creative play, 69, 136, 139
The Crossings, 125–154
Cultural democracy, 5, 6, 17, 19, 21, 30–33, 39, 48, 54, 83, 197
Cultural livelihoods, 5, 81–120
Cultural policy, 17, 19, 22, 26–29, 36, 37, 48, 49, 54, 54n3, 56, 84, 162–165, 168, 169
Cultural rights, 39, 82
Cultural turn/culturalist, 19–24, 31, 32, 36
Cultural vitality, 40, 119
Culture, 1, 4, 8, 15–21, 23, 24, 26n6, 27–36, 39, 40, 42, 54, 58n9, 63, 65, 82–84, 87, 92, 107, 112, 117, 119, 120, 126, 129, 130, 151, 162, 164–166, 193
Cycle of engagement, 47–78, 195

D
Democratic cultural policy, 17, 19, 26–29
Documentary theatre, 50, 66
Drama Box, 38, 44, 157–189, 197
Dynamic community, 19, 21–23, 30–33, 36

E
Emancipated spectator, 133
Ethics of care, 92
Exclusive corporate governance, 164

F
Forced social exclusion, 196

G
Gas Girls, 48, 57–59, 65, 67–69, 71, 77
Global City/globalisation, 64n14, 162, 164
Grassroots theatre, 16, 19, 21, 33–36, 40

H
HDB nation, 157–189
Hegemonic consensus, 160
Hegemony, 19, 24, 26, 29, 32, 36
Hipbone Sticking Out, 82, 83, 89–93, 111–117, 120
Housing Development Board (HDB), 159–162, 160n4, 169, 171, 173, 176, 178, 181, 184, 186–189, 197

I
Ideological transaction, 19, 23–26, 32–36
Imagination, 5, 53, 57–59, 67, 69–75, 77, 129, 136, 139, 177
Inclusive corporate governance, 158
Islands of Milwaukee (IoM), 44, 125–154, 196

K
Kampong nostalgia, 161, 173, 188

L
Layered approach, 81, 83, 85
Local acts, 16, 37, 66

M

Marinos, Sophia, 85, 87, 93, 97–99
Memory, 53, 57–59, 61–63, 65, 67–70, 77, 116, 129, 162, 170, 175–184, 189, 195, 197
Modernisation, 160, 164, 179
Myers, Debra, 82, 93, 96–102, 106, 119

N

Ngarluma, 81, 90–92, 94–96, 105–107, 109–114
Nostalgia, 9, 26–29, 69, 151, 161, 197

O

Oral history, 35, 58, 59, 66, 67, 86, 108, 114, 162, 169, 170, 176, 182, 184

P

Participatory arts, 10, 10n6, 16, 18n2, 22, 37, 40n10, 48, 55, 132, 133, 135, 194
The Penelope Project (PP), 126–130, 129n8, 132, 135, 136
Play, 10, 22, 25, 31, 40, 42, 49–56, 60–62, 69, 72–76, 87, 89–92, 103–105, 112, 116, 131, 133, 135, 136, 139, 147, 148, 166, 166n10, 167, 175–178, 180, 195
Practical principles, 42, 87–93

R

Radical welfare, 27, 39, 194
Rankin, Scott, 39, 81–86, 88, 96, 100–105, 108, 110

Regional documentary, 50
Renaissance city, 163
Rohd, Michael, 44, 126, 128–135, 142, 147

S

Singapore, 158–160, 159n2, 160n5, 162–171, 173, 175, 178, 181, 183, 188, 197
Social exclusion, 43, 48, 54, 86
Social history, 170
Social memory, 195
Social practice, 128, 129, 132, 133, 194
Social welfare, 22, 30, 31, 40, 84
Socio-economic marginalisation, 86, 94, 95
Sojourn Theatre (ST), 40, 126, 129–132
Structure of feeling, 19, 21, 33–36

T

Ticky Picky Boom Boom (TPBB), 48, 57–65, 77
TimeSlips (TS), 129, 130
Traffic calming, 139, 140

V

Verbatim theatre, 50, 66, 69
Village (*kampong*), 159–161, 170, 173
Virtuosity, 83, 86
Voluntary social exclusion, 196

Y

Yijala Yala, 81–120, 195
Yindjibarndi, 81, 90–92, 95, 95n6, 96, 105–107, 109, 111, 112, 114, 115

Ingram Content Group UK Ltd.
Milton Keynes UK
UKHW020812180623
423483UK00017B/627

9 783030 957568